Powerful Problem Solving

Max Ray of the Math Forum @ Drexel

Powerful Problem Solving

Activities for **Sense Making** with the **Mathematical Practices**

HEINEMANN
Portsmouth, NH

Heinemann
361 Hanover Street
Portsmouth, NH 03801–3912
www.heinemann.com

Offices and agents throughout the world

The author and publisher wish to thank those who have generously given permission to reprint borrowed material:

"Blanket Challenge" and "Clarifying Questions Mingle" developed by Training for Change, http://trainingforchange .org. Reprinted with permission.

"The Grade 6 $1,000,000 Unsolved Problem" developed by Dr. Gordon Hamilton of MathPickle, http://mathpickle .com. Reprinted with permission.

"The Take-Away Game" developed by Bob Lochel from mathcoachblog: Ramblings of a Math Coach, http:// mathcoachblog.wordpress.com, posted November 20, 2012. Reprinted with permission.

Excerpts from Common Core State Standards © Copyright 2010. National Governors Association Center for Best Practices and Council of Chief State School Officers. All rights reserved.

"Charlie's Stamps" from *Crossing the River with Dogs: Problem Solving for College Students* by Ken Johnson, Ted Herr, and Judy Kysh. Copyright © 2012 by John Wiley & Sons, Inc. This material is reproduced with permission of John Wiley & Sons, Inc.

Acknowledgments for borrowed material continue on page vi.

Library of Congress Cataloging-in-Publication Data
Ray, Max.
  Powerful problem solving : activities for sense making with the mathematical practices /
Max Ray of the Math Forum @ Drexel ; foreword by Susan O'Connell.
      pages   cm
    ISBN-13: 978-0-325-05090-4
    1. Problem solving—Study and teaching—Activity programs.   I. Title.

QA63.R29 2013
370.15'24—dc23   2013018842

Editor: Katherine Bryant
Production: Vicki Kasabian
Cover and interior designs: Monica Ann Crigler
Cover photographs: © Ocean/Corbis
Typesetter: Kim Arney
Manufacturing: Steve Bernier

Printed in the United States of America on acid-free paper
17 16 15 14 13 EBM 1 2 3 4 5

CONTENTS

FOREWORD

Susan O'Connell

Learning mathematics is about more than memorizing facts and algorithms. Proficient mathematicians *think* mathematically. They develop mathematical reasoning and apply their computational skills and conceptual understanding to solve math problems. The Common Core State Standards place great emphasis on developing students' problem-solving skills. Standard 1 of the Common Core Standards for Mathematical Practice affirms that mathematically proficient students make sense of problems and persevere in solving them. And throughout the content standards, we repeatedly see references to students solving problems using whole numbers, fractions, measurement, or other content strands.

Have your students internalized the problem-solving process? Have they acquired a repertoire of strategies to solve varied types of problems? Have they developed enough confidence in their problem-solving skills to allow them to persevere when problems become challenging?

How do we support our students to promote the development of their problem-solving skills? How do we help them think like problem solvers? This book, *Powerful Problem Solving*, will serve as your guide. Max Ray has developed an understandable, practical, and insightful book to guide you as you explore math problems with your students. In the rich tradition of the Math Forum, which has been posing challenging problems and guiding students in the development of mathematical thinking for twenty years, this book provides rich problems and invaluable tips for building your students' problem-solving skills. The importance of math talk, the critical nature of reflection about our own thinking (metacognition), the ability to struggle while finding paths to solutions, and the benefits of exploring divergent methods for solving problems are all explored.

While standard 1 in the Common Core Standards for Mathematical Practice specifically highlights problem solving as a goal, *Powerful Problem Solving* explores the links between problem solving and the other math practice standards. Other Practice Standards (e.g., constructing viable arguments, looking for and making use of structure, using models, selecting tools, exploring repetition) are identified at the start of each chapter, and then links are made between that standard and problem solving. The interdependence of the Practice Standards, and their connection to building confident problem solvers, is clearly evident as each chapter is developed.

In addition to a clearer understanding of what makes an effective problem solver and how problem solving is linked to the Practice Standards, you will love the many practical tips and classroom activities described throughout this book. Each chapter targets a specific practice standard and highlights several activities that can be easily integrated into your math classroom and will serve to strengthen your students' skills in that critical practice. The book's companion website is filled with numerous problems that will engage and excite your students, while challenging them to think mathematically! There are also reproducibles that you can use with your students.

Our students learn to be problem solvers by solving problems. We must pose problems that challenge them to analyze, interpret, plan, check, and reflect on their approaches and solutions. We must help them develop foundational thinking skills, including modeling strategies, ways to simplify problems, and ideas for organizing data and selecting helpful tools. In addition, we must develop a classroom climate in which students feel free to talk about their efforts, listen to each other, develop arguments to support their decisions, take risks, and have enough confidence to persevere when solutions are not immediately apparent. Through this book, Max Ray shares a wealth of resources, tips, insightful anecdotes, and specific activities for developing students' skills and habits of mind. *Powerful Problem Solving* will help you envision the key components of a problem-rich classroom and guide you in creating a classroom environment that fosters the development of problem solving.

Whether you read this book from front to back (which I would recommend so you don't miss any of the important insights) or simply dive into chapters that address the needs of your students at the moment, you will find it practical, understandable, and enlightening. It provides clarity to an often-confusing and definitely complex area of mathematics, and helps us make sense of and simplify the teaching of math problem solving.

Don't wait another minute—dive into it!

ACKNOWLEDGMENTS

While Max Ray is the official author on the cover of this book, the book was a true collaboration among the entire Math Forum staff, past and present. In particular, Steve Weimar, Mai Sidawi, and Troy Regis were the original authors, along with Max, of the Problem-Solving and Communication Activity Series, without which this book would not exist. Colleagues Ellen Clay and Valerie Klein's input on topics like what mathematicians notice and wonder about and what gets hard for teachers and students while noticing and wondering was invaluable. Annie Fetter, in addition to keeping track of the entire history and philosophy of the Math Forum from before it was born to the present (and beyond!) and writing it up for the Introduction and Conclusion, and first inventing I Notice, I Wonder™ as a tool for getting students started problem solving, also contributed stories and insights that brought the activities to life. Also thanks to Bruce Levine for securing the publishing contract, and to Gene Klotz for everything he's done for the Math Forum.

Suzanne Alejandre gets a paragraph all to herself, since her contributions are almost too numerous to list: moral support, being a great boss, taking on lots of tasks so I could concentrate on writing, reading every word with her eagle eye for inviting tone and classroom practicality, contributing the handouts for students and teachers, sharing stories, collecting videos, field-testing activities, collecting student work, and writing great, pithy blog posts about her personal philosophy of student learning and how it's woven into everything the Math Forum does. And for occasionally handing me the purple pen and saying, "Just write it, dude!"

And everyone at the Math Forum gets a hearty and much-deserved "Thank you!" for the work they took on to free me up to write, especially Valerie, who shouldered the teaching load, Annie and Steve Risberg for highlighting great submissions to the Problems of the Week (PoWs), and Brianna Guidos, who did an awesome job writing the Trig/Calc PoW Packets (and who is welcome to keep doing so as long as she'd like the job!).

A special thank-you to the schools we collaborated with, and whose stories and students are reflected in this work, especially the students, teachers, coaches, and administrators at William Penn High School and McCullough Middle School in the Colonial School District; at Vare, Bluford, and Universal Institute Charter School (UIC) in the Universal Family of Charter Schools (especially Amanda Guille for the loan of her fabulous fourth grade); George Meade Elementary School, Christopher Columbus Charter School, and Arise Academy Charter High School in the Philadelphia School District; Heidi Rudolph at Orange High School in the Orange City School District; and Chris Yeannakis at Pinecrest School. Thanks also to the teachers from Montgomery County Public Schools, Kristina Nicholson and Java Robinson, who shared their classroom stories through Suzanne's online professional development course.

Thanks to Jon Manon and his colleagues at the Mathematics & Science Education Resource Center (MSERC) at the University of Delaware for fruitful collaboration and their insight on what the "new normal" in math classrooms might look like.

The teachers whose students submitted to the PoWs, and the students who shared their innermost math thoughts with us online, deserve a huge thanks as well. Reading students' submissions to the PoWs is the highlight of my week and the basis of much of this book. A special thanks to Laurel Pollard and her students at Hanover Street School whose "Voter Turnout" video we are proud to link to in the book. And to the Math Forum Teacher Associates who have been involved in giving feedback on these problem-solving activities since we first started them: Glenys Martin, Barbara Delaney, Ashley Miller, Marie Hogan, Peggy Mc-Closkey, Seth Leavitt, and Craig Russell.

Special thanks to my online Personal Learning Community of tweeting and blogging math teachers. Those whose work is explicitly named in this book or on the companion website (Karim Kai Ani, Sadie Estrella, Matt Lane, Bob Lochel, Chris Lusto, Brian Marks, Bryan Meyer, Dan Meyer, Fawn Nguyen, Kate Nowak, Nora Oswald, Julie Reulbach, Sam Shah, Andrew Stadel, and Elizabeth Statmore) and those who aren't, know that your thoughts and feedback and stories and insights and questions pushed my thinking forward and made me want to write this book. Thanks especially to those who participated in the Global Math Department chat about the Notice and Wonder strategy in February 2013, to James Cleveland for nominating me and Megan Hayes-Golding for organizing it, and to everyone at Twitter Math Camp 2012 for being awesome and for wanting to hear more about the Math Forum problem-solving strategies and noticing and wondering, especially to Lisa Henry and Shelli Temple for organizing the event, and to Sarah Bratt for immediately making noticing and wondering a special part of middle school math in the Gahanna-Jefferson Public Schools and then telling me all about it on Twitter. In many ways this book is especially for you, teachers of the mathtwitterblogosphere, as a sort of apology for not writing more on my blog.

Special thanks to everyone at Heinemann and especially Katherine Bryant, our awesome editor, for helping us make sense of just what would make this book interesting and useful, and for having a great eye for everything from details of classroom implementation to staying consistent with our philosophy and vision.

Personally, I'd like to thank the math teachers and math education professors who exposed me to math in a way that was joyful and empowering and helped me realize I had mathematical ideas worth listening to. Thanks to Ms. Allen at the Harley School in Rochester, New York, for handing me that green marker without which I would not have written this book, and to each math teacher I've had since then in the Charlottesville City Schools (you all helped me believe in myself and my math ideas): Ms. Walker, Ms. Thomas, Ms. Overton, Ms. Burke (and for being my friend on Twitter now!), Mr. Wainwright, Ms. Perkins (who said, "Of course you did," when I told her I had chosen math education as my major), and to my professors in math and education at Swarthmore, especially Cheryl Grood, Steve Wang, Don Shimamoto, Diane Anderson, and Ann Renninger.

And thanks to the long line of educators in my family, especially my parents, Howard Singerman and Janet Ray. Finally, thanks to Kaytee Riek for putting up with me disappearing to do nothing but type . . . even while we house-trained Whim, future service dog and current noisy puppy. I hope I managed to do my fair share of 3 am trips outdoors in the cold!

Powerful Problem Solving

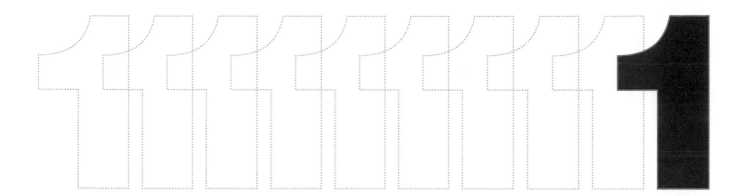

Introduction

This book represents the collected wisdom of the Math Forum @ Drexel University, an online community of math students; their teachers, coaches, and curriculum developers; education policy wonks; math education researchers; and mathematicians. Specifically, we set out to write a book that gathers what we've learned about helping students become powerful problem solvers, focused through the lens of the Common Core Standards for Mathematical Practice. This book is about what we as a community know and believe about:

- ▸ how students develop their abilities to make sense of mathematics
- ▸ how students develop the habits of mind outlined in the Standards for Mathematical Practice
- ▸ how the practices contribute to students' learning to make sense of mathematics
- ▸ how the practices align with problem-solving strategies students and teachers already use, and
- ▸ specific activities teachers can use to support their students in engaging in the sense-making behaviors described in the Standards for Mathematical Practice.

Meet the Math Forum

The Math Forum @ Drexel launched on June 15, 1992. At the time, it was known as the Geometry Forum and was based out of Swarthmore College. We are both a large online community and a small group of hardworking staff members who maintain our online services, such as Ask Dr. Math (http://mathforum.org/dr.math/), our Teacher2Teacher question-and-answer service (http://mathforum.org/t2t/), the Math Tools digital library of technology resources for teaching math (http://mathforum.org/mathtools/), and our Problems of the Week (PoW) services (http://mathforum.org/pows/).

The Math Forum PoWs are challenging problems, everything from applications of math we notice in our daily lives (storing cords of wood, patterning shotguns, commuting to work, baking cobbler) to wild stories we cook up just for fun (buying snacks from a vending machine . . . in another galaxy!). We publish problems on a two-week cycle (to give plenty of time for reflection and revision), in six "services": Primary, Math Fundamentals, Pre-Algebra, Algebra, Geometry, and Trigonometry/Calculus. In addition, we maintain a library of more than one thousand problems we've published between 1993 and the present. The PoW software allows students to submit their thinking (in writing, plus any images they want to upload), as well as makes it possible for teachers, volunteers, and Math Forum staff to write back to students with feedback to support their revisions. In fact, from 1993 to 2001, Math Forum staff wrote back to every student who attempted to solve one of our PoWs. This created a huge archive of student work and the mentors' responses that helped students learn. Since 1993, we've been studying this archive and making it available to teachers for their own learning. We've discovered a lot about the conditions that enable students to learn how to solve interesting problems and to learn mathematics through this process, such as:

> ▸ When students reflect on their work and revise, their learning skyrockets, especially for students who have been struggling with problem solving.[1] It's not enough just to focus on getting answers; we need to support them thinking about their thinking and learning from the problem-solving process.

> ▸ The problem-solving process and mathematical practices should be an explicit part of the curriculum. Too many students struggle to learn math because they don't have strategies to make sense of math scenarios or to work toward solutions on novel, challenging problems.

> ▸ Students who are successful problem solvers have big picture *concepts* that they use to monitor and launch their understanding; they have lots of *methods* in their toolkit to explore and apply concepts, and they recognize patterns and repeated steps to develop generalizations and *procedures* to solve similar problems fluently. We help teachers learn to recognize and support students on all of these levels.

> ▸ To support students to make sense of and learn mathematics, it is vital to listen to their current thinking, value their ideas, and provide interesting follow-up questions or ideas that support them to reflect, revise, and reengage.

The key philosophy behind everything we try to do in the Math Forum community is to ask questions and listen to the answers we hear—and then make those questions and answers available to the public. Our volunteer PoW mentors, our "math doctors," and our Teacher2Teacher Associates all commit to responding to community members' questions

---

1. Renninger, K. Ann, Laura Farra, and Claire Feldman-Riordan. 2000. "The Impact of the Math Forum's *Problem(s) of the Week* on Students' Mathematical Thinking." Presented at ICLS 2000. Available at http://mathforum.org/articles/Renninger2000.pdf.

with a mix of expertise, honest reflection, and questions to stimulate more thinking. PoW mentors ask questions to learn more about the student's thinking and help the student reflect and revise.

Why We Wrote This Book

The Math Forum education staff (in order of appearance), Annie Fetter, Steve Weimar, Richard Tchen, Suzanne Alejandre, Tracey Perzan, Ellen Clay, Max Ray, and Valerie Klein, collaborated on this book (which Max wrote) to collect what we have learned about supporting students to become problem solvers and sense makers. We're constantly learning more about what it takes to effectively facilitate students' problem solving, and now it's time to reflect, revise, and communicate our thinking.

This book grew out of the Math Forum Problem-Solving and Communication Activity Series, which we developed from 2008–2010. Writing the Activity Series gave us a chance to collect the various classroom activities and reflection questions that we'd been using with students and teachers online and in classroom coaching visits. It also gave us the opportunity to write and solve lots of problems, using as many problem-solving strategies as we could. Solving problems ourselves and with students and then reflecting on what happened and why, was really powerful. Through applying different problem-solving strategies at different grade levels, we noticed what was common across the strategies at all levels and what developed over time and with practice as students became more sophisticated. Through solving and reflecting on problems, we began to get better at noticing the problem-solving strategies of the students we worked with, as well. We would read PoW submissions and notice the wide range of tables students used and wonder, "What made that table more effective for that student?" and "How could we help all these students use their tables to show more patterns?" We would visit classrooms and hear students say, "This problem is *too hard*!" and instead of thinking, "Darn, they're stuck," we would be thinking, "Oh boy, this student is about to brainstorm some different Solve a Simpler Problem approaches. They just need some support knowing that it's okay to start with a simpler version."

Why Now Is the Time for Focus on Problem-Solving Practices

When the Common Core State Standards were released, including the eight mathematical practices, we began working to figure out how our problem-solving strategy activities could help students be more aware of and develop each of the mathematical practices for themselves. The publication of the Common Core became the impetus for us to get everything written down in one place for teachers to use!

As we talked to teachers, principals, and district leaders about what their professional development goals were in light of the new Common Core, problem solving became a bigger and bigger theme. Looking at some of the sample tasks released by the various assessment consortia helped solidify for math educators that students were going to be assessed on their ability to make sense of mathematical situations, find relationships, "mathematize" those relationships, solve problems about the relationships, and communicate and justify their thinking. Teachers are feeling like they need support understanding how the Common Core relates to what they already know about problem solving and sense making, as well as ways to push themselves and their students to get better at problem solving, sense making, and communication.

Math Practices: Uniting Conceptual Understanding and Procedural Fluency

In addition to the new requests for support helping students demonstrate their ability to model with mathematics, solve challenging problems, and communicate and justify their thinking, we feel that this book has an important role in helping teachers bridge the gap between conceptual understanding and procedural fluency. The piece that is often missing from the middle, which connects conceptual understanding to procedural fluency, is learning *methods*, the practices or habits of mind that mathematicians use to actually do math. What does it mean to *do math*? And what does it mean to be a novice doer of math, and how does one get better at doing math?

We believe shifting our focus from the "nouns" of mathematics to the "verbs" is a compromise in the traditional dichotomy between concepts and procedures.

We informally define doing mathematics as seeking to understand new ideas to create powerful tools to understand even more mathematical ideas, and generating and solving interesting problems using those ideas and tools (whether those domains are application domains, such as modeling the weather, or mathematical domains, such as understanding operations that are associative but not commutative).

How does this help us think about the chicken-or-egg question of whether teachers should focus first and mainly on concepts or procedures? If, in fact, mathematics is about studying and applying both concepts and procedures, the focus shifts from which of the objects of mathematics (concepts and procedures) we should study first to how to engage students regularly in both *studying* and *using* the objects of mathematics. The mathematical practices give us glimpses of how it is that students learn to do mathematics. Students learn to understand and apply mathematical concepts and procedures through problem solving, making connections, reasoning and proving their hunches, and communicating those ideas to themselves and others. They learn to both generate and understand mathematical procedures through looking for patterns in repeated reasoning and making use of structure. As students learn to attend to precision and use appropriate tools strategically, and they come to appreciate the values of rigor and elegance, they master algorithms. They value and strive to learn standard algorithms as the crystallization of mastered concepts and efficient procedures for solving future problems with hardly a thought.

In many other subjects, students are engaged in not just learning about the subject but are actually doing it. Young students read important things and write original texts. In music class, they don't just listen to others and practice reading music, they perform and sometimes even compose their own music. In science classes, students don't just learn about theories and results of others' experiments, they design their own experiments to test their own hypotheses. In those subjects, we have learned to recognize and value novice versions of the adult practice. We listen to students' poetry excitedly, even though we don't expect Shakespeare.

We admire and give constructive feedback on their singing and their science projects. In this book we hope to help teachers engage students in doing math and support teachers to value the novice version of mathematics that students can do. We believe shifting our focus from the "nouns" of mathematics to the "verbs" is a compromise in the traditional dichotomy between concepts and procedures.

About the Book

We hope this book helps you to:

- ▸ understand the coherence among the Common Core Standards for Mathematical Practice in that they all support students to make sense of mathematics
- ▸ support students to engage in and develop their mathematical practices
- ▸ learn specific activities you can use to support students as they develop their mathematical practices and ability to make sense of mathematics.

As you read this book, we hope that you'll also notice some themes that we've woven throughout the chapters:

- ▸ Problem solving is a process: the goal is not to be over and done, the goal is to reflect and revise.
- ▸ Unsilence students' voices: make space for student-to-student talk as well as student-to-teacher talk, by limiting teacher-to-student talk.
- ▸ Give students space to think for themselves, struggle, and come up with their own ways to approach problems.
- ▸ Take lots of opportunities to listen to students and learn about their current thinking.
- ▸ Use communication and comparison of student ideas as learning opportunities, more often than the presentation of teacher ideas.
- ▸ Facilitate students' thinking to help students learn habits of mind versus training students in processes to help them learn routines and practice skills.

How to Use the Book

This book is both a collection of activities, each of which could stand alone, and a sequence of classroom practices that builds toward student independence and success in solving math problems. Each activity in the book offers you a chance to support student development, as well as to learn more about your students' current problem-solving skills. We hope it serves as a resource for classroom teachers of grades 3–8 (and their coaches and administrators). We attempt to illustrate in useful ways how students get better at sense making and specific problem-solving strategies by providing classroom stories and sample student work, and we provide classroom activities that help students focus on the problem-solving strategies and mathematical practices.

One resource that we hope you will find particularly helpful as you read this book is the companion website (http://mathforum.org/pps/). There you will find additional problem-solving activities and student handouts to print, as well as Math Forum PoWs aligned to the problem-solving themes and strategies in each chapter that we are providing to readers of this book—complete with versions of the scenarios both with and without the question asked, teacher packets with support materials, scoring rubrics, and documents from the Activity Series mentioned previously. The companion website also has classroom videos of some of the activities described in the book, as well as links to other resources from the Math Forum and around the web to supplement and extend what you'll find in the print book.

Read beginning to end, this book explores the whole developmental sequence: from building a classroom culture of students who can communicate their ideas and listen to others, to supporting students to begin to make sense of math problems, to helping students see the big picture and using their estimating and reasoning skills to really make sense of problems, through supporting students to develop skills of organizing information, building mathematical models and representations, learning a variety of problem-solving strategies, planning and engaging in the full problem-solving process, and finally reflecting on, revising, justifying, and extending their work.

I hope the classroom stories and samples of student work and student thinking from across the grade levels we've focused on (third through eighth grade) might make you wonder, "How would my students do with this prompt? Is that what happens in my classroom as well?" and help you pick specific activities to try with your students. As you learn where your students are with regards to the habits of mind and strategies discussed in the book, you can start to use this book as a reference. When you encounter a problem in your curriculum that you're not sure your students will have the tools to approach, or if you notice, that, say, they're not really doing anything to organize their problem-solving work and so their Guess and Check approaches are inefficient and frustrating, you can turn to a specific chapter to try to help your students build up their skills.

We've tried to provide examples of problems and prompts to use with a particular activity within the text as well as on the companion website and through the list of additional readings and links referenced in Chapter 9, so that if you are supplementing your curriculum with additional problem-solving resources, you'll find some for each habit of mind or problem-solving strategy. We also encourage you to use the habits of mind in this book as a lens to look at problems from your own curriculum. If your own curriculum is problem-based, this book can help you support your students with the skills and practices needed to make sense of, persevere through, solve, and learn from those problems. If your curriculum is not problem-rich, we've often found that the word problems, projects at the end of chapters, introductory hooks, and other little nuggets woven into even the "driest" of textbooks can serve as great scenarios for students to explore and wonder about and use to practice exercising their math imaginations and problem-solving skills while keeping on pace with

The companion website (http://mathforum.org/pps/) uses a passcode for book purchasers only. You'll be asked to log in with a specific word, which you'll find in the text.

your curriculum. Also, even in the most traditional of math programs, there are still moments when students are called upon to make sense, to guess and estimate, to organize, to model, and to solve problems using a range of strategies. We hope that the activities in this book help you recognize those practices, notice your students' readiness for those practices, and support them explicitly in using the practices as they do mathematics.

Finally, we want to invite you to use this book to start and join conversations. Whether it's within your school, at a Math Teacher's Circle, or online through Math Forum discussions, Twitter, or your own blogs and the blogs of others,[2] we hope that the stories, problems, student work examples, and accompanying online materials can be part of larger conversations about implementing the Common Core Math Practices, about mathematical habits of mind, and about supporting students to become independent math problem solvers.

---

2. Learn more at the website Sam Shah created, http://mathtwitterblogosphere.weebly.com/.

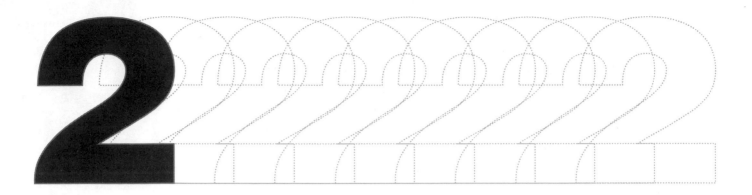

Communication and Community

Focal practices:

3. Construct viable arguments and critique the reasoning of others.
6. Attend to precision.

This chapter introduces activities and routines to support students to communicate their ideas and work together. It also provides examples of how students' communication develops, to help teachers meet students where they are and provide students with authentic communication opportunities that stretch students without being too frustrating.

The inspiration for beginning with two chapters on communicating and listening in math class comes from a school district that the Math Forum has worked closely with for several years. The district is committed to using problem-based learning in math classes and has been excited at their students' rising test scores, especially on items that require reasoning and problem solving, as well as their students' increasing self-reliance and belief that they can find answers without being told. In thinking about what they wanted to continue to work on, one of the teachers told me that he felt that his students were getting good at solving individual problems but that they weren't making connections across topics and sometimes even struggling to see the connections from day to day. When I asked him what it would look like if his students were making those connections, he described students who:

- asked questions of him and each other, questions that led to further exploration
- used their mathematical reasoning to debate and come to consensus about their questions and ideas
- spontaneously offered up ideas about how the math they were studying was like other topics.

It struck me that all of the things he was looking for had a communication aspect, in addition to a mathematical reasoning aspect. Learning to wonder well and ask questions that lead to math explorations is certainly a mathematical habit, but learning to ask questions at all is a communication habit. Learning to use mathematical reasoning in a debate takes not just math skills but the ability to put your ideas into words. I visited the teacher's classroom to listen to his students communicate and learn what support they might need.

The students were sitting, as usual, in groups of four, talking with their elbow partners (the person sitting next to them, as opposed to their face-to-face partner). I heard students asking each other good questions like, "How do you know?" and "Why did you do that?" I also heard students responding to those good questions rudely: mocking their peers for asking questions and refusing to respond. Deflecting a response to a math question, even rudely, is quite normal for novice math communicators. After overhearing one student tease her elbow partner for asking a question, I went over to talk to her about the way she'd responded. I was a little surprised by her candid confession: "I didn't like that she asked me that because I don't know how I know. I just know. I can't explain it."

After hearing her confession, I walked around the room to check in with several groups. It seemed like most of the students in the class shared her feeling of "I know it but don't ask me to explain it." Not knowing how to talk about their thinking meant they didn't like to be asked questions or work collaboratively. That shut down the students with questions, and certainly closed any possibility for having mathematical debates (at least ones that didn't devolve into put-downs).

Students blossom as math communicators when they feel heard.

The story is typical of many, many classrooms. Not feeling comfortable putting mathematical ideas into words or writing is frightening to students and makes it hard for them to want to collaborate, ask questions, share ideas, or articulate things about math besides the steps they already know how to do. However, it is also typical of many, many math classrooms that students do find they have a mathematical voice, and once they've experienced having their ideas heard and valued, they come to enjoy sharing them. We've always found listening and showing our appreciation to be a simple, effective way to start students as mathematical communicators. Whether it's the elementary students who run to greet our coworker "Miss Annie" when she visits their school so they can tell her about their math homework, to the eighth-grade student who wrote to me to tell me that her math-imagination saw things other people never dreamed of, we've always found that students blossom as math communicators when they feel heard.

In this classroom, we found some very simple opportunities to help students practice their math communication in extremely nonthreatening ways. I Notice, I Wonder™, a brainstorming activity we introduce in Chapter 4, helped all the students realize they had at least one math idea to contribute every day. Mathematical games that brought a challenge combined with highly structured ways of communicating helped students take the risk to talk (it was worth it to try to win a game) and focused them on their communication. Seeing different examples of ways to explain the same thing and then getting a chance to revise and improve their own explanation helped students practice and notice how they were getting better. By the end of two years working on student communication about math reasoning, the students were engaging in student-led problem-solving sessions that brought most voices into the room and ended with students experiencing how sharing and comparing their ideas meant they could solve *and explain* math problems without a teacher telling them anything.

How Math Communicators Develop

Getting students from a place where they feel incapable of putting their ideas into words (and so react with fear or anger when asked to) to being willing to share ideas with peers and even have those ideas critiqued is a long road. And it's yet another long road between sharing orally and writing a formal solution such as students might have to do on a Problem of the Week or constructed response problem on a high-stakes test. Even though as teachers we know it takes perseverance to get students from A to B to C, it's still easy to expect too much from our students as math communicators. Too often, we are so eager to hear our students' ideas that we expect novice problem solvers to thoroughly explain all the details of the novice thinking that they are doing. We wish that students who have learned how to get themselves from problem to solution will be able to turn and teach a partner exactly how they did it. "They thought it," we wonder, "why can't they say it?"

The reality, of course, is that students come with a wide range of skills, abilities, and preferences when it comes to communicating in math (just like when it comes to doing math) and finding a way to recognize and honor growth in many ways is important! For example, in some classrooms students are much more comfortable expressing themselves orally, and when asked to do written work, they seem to regress in their thinking as well as their communication. On the other hand, there are classrooms where students would much rather write about what they are doing than have to say anything out loud, whether to a partner, a teacher, or (yikes!) the whole class.

Also, some students come to math class already accomplished at writing and speaking in general. These students know how to construct an argument, how to be convincing, and how to check if their arguments make sense. Applying these skills to math class may be new, but once they make connections among writing or speaking they do in other contexts, they are quick to pick up on the need for precision, logical argument, organization, and so on. Other students who are equally good problem solvers may not have practice communicating in academic settings. They might have more trouble with the mechanics of writing, as well as making their arguments flow, their presentation clear, or their details precise enough. These students will need more support to make their expression clear—but this doesn't mean they aren't brilliant problem solvers!

Supporting the Development of Math Communication Skills

Following is a table of some different purposes and styles of communication that students eventually need to master and some paths through them for students with different experiences and skill levels. We hope this helps teachers select writing and speaking tasks that are a stretch for students but not so hard that they don't have a chance to succeed.

	Oral	Written
Communicating to organize your thoughts and explore	• Working on problems in small groups • Group brainstorming • Reaching shared understanding of a situation	• Writing noticings and wonderings about a problem scenario • Highlighting or circling key words • Carrying out calculations • Making a table • Testing values
Communicating to ask questions	• Asking peers what they did • Asking a teacher for help (beyond saying "I don't get it.") • Asking a peer for help • Asking for clarification	• Writing questions in the margin • Writing a list of wonderings • Writing a note to a peer • Writing a note to the teacher
Communicating to tell your point of view	• Stating a position on a question • Making oral predictions • Telling the group about something you noticed • Telling if you think the problem is hard or easy • Explaining how you interpreted the problem • Suggesting a strategy or approach to the group • Explaining your assumption	• Writing an answer to a poll or opinion question • Writing the answer to a prediction • Writing down something you noticed about the problem • Writing about whether a problem seems hard or easy to you • Writing about your interpretation of a problem • Writing about how you plan to approach a problem • Writing about assumptions you made
Communicating to tell what happened	• Telling the teacher about your "aha!" moment • Explaining to a peer what steps you did to get the answer • Explaining to the class what steps you did to get the answer	• Writing about your "aha!" moment • Writing down the steps you did • Writing a guide to show someone else the steps to take
Communicating to explain	• Telling a peer how you thought about the problem • Showing a peer how you solved the problem and telling how you knew • Telling the class or the teacher what steps you did and how you thought to do them	• Writing a personal account of how you thought to solve the problem • Writing about how your steps connected to your understanding • Writing a guide to help someone who is stuck think through the problem
Communicating to justify	• Telling why you are confident in your answer • Debating with another student about which answer is correct • Giving a counterexample to someone else's argument • Explaining why there can only be one answer to the problem (or why there are definitely multiple answers) • Using definitions to show that your reasoning is right • Proving that your answer must follow from the definitions/assumptions	• Writing about how confident you are • Writing an argument for why you are correct • Writing a counterexample to disprove an argument • Writing an explanation of why there can only be one answer to a problem (or why there are definitely multiple answers) • Using definitions to write a justification of your answer • Writing a two-column proof • Writing a paragraph proof • Writing an article for a mathematical journal

Within each cell, there is a continuum of activities, so even though writing to justify is often harder than writing to ask a question, students might be ready to argue with a peer about whether they are correct before they can formulate a written question that will help a teacher give them just the help they need.

The table can help you pick sequences of activities that match your students' preferences, aren't too far ahead of where they are and what they've done, and are authentic to the task. For example, students who love to talk and argue but don't like to sit down to write should have a chance to explain their work to a peer or teacher out loud and get some support and feedback before writing it down. Students who are more comfortable talking than writing are often helped by having a real audience to write their thinking to, just as they would have if they were talking face-to-face. Ideas like posting their work on a blog, emailing it to a student or teacher in another class or school, or writing an explanation that will be used to help a different student in the class can help students focus on their audience and write more clearly. On the other hand, if you have a class with lots of students who are hesitant about speaking up in class and feel more comfortable organizing their thoughts on paper, privately, it makes sense not to ask them to defend their answers orally in a small group until they've had a chance to write their arguments on paper, and maybe even exchange papers with other students.

Really, the point of the chart is that communication should always have a purpose.

In general, students usually prefer authentic tasks and communication tasks that are motivated by the math they are trying to solve. Having to write out explanations of how they solved a simple arithmetic problem is rarely popular—you get a lot of "I did it in my head!" But if that same problem is really being used with a younger class down the hall and your students will be explaining their steps to their younger partners, suddenly the task has a purpose and audience and is more engaging. Also, most people like telling about their ideas, especially if they are going to be listened to and appreciated for their thinking. The tasks in the "Communicating to tell your point of view" row are frequently popular, especially when students are writing or speaking to people whose thoughts they value—writing or talking to the teacher for a quick "Whoa, that's cool, I never thought of that!" or writing a note to a pen pal who will write back with an in-depth response, or even reflecting on a mathematical achievement they're proud of.

Really, the point of the chart is that communication should always have a purpose. When we ask students over and over to "show their work" and tell them that it's good for them, or it helps them get partial credit, or that their employers will expect them to be able to explain their steps, they start to tune us out. Instead, we can remember that there's a whole menu of communicative tasks *that serve real, immediate purposes*. For example, if your students are solving problems in groups then they're communicating math, and that can be praised and improved and built on! If you want them to write out their solutions, then you are asking them to communicate their opinions in writing—it gets interesting when other people have different opinions! How could they decide who is correct? Why does having the different examples in writing help them decide that? If your students hate writing their work clearly, you can give them a problem with lots of steps and let them fail to solve it. Then if you reflect with them on what made the problem so hard, and show them some tools for organizing their calculations, when you give them another problem with lots of steps they might find it's just a little bit easier using a nifty way of writing out your steps clearly. If your students struggle with one cell of the chart, you can put them in a situation where they need to do the purpose of that cell—for example, maybe they have to ask you a question about the homework via email, Facebook, or Twitter. The point is, they are practicing writing questions to get help.

A Culture of Communication

The activities in this chapter are designed to support students to communicate their mathematical ideas. This means creating a classroom culture in which students need to talk to each other about math ideas, know what it means to have a respectful mathematical conversation, and have tasks that require them to write for real communication with a real audience.

A classroom with productive math communication happening will have many of the features in this list:

▸ Students talk to one another, not just to the teacher.

▸ Students solve math problems or compare solutions to math problems in small groups, requiring them to explain their own and listen to others' mathematical thinking.

▸ Students communicate both orally and in writing with the teacher about their mathematical thinking.

▸ When students communicate, they are respectful of one another, using a polite tone and questions and feedback rather than put-downs.

▸ Students listen to other students as well as the teacher.

▸ Students are able to make themselves understood in their peer group.

▸ When discussing their ideas, students justify their thinking, using personal experience, referring back to given information, recalling past work, or mentioning definitions.

▸ Students ask other students to justify their ideas, asking, "How do you know?" or "Are you sure?"

▸ Students can explain what they did step-by-step.

▸ Students say why they did what they did.

▸ Students use writing to organize their thoughts.

▸ Students use writing to collaborate and share ideas with an audience.

▸ Students use writing and speaking formally to present finished ideas.

▸ All students contribute ideas to the large group over the course of several lessons.

▸ Small groups make sure that all members are heard from.

▸ Small groups check that all members understand what's going on.

▸ Students are able to work in small groups or alone and stay on task.

▸ Students ask questions of one another when they are stuck.

> ▸ Students ask questions of the teacher when they are stuck.

> ▸ Students collaborate in different ways depending on the task (e.g., the students work in larger groups when many ideas are needed and in small groups or on their own when students need to explore or practice independently).

Activities

Activities Focusing on Group Communication

ACTIVITY Blanket Challenge[1]

While this activity doesn't directly relate to mathematics (except perhaps some advanced topology?), it does require group oral communication and weighing multiple peoples' ideas about strategy and tactics for solving a problem—in this case, a physical challenge.

Format: Students working in groups of 8–10, or one large group if you have a blanket large enough.

Materials: One blanket for each group of 8–10 (large enough for all ten group members to stand on with room to maneuver, but not much larger), and enough space for the groups to spread out their blankets and not be distracted by one another—for example, a cafeteria or outdoor space or large hallway.

Step 1: Place a blanket on the floor. Have the group members stand on the blanket (they should be only slightly packed on the blanket).

Step 2: Give students the challenge: turn the blanket over (flip it over) without anyone stepping off the blanket (so no leaving the blanket, leaning on walls, etc.). Some groups may take longer than others; allow the group to take as long as it takes. If the group steps off the blanket, or someone steps on the ground, start over again. It's a very doable task!

Note: As groups finish, have an additional challenge prepared so students don't distract other groups—it could be as simple as silently sharing and eating a snack. If they make noise, no more snack! Or students might quietly make a plan for if they knew they would be making a time-limited video recording of doing the Blanket Challenge. In other words, have them refine their strategy for completing the task and, perhaps, practice it to get good and fast.

Step 3: After the group completes the task successfully, help the group self-reflect by asking students:

> ▸ How did the challenge feel—was it fun? Frustrating? Scary? Confusing? Exciting?

> ▸ How did you feel about having to work together to solve the problem?

---

1. This activity is used with permission from the organization Training for Change (http://trainingforchange.org).

- Was it hard or easy to get the group to understand different ideas?

- Did you debate or argue about which ideas to try?

- What went well?

- What are some ways that you helped others understand your ideas?

- What are some ways you convinced other people to try your ideas?

Note: This reflection could be done in writing after small groups discuss the bullet points orally. Having a chance to write about an activity can help students get into the habit of written communication and reflection, too. One teacher we know who has a class set of tablets has her students add their reflections to a Google Doc. Then they sometimes view the document and discuss as a class any common themes they noticed.

Step 4: After reflecting on what happened, support the students to generalize. Record a list of what good group communication looks and sounds like. If students are having a hard time thinking about good group communication in general, have them turn and tell a partner what a really good group would have looked and sounded like as they solved the blanket challenge.

The Blanket Challenge helps students experience effective group work skills and effective communication, in situations where mathematics isn't a hurdle to communication, since students likely have some common vocabulary about flipping blankets. The key in using games like this one to help students become mathematical problem solvers is to help them *generalize* and *apply* this experience to mathematical tasks, so that they develop a repertoire of ways to talk mathematically and understand others' mathematical talk. An added bonus of focusing on communication with games like this is that they are also team-building games; they can help build a classroom environment that is safe for risk taking, sharing and comparing ideas, and publicly airing mistakes, where students don't use as many put-downs to deflect math questions or make fun of students they think are wrong. Having a supportive environment is also key to helping students be confident communicators.

You can end these team-building games with some self- and group reflection. One very handy tool that we alluded to is ending the game by making a "what worked" list—perhaps a list of what good groups look and sound like, or a list of things that help other people understand your ideas, or a list of good clarifying questions.

For example, I worked with a group of students at a local alternative school to brainstorm a list of what was needed for good group work in math. The students came up with:

- cooperation
- communication
  - staying on task
  - talking about math
- keeping your composure
  - dealing with frustration.

After we did a group problem-solving activity, I asked the students what they had done well relating to group work, and they come up with this (pretty impressive) list:

- used teamwork
- worked together
- kept an open mind
- listened to one another's ideas
- checked one another's work
- kept their composure (most of the time)
- stayed on task for almost an hour
- talked about math.

Stating their goals beforehand, and designating some students the job of paying attention to how well the team was doing and helping them remember to use teamwork, really helped the students stay focused. When one student grabbed the whiteboard marker from another, everyone said "Hey, teamwork!" and the students tried to quickly rein themselves back in. I was especially impressed because this group at the alternative school is particularly volatile, with many students constantly in fight-or-flight mode. The task of focusing on stated teamwork goals helped the students communicate what they needed from their groups and keep their composure during frustration.

Brainstorming lists of what we want to see before activities and/or what worked during the activities, and keeping these lists visible around the room, gives students gentle ways to remind each other how to make themselves understood, understand others' ideas, and be effective in learning from one another. When small groups or partners aren't functioning well, simply pointing to the students' list or asking them, "What kinds of behaviors helped you win the blanket challenge?" can help them refocus and remember that even in math class, they know how to talk to each other and get and give help.

The Blanket Challenge format can be used with a variety of mathematical puzzles and group challenges, and each one can be debriefed slightly differently, to help build lists around a range of helpful communication skills:

- strategies for coping with frustration (e.g., take a deep breath, get a drink of water, move to a different seat, ask someone to recap what you've done so far, ask for help)
- ways beyond words to share your ideas (e.g., draw a picture, use gestures, act it out, use math symbols)
- good clarification questions to ask when you don't understand someone (e.g., Can you tell me what you meant by this word? What did you notice that made you think of that? Could you show me what you mean with a picture? Could you point to what you're talking about?)
- how to talk so people can understand you (e.g., talk in an indoor voice; don't use words like *that one*, *stuff*, or *junk*; look at the person you're talking to; use descriptive words; give examples and counterexamples).

To find more mathematical puzzles and challenges for students to work on in groups and debrief their group communication, please visit the companion website for this book: http://mathforum.org/pps/. You'll find cooperative mathematical challenges such as trying to stretch a loop of rope into a perfect square (while blindfolded!), trying to build a square puzzle collaboratively without talking, or trying to master a human-sized version of wooden peg games played at truck stops and family restaurants.

Activities for Explaining Your Thinking and Learning from Others

One very common challenge in math class is that students struggle to use language that is precise enough to communicate their ideas. We'll address the role of precision in problem solving in later chapters, but since it's also a challenge that gets in the way of students even starting to work together to solve problems, compare multiple strategies, or reach consensus on a new understanding, we offer a few activities to help students surface the idea that precise language is important for successful problem solving and group work and that it's something they need to get better at.

ACTIVITY Mission Control

>   **Format:** Students working in pairs or groups of four.
>
>   **Materials:** Cardboard or manila folders to serve as dividers and pattern blocks or tangram sets.
>
>   **Step 1:** Determine which blocks will be used for Game 1.
>
>   *Suggestion:* Start with two each of two different polygons.
>
>   **Step 2:** Using the cardboard or manila folder to block others' views, one student in the group (or pair or class) constructs a pattern using the specified number of blocks.
>
>   **Step 3:** Set the scenario explaining that the person making the pattern using the specified number of blocks is Mission Control and all others participating are Space Ship Crew Members. The Space Ship Crew Members are on a mission and have encountered problems—they have only one-way communication with Mission Control! To find their way home, they must follow Mission Control's orders exactly to rebuild their panel of controls.
>
>   **Step 4:** Remind all students that there is only one-way communication, which means *only* Mission Control may speak!
>
>   **Step 5:** Looking at the "panel" of shapes, Mission Control carefully describes the position of the shapes using as precise vocabulary as possible to assist the crew in constructing the panel, which will enable them to return to Earth.
>
>   **Step 6:** As Mission Control speaks, the Crew Members listen and construct the panel using Mission Control's description.

Step 7: All students compare their control panel to that of Mission Control. If it is exactly the same, they return to Earth. If it is not exactly the same, they are lost in space!

Step 8: Discuss how precise vocabulary can be very helpful. Make a list of useful words (available for everyone to see) to assist in subsequent games.

Step 9: As skill in describing the configurations improves, add more blocks to the panel until all six different polygons have been used.

Note: If you have access to computers, you can use the pattern blocks virtual manipulative from the National Library of Virtual Manipulatives (http://nlvm.usu.edu). Students can use a program like Jing to record their work with the virtual manipulatives on their screens and the audio of Mission Control giving directions. Then later they can play them back and reflect on how they did. It might be fun for Mission Control to see too!

In debriefing this game with students, one of the key aspects we like to bring out is how their language changed over the course of the game. Most students start out by saying things like "Put the red in front of the blue," "Put the yellow on the edge of the table," and "Put the green next to the red." Then they start to realize things like:

- ▸ Color isn't as precise as geometric shape names, particularly if any students are color blind, or you play the game again with shapes of all one color such as tangrams!
- ▸ "Next to" doesn't take into consideration the orientation of the shape.
- ▸ Phrases like "long edge" or "vertex" or "rotate so that . . ." can make the direction more precise.

Students at first struggle with the precise language, the one-way directions (no questions allowed!), and listening to the directions from Mission Control. Many students don't think to use words like *rhombus*, *trapezoid*, or *hexagon* to describe the shapes. It's interesting to find out from them how they came to decide on names for the different pieces, and once they did, how they communicated about it.

Once students have played Mission Control, listen carefully to their reflections. Did they notice that it was hard to understand their classmates' descriptions and make the matching panel? Were students frustrated by their own inability to either articulate or understand others? Some great *generalizations* to take away from the Mission Control activity are:

- ▸ a list of precise math words to use to talk about shape, orientation, and location
- ▸ a list of clarifying questions to use to get more information about shape, orientation, and location
- ▸ a list of what good explainers did, or what made for a good explainer
- ▸ a list of what good listeners did, or what helped people understand their group mates.

Another classic "how to be precise" activity is the famous How to Make a Peanut Butter and Jelly Sandwich activity, in which students write or dictate instructions to a teacher who takes their words as literally as possible. *Note*: If peanut allergies are a concern, making a cheese sandwich is a fine alternative. We recommend those wrapped single slices; they're fun to mess with. Other nonedible alternatives are loading and using a stapler, creating a Facebook event, or putting a letter into an envelope, addressing it, and stamping it (assuming your students have ever done this!).

ACTIVITY Making a Peanut Butter and Jelly Sandwich

Format: Students working alone, then whole group, and then working in groups of four.

Materials: Enough containers of peanut butter, jelly, and bread for each pair of students to have one; plastic knives for each pair of students; plastic gloves and (optional) trash bags for students to make aprons from. Hotels, diners, and convenience stores might be able to sell or give you some single-serving packets of peanut butter and/ or jelly.

Step 0, the day before: Have each student write a description of the steps they would take to make a peanut butter and jelly sandwich. You might tell students that these directions are for an alien or a Neanderthal.

Step 1: Select some typical or interesting student descriptions and prepare in advance how you will act them out. Feel free to don a Neanderthal or alien costume but definitely wear an apron and gloves, as this can get messy! Take the students' instructions as literally as possible, and play up times when they skipped steps (e.g., put the peanut butter on the bread might be interpreted as balancing the jar of peanut butter on the loaf of bread). Model at least two sets of instructions. If you'd like to see some examples, searching YouTube or SchoolTube for "peanut butter jelly follow instructions" yields some good results (though you have to wade through some actual recipes for making PB&J) or visit the companion website for this book: http://mathforum.org/pps/.

Step 2: Put students into groups of four and give each group two sets of instructions that you modeled publicly. Working in pairs within their group of four, students revise the instructions so that someone as literal and silly as you modeled could successfully make a sandwich.

Step 3: Pairs swap their directions and use the materials provided to follow them literally. After attempting to make a sandwich, they give feedback on places the directions could have been clearer.

Step 4: The group of four puts their sets of directions together to make one set they're confident is foolproof.

Step 5: Collect each group's directions and randomly choose one to act out. Celebrate the increased success and precision!

Step 6: Debrief. Hear students' *reflections* on the process, and then support them to *generalize* their experience by thinking about (and making a list for) one of the following:

- ▸ how to write clearly for different audiences (aliens/Neanderthals versus friends versus teachers, for example)
- ▸ good words to use when writing step-by-step processes
- ▸ what works when editing other peoples' work
- ▸ what makes an explanation good.

One of the key features of the Making a Peanut Butter and Jelly Sandwich activity is the opportunity students have to edit other peoples' work and make a revised, improved version. We've found that for students who struggle to articulate their own ideas, the opportunity to use feedback to make an already-written explanation better can be a huge help. It's hard to come up with an explanation from scratch, so the process of improving someone else's work in light of specific feedback both exposes students to how other students explain mathematical ideas and also encourages them to think hard about what makes a good explanation.

Activities for Revising Your Thoughts

We've found that for students who struggle to articulate their own ideas, the opportunity to use feedback to make an already-written explanation better can be a huge help.

Remember the classroom we described at the beginning of this chapter? With the students who struggled to explain themselves, to such an extent that they ended up insulting each other? One of the most successful experiences the students had with explanations was when their teacher had them do an oral activity about classifying polygons (in pairs), then talk as a whole group about some of the polygons that had been hard to classify, and then finally work individually to write about each polygon based on the examples they heard in the group discussion. What made that series of tasks effective, we hypothesized, was that students only had to write on their own after having multiple layers of discussion and models, and that after hearing examples, they had a chance to try the task on their own. Doing some writing and then seeing examples isn't sufficient, and writing based on examples isn't quite enough either: students need to wrestle with the ideas, encounter feedback and examples, and then write or explain again (revise) based on the feedback. Revising others' work is a good start for struggling students; revising their own communication is a vital part of learning to become a mathematical communicator.

ACTIVITY Team Revision

Format: Students working in groups of two to four.

Step 0: Collect written explanations from each student about a problem she solved or topic she is learning. Group together papers that display similar understandings/explanations. For each group, choose one student's work that is representative and write (on a sticky note) one thing you *noticed* (and valued) about the student's work and one thing you are *wondering* (and would like her to address).[2] Make a copy of the work and feedback for each student in the group.

---

2. For more information on giving I Notice, I Wonder feedback and more strategies for helping students revise their thinking together, see Chapter 11.

Step 1: Let students know with whom they will be working. Have them sit in their groups. Give the student whose work you responded to their paper and feedback, and give everyone else their copy.

Step 2: One student in each group volunteers to read the feedback out loud to the group. The students discuss what they think the feedback means and what the author could do to address it.

Step 3: The group works together to answer the teacher's question.

Step 4: Each student uses his copy of the work the group focused on to rewrite the response in light of the group's answer to the teacher's question. The goal is to rewrite and revise, not just add on another paragraph. Think about how the writing could be improved.

Building Student Independence in Communicating

Mathematics is, in many ways, a foreign language. My Math Forum colleague Suzanne, who has taught conversational English in Spain and Germany in addition to teaching math and computers to middle school students, has noticed many parallels between learning to speak math and learning to speak a foreign language.[3] One parallel is that people tend to speak to one another in the language they first were introduced in. Our students come to us already speaking to one another in nonmathematical languages. Building student independence in mathematics can be a kind of foreign language immersion program: put them in situations where they need to make themselves understood about mathematics, in increasingly formal ways. Like tourists, they will start with gestures, pictures, pointing, and using their home language interspersed with key words. As they are asked to make themselves understood over and over again, and as they hear examples of people speaking at other, more fluent levels, they begin to pick up on the vocabulary and structures that make their task easier.

The chart at the beginning of this chapter is a very useful tool for both building student independence and tracking their progress. As we mentioned earlier, students need experiences writing and speaking in authentic tasks that give them natural feedback and are just outside their comfort zone. Goal setting and reflection on success, in the form of making lists of goals and what worked, can support students to focus on their communication skills while doing math. In the beginning of the year, the goals may be to use polite tones and ask questions instead of using put-downs. Later in the year, the goals can shift to asking good questions, using appropriate math vocabulary, telling why and how you know, and so on.

In addition, students learning to "speak math" need lots of opportunities to get feedback, hear/read examples, and make revisions based on what they saw and heard. Students develop their skills by attempting to communicate, hearing from someone else what was clear and unclear, and revising. This can be facilitated by new technology that allows students to use

Building student independence in mathematics can be a kind of foreign-language immersion program: put them in situations where they need to make themselves understood about mathematics, in increasingly formal ways.

Students need experiences writing and speaking in authentic tasks that give them natural feedback and are just outside their comfort zone.

---

3. You can see a video of her giving a talk about these ideas on the companion website, http://mathforum.org/pps/.

computers, tablets, and smartphones to capture their work and have it reviewed by peers. One teacher we know assigned his students homework of watching *one* of their peers' podcasts of how they solved a problem, and when they came in the next day all students had watched every single other video and were full of insights into the math and insights into how to improve their mathematical communication!

Using Communication to Get Unstuck

A common refrain in math classrooms is students who have stopped working on a problem and when they are asked, "What's up?" they answer, "I don't get it!" When their teacher asks "What don't you 'get'?" the student invariably replies, "The whole thing!" But then, on further questioning, the student often reveals quite a bit that they do understand about the story, what the question is asking, and what mathematics they might use to solve the problem. Something has certainly derailed them, but they aren't communicating what, specifically, is the problem. Here are some of our favorite prompts for helping students communicate about where they are stuck and ask for help in a more specific way:

- ▸ What's going on in the problem? What's it about?
- ▸ What's making this problem hard for you? Tell me everything you can that looks hard.
- ▸ On a scale of one to ten, how hard do you think this problem is? Why?
- ▸ What's one thing that you noticed when you read the problem? What stood out to you?
- ▸ What are you wondering about the problem?
- ▸ Can you tell me one thing you *do* get about the problem?
- ▸ If your math fairy godmother appeared right now and she could tell you one thing to help you get started, what would you ask for?

As students get used to the fact that any complaints of "I don't get it!" will be met with probing follow-up questions that get them talking and thinking about the problem, they often start to anticipate and tell you more about the problem in hopes of getting to your help fast. Instead of hearing, "I don't get it!," you might hear, "I don't get it . . . I mean, I get that it's about ostriches and llamas and we know how many heads and how many legs there are together, but I don't understand how we can use that because ostriches and llamas have different numbers of legs so we can't just divide and I don't know what I would divide by anyway—can you help me?" As you start to establish the expectation that students need to give you some details about their thinking for you to give them effective support at getting unstuck, you can also remind them of some of the communication norms you've been establishing. "This is sort of like the Mission Control game. I can help you best if you can tell me clearly what you're thinking so far, using your best math words." As students become better at telling you where they're stuck, you just might hear that music-to-math-teachers'-ears phrase: "Oh, wait, never mind! I just figured it out while I was explaining it to you!"

Conclusion: The Role of Communicating (and Listening!)

In this book, much of the learning about problem solving, sense making, and developing the mathematical practices will be through students trying to solve problems in particular ways, comparing their methods and thinking with others using structured comparison activities, reflecting on what happened and what they noticed, generalizing this one experience into a concrete idea about how they could improve, and finally applying that new idea or deepened skill to a new challenge.

This kind of learning is not what many students are used to at school (or even outside of school) and presents some challenges, such as learning to:

> ▸ "hang in there" and persevere as they encounter the initial challenge that they will reflect on and eventually learn from
>
> ▸ share their own ideas so others can make use of them
>
> ▸ use resources to evaluate ideas
>
> ▸ come to consensus.

We hope some of the challenges in this chapter help students experience persevering, communicating, working with a group, and coming to agreements. But the other half of communication is listening. To be someone who learns effectively from communicating with teachers and peers, students also need to:

> ▸ listen to alternate ideas and make sense of multiple student viewpoints (and notice when others' ideas don't make sense!)
>
> ▸ compare their thinking with the thinking of others
>
> ▸ handle the ambiguity of entertaining multiple possible correct and incorrect ideas until the problems are resolved.

In the next chapter, we'll focus explicitly on the listening portions of learning through working together.

3

Learning Through Listening

Focal practices:

3. Construct viable arguments and critique the reasoning of others.
6. Attend to precision.

Students can get pretty far in many math classes only listening to the teacher and only listening for step-by-step instructions on how to get to the answer. Most of us will recognize the description of the student (often quiet, hardworking, and with good grades) who sits patiently in math class, doodling or daydreaming, until the teacher (or an acknowledged "smart kid") starts going over how to get the answer. Then our doodler springs into action, copying down each step, creating a template to apply to that night's homework, tomorrow's class work, and next week's test.

Listening and Sense Making

What's wrong with that picture? Students who aren't working on active listening skills are missing a huge opportunity for practicing their sense making. One of the main differences we witness when we enter a classroom where students are learning math at high levels is that most of the students in the class are exhibiting signs of active listening and sense making. When their teachers or peers make statements, they ask for clarification or illustration, make a comparison to another idea, or ask how this idea fits into something they already know. We witness students who have a belief that math should make sense and they can make sense of it. When they hear something, they work to understand it.

When we walk into classes that have been labeled as "low-level" or "underperforming," we often witness students who seem to be taking everything in passively. They copy down everything that's on the board, without asking questions or asking for clarifications. We rarely hear students ask questions that help them figure out, "How does this fit with what I already know?" Students who are underperforming in math are often stuck in the belief that they can't make sense of math, and that it's something they receive from others ("smart people") and have to memorize and mimic. Although they might learn, through passive listening and lots of memorization and repetition, many of the procedures mathematicians use to solve problems, it's likely that they're struggling to understand how and when to apply those tools, how to use their tools in novel problem-solving situations, and worst of all, how to come up with new tools in situations that they don't yet know how to solve. When we don't hear students actively engaged in sense making as they listen to others speak, we instead hear questions like "Is there a formula for this?," "How will I ever memorize all this?," "Do we have to know this for the test?," and statements like "I don't get how I'm supposed to know what to do" or "None of these questions looks like the examples you did."

The Role of Listening in Building Thinking Skills

People often criticize problem-based learning in math classrooms, claiming (not unfairly) that it tends to devolve into disorganized work on a series of problems and doesn't lead to firm conceptual understanding and procedural fluency. In other words, students work in groups on math problems, but they never take what they've done and turn it into thinking tools. For example, you may have heard that elementary students using problem-based curricula invent all sorts of ways to solve multiplication problems, but those methods are slow and complicated and bog students down when they need to use multiplication quickly in the context of harder problems. We often find that students who are solving lots of problems without solidifying their results into efficient skills are also students who don't have opportunities to listen to multiple approaches and compare them. They aren't taking their approach, actively comparing it to other approaches, and coming up with a best approach. Reflecting on the mathematics that's been done, comparing and understanding multiple approaches, and coming to conclusions about good approaches and tools to use in the future are not just good habits of mind for problem solving, they're key elements in supporting students to learn mathematical skills and content from solving problems.

> *In a classroom with lots of listening, some important work **begins** when students get an initial answer, because that's a moment when they're ready to listen to other ideas and start to learn from their answer.*

In a classroom with lots of listening, some important work *begins* when students get an initial answer, because that's a moment when they're ready to listen to other ideas and start to learn from their answer. And there are lots of moments in the problem-solving process when good, active listening can take the experience from a get-to-the-answer experience to a learn-some-serious-math experience.

In many science, and particularly physics, classrooms, teachers are adopting a classroom approach called "Model-Based Physics." In these classrooms, students design and carry out initial physics experiments, such as predicting what will make a car roll down a hill faster, and then collect data from their experiment. They create a conceptual or mathematical model to account for their data (such as explaining whether adding weight to the front of the car made it go faster than adding weight to the back of the car, and why), and then they compare their models. Once they come to consensus on a model that explains the data, they run further experiments to prove or disprove their model, such as experimenting with reducing friction, increasing the angle of the hill, and so on to make sure their model accurately accounts for all those variables.

In the Model-Based Physics classrooms, the students don't just carry out experiments and learn about isolated results, they synthesize the results of multiple experiments into accurate conceptual understanding of the physical world, understanding that allows them to answer typical physics problems from a traditional course. The key features are that students base their work on actively seeking to build on what they currently understand, they must compare and come to consensus on the best model out of many possible models, and once they have done something, they reflect on it, relate it to their current understanding and work hard to turn their new thoughts into useful tools they can apply to solve more physics problems. Active listening skills are such an important component of Model-Based Physics that the first lessons in these classrooms in September are on group listening skills, coming to consensus, and comparing ideas.

Encouraging Active Listening

The first step in creating a classroom in which students actively listen to one another is to convince students that what their classmates are saying is worth listening to. It sounds obvious, but students come to us with a lot of experience suggesting that peers don't have anything to say. A common belief among teachers in the United States is that hearing a peer say something will only confuse students—students are certainly much less likely than teachers to be consistently clear and correct with precise language. And so when our students talk, we often rephrase what they say. We revoice for students who are quiet, we reword for students who aren't precise, we reframe for students who aren't correct. The long-term effect of this reasonable strategy is that students learn that they don't have to pay attention while another student is speaking, they can just wait for the teacher to say it again, louder. Similarly, as teachers we often get in the habit of calling on students until we hear the answer we're listening for. Kids are astute social observers and so they learn to wait for "the smart kid" to be called on, or for the answer that the teacher smiles and nods at, or the answer the teacher repeats.

The first step in creating a classroom in which students actively listen to one another is to convince students that what their classmates are saying is worth listening to.

Think of a conversation at an animated dinner party. You are excited to be hanging out with all of these interesting, smart, funny people. There's a topic that's been on your mind lately, and so you ask the group of people you're sitting with about it, perhaps saying, "Has anyone here seen the new movie adaptation of that really popular book? I want to see it but I haven't read the book. Should I read the book first?" Because you value the opinion of your fellow dinner guests, you're likely to listen to each of their opinions in turn. Even if you really want to hear someone say, "Go ahead and see the movie. Both are so good that it's worth seeing the movie even if you plan to read the book later," you're not going to wait until you hear that and then say, "Very good, John! Did everyone hear what John said about the movie?" If you did that repeatedly at dinner parties, you wouldn't be invited back—or if you were, no one would answer your questions and even if they did, no one would listen to other people's answers. Scintillating conversation comes when someone asks a question that she is interested in multiple answers to, and everyone listens to and is accountable to each other's answer.

Some suggestions for making whole-group conversations in math class more like conversations at a dinner party:

▸ Don't repeat or rephrase what students say—it takes up class time and gets students out of the habit of listening to others.

▸ If a student is speaking too quietly, invite him to repeat himself rather than repeating for him.

▸ Make sure multiple students respond to each question before asking another.

▸ Ask questions that you don't already know how your students will answer. (You might have anticipated multiple possible answers while planning the lesson, but the key is that you are listening to and learning about what your students think, not listening for and confirming what you told them.)

▸ Occasionally, ask questions that you don't know the answer to (but that you and your students might have ideas on how to investigate).

▸ Ask questions that have multiple possible answers, such as "What do you think is the most useful way you could represent this, and why might someone else want to represent it differently?"

▸ When students respond to each other through you, remind them to turn and talk to the person whose idea they are addressing.

▸ Encourage students to reflect back what they are hearing or offer alternate ways to say the same thing, as well as asking, "Is this another way to say what you're saying?" or "Am I understanding you correctly to mean this?"

▸ Rotate the task of facilitating the discussion   let students lead activities they are familiar with, such as an I Notice, I Wonder brainstorm.

▸ Give students the role of summing up the discussion.

▸ Listen *to* students' ideas, don't just listen *for* correct thinking.[1]

Modeling good listening skills and acting like a dinner party host (bringing together interesting people with good ideas, asking questions or providing activities to help them start talking, and then backing out of the way and encouraging them to talk to one another) go a long way in helping students pick up on the idea that their peers have useful things to say. Another way teachers can act like hosts, support peer-to-peer communication, and maximize the time for student talk is by supporting more small-group conversation. After all, at a successful party, many small conversations are going on at once. Eavesdropping here and there, or stepping back to listen to the overall tone of the room, lets the host know that the guests are having a stimulating, enjoyable time, but the host doesn't need to be facilitating every conversation to know they are worthwhile. Of course, what host can resist asking a few guests for a recap from time to time—but it doesn't always have to be right after the party either. The host might check in a day or two later, or just pay attention for later evidence that

---

1. I tackled this topic further in an Ignite talk at the National Council of Teachers of Mathematics conference in 2011. You can find a link to the video at the companion website: http://mathforum.org/pps/.

her guests enjoyed and learned from each other's company! Similarly, the classroom teacher can be a good host by allowing students to have small-group conversations, eavesdropping or watching the "hum" of the room to ensure they are productive, and only checking in briefly as a whole group if it seems necessary to get broader input on the topic.

Suzanne has been working with middle school teachers in a nearby district, helping them be good "conversation hosts" in their classrooms. She recently shared a story of a day when everything came together and the students and teacher had a lot of great conversations together: conversations that supported learning as students heard ideas that challenged their current thinking, conversations that supported the teacher to do formative assessment and learn where her students struggled and where they were successful, and conversation that supported students' engagement and self-concept as they had interesting conversations and felt successful in math class.

The students were working on a neat problem from their curriculum about making chocolate leaves. They had some different leaf shapes and graph paper to use as tools to help them figure out how much chocolate they would need to pour to make each leaf. Their teacher had read carefully through the teacher's guide and student materials to think about the key experiences she wanted the students to have and what she wanted to hear them talk about to assess their current understanding. She also thought about how to provide some different activities to help keep students alert and engaged throughout the ninety-minute math period and to have multiple opportunities for students to converse and multiple ways for her to listen.

They started with an opening exercise in which students listed three things in their classroom that had area, and then they shared out and made a class list on chart paper. This helped the students remember the unit topic and connect to their current ideas of area. Then the teacher led a whole-class discussion on the topic of "What is area?" She was excited to see that her students were starting to respond directly to each other, asking for clarification or answering each other's questions, instead of always only speaking directly to her. In addition, by asking the open-ended question "What is area?" she was able to hear students' wide range of thoughts, including some confusion about the relationship between area and perimeter. She did not know how her students would describe the concept of area, and welcomed each student's attempt to articulate their thinking—there was not a correct definition that she had in mind she was hoping to move students toward. Instead, she was interested in listening to their current thinking to plan how she might respond to students later in the period. Suzanne, who was observing the lesson, noticed that the teacher did not try to rephrase or push her students in one direction, nor did she respond to some attempts to answer more positively than others. Suzanne could tell that this helped more and more students risk answering this difficult question!

Next, the teacher wanted to get even more students talking and listening. She explained to the students that they would turn and talk to their elbow partners, and they briefly discussed the expectations for what "turn and talk" looks and sounds like: only talking to the person next to you, taking turns, listening to each other's ideas, and facing one another. The teacher displayed the chocolate leaves story and images from the students' textbook and the groups began talking. At first the students were very focused on the story context and less on the math behind it (they talked a lot about chocolate!), but as the groups continued to talk, they began to focus more and more on the question of how much chocolate, and by extension, the area of each leaf shape. Again the teacher circulated and listened to the groups, getting a sense of how even more of her students were making sense of area. She heard a wide range of effective and ineffective strategies, from counting how many squares of the grid paper were covered and using estimation and fractions to count partial squares to trying to figure out the perimeter and somehow use that to find the area.

She moved from the first turn-and-talk activity right into a second one. She didn't feel that the group needed to debrief as a whole yet because they were still just starting to grapple with the idea of area of irregular shapes and she didn't think the groups were ready to compare strategies yet. Instead, she displayed another irregular shape on grid paper that she asked students to find the area of. She noticed that this time, students used a wider range of counting-based strategies, such as counting the area *not* covered by the image, or thinking about breaking apart and rearranging the image to make a more regular shape.

At this point, she decided to debrief as a whole group because she wanted students to begin to consider the range of strategies for finding the area of an irregular shape. The main theme of this unit was strategies for breaking apart and rearranging figures to consider their area, and so she wanted the students to reflect on some of those ideas. She asked a few of the groups to share how they had thought about the second turn-and-talk prompt and was pleased to see that her students seemed interested and engaged in hearing how their peers had approached the problem and that they were starting to make sense of the idea that multiple approaches could work for the same area question. Ending the period with an exit question about area gave her one more chance to check each student's understanding and look for ways their thinking might have changed through the many rich conversations about area they had.

The activities that follow offer some more ways to help students work independently in small groups while focusing on their active listening skills. They also provide some structure for students to actively organize and make use of what they hear.

Activities

Activities for Encouraging Active Listening

One way to encourage active listening is to give students a challenge that requires each team member to understand the whole team's strategy. This challenge does put individuals on the spot, but, like professional cycling, those individuals really reflect the performance of the whole team. Help students see that if their teammate doesn't follow the team's strategy, then it was the team's collective failure to ensure each member was ready to shine.

What follows are two different possible games you could use in the team challenge. The first, which I call Red Versus Blue, is the leading candidate for the Grade 6 $1,000,000 Unsolved Problem on the site http://mathpickle.com, run by Dr. Gordon Hamilton, which has a great collection of games and activities for "hard fun." Most of the activities are accessible to students in grades K–8, and yet they connect to some of the greatest unsolved math problems of all times! The other, The Take-Away Game, is a version of a pretty common type of strategy game (sometimes called "Nim") that's been analyzed by mathematicians and game theorists for years. But it was math coach Bob Lochel's blog post "The Takeaway Game" on his Math Coach Blog (http://mathcoachblog.wordpress.com/2012/11/20/the-take-away-game/) that convinced me that third-grade students could develop strategies and play the game competitively.

I've played Red Versus Blue with a wide range of ages, from elementary students who only recently learned about prime and composite numbers to college students. The game has almost infinite levels of challenge. (Red can choose easier or harder numbers to start with, both teams can have time limits imposed or take as long as they need but even students who need a reminder about prime numbers catch on quickly and start to think strategically.) The first time I played this game with students, I had them playing two-on-two. I noticed that often one teammate in the pair would figure out a strategy—I could tell by the student's confident answers that always gave their team the advantage—but then they would gallantly say to their teammate (trying to be a good partner!), "Why don't you pick the numbers for this round?" Their teammates would hesitantly offer a number and usually lose the round. As I reflected on the "teamwork" being displayed, I realized that just taking turns and making sure everyone talks isn't enough. To be a successful team, every member has to be responsible for the whole team's understanding. People who are having success have a responsibility to explain their success to their teammates, and their teammates have a responsibility to ask clarifying questions until they too understand the strategy. As Suzanne would say, everyone has a responsibility to *facilitate*. It was from that experience that the team challenge activity was born.

ACTIVITY Team Challenge

This activity can be used with a variety of mathematical strategy games (Mastermind, Nim, etc.). We share two examples here, one (Red Versus Blue) for students who are familiar with prime and composite numbers, and one (Take Away) suitable for all levels. The key is to focus students on debriefing the experience, and particularly how listening was part of both understanding and explaining the team strategy.

Format: Students preparing in teams and then playing one another individually.

Step 0: Teach the whole group the games (rules for each game follow). Then, break students into teams of four. Have them play several two-on-two rounds of the games until they feel that they have a strategy for playing the games well.

Step 1: Each team chooses a strategy. Players should ask clarifying questions and practice to be sure they're confident that everyone understands the strategy. (For Red Versus Blue, they'll need to have a strategy to play as Red and as Blue.)

Step 2: Using a single-elimination tournament-style competition, pair teams up to go head-to-head. The catch: Each player on a team takes turns playing, and teams cannot comment or help teammates at all. So the teams win or lose based on how well all the teammates understand the strategy, as well as how good their strategy is.

Step 3: Finally, bring all the team members together to debrief how they learned and explained their strategy. In addition to reflecting on what happened and how it felt, make a class list of either good listening skills or good clarifying questions. If students want to talk about what they did to explain well, or how their teammates weren't good explainers, shift the talk to what they did to *listen* well, and how they could have used questions to get better explanations. For example, good explainers have to listen to be sure their ideas are understood—how did students tell if their classmates understood them?

Rules for the games:

Red Versus Blue: In this game, players write two multiplication problems. The Blue team represents peace, harmony, and equality. In other words, they want the multiplication problems to be equal. The Red team represents conflict, mischief, and inequality. In other words, they want the multiplication problems not to be equal. Each side will take turns choosing the numbers for their problems, with the Blue teams trying to make equal products, and the Red team trying to make unequal products. (If needed, review prime and composite numbers.)

Write a blank multiplication problem on the board, like this:

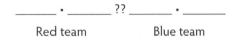

_____ • _____ ?? _____ • _____

Red team   Blue team

You might ask, "Which team wants the question marks to be an equal sign? Which team wants it to be a not equal to sign?" to check for understanding.

Move 1: The Red team chooses first. The members choose a *composite* number for the first number in their multiplication problem. Have the students toss out a composite number. Fill it in the first blank for the Red team.

Move 2: The Blue team chooses next. The members choose a *prime* number for the first number in their multiplication problem. Have the students toss out a prime number. Fill in the first blank for the Blue team.

Move 3: The Red team chooses again. The teammates choose a *prime* number to complete their multiplication problem. Have the students toss out a prime number to complete Red's moves. Fill in the last blank for the Red team.

Move 4: Remind students of the goal: the Blue team wants the two products to come out equal. Ask students, "Is there a *composite* number that Blue members could pick so that their product will equal the Red team's product?" (Usually the answer will be no, if students were just tossing out their favorite numbers in previous steps.) If the Blue team members can find a *composite* number to make the products equal, they get a point. If not, the Red team wins a point.

Sample Round:

Red team chooses first, a composite number:

<u>   14   </u> • <u>   </u> ?? <u>   </u> • <u>   </u>
      Red team   Blue team

Blue team chooses second, a prime number:

<u>   14   </u> • <u>   </u> ?? <u>   3   </u> • <u>   </u>
      Red team   Blue team

Red team chooses third, a prime number:

<u>   14   </u> • <u>   5   </u> ?? <u>   3   </u> • <u>   </u>
      Red team   Blue team

Blue team chooses last, a composite number. If the members can make the products equal, they win:

<u>   14   </u> • <u>   5   </u> ?? <u>   3   </u> • <u>   X   </u>
      Red team   Blue team

Blue teammates figure out that they can't win this round. There is no composite number that you can multiply by 3 to get 70 (14 • 5). They would have to use a fraction and fractions aren't composite numbers. Red wins! What could Blue members have done differently on their first turn to give them a better chance at winning? What could Red have done to make Blue's job harder or easier?

Take Away: In this game, the winner is the person who takes the last piece. In each turn, players may choose to take away one, two, or three pieces.

Write thirty-five dots on the board, like this:

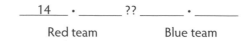

Move 1: Player 1 crosses out one, two, or three dots. For example, the board might look like:

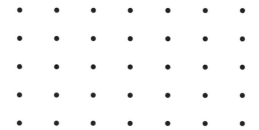

Move 2: Player 2 crosses out one, two, or three dots.

End: Play continues until one of the players can cross out the last dot. The player that crossed out the last dot is the winner.

ACTIVITY Clarifying Questions Mingle[2]

Another activity that supports students to get better at asking questions (and involves moving around, too!) is an activity structure called a "Mingle."

Format: Students walking around the classroom.

Step 0: Using a topic that you've been studying, ask each student to write or think of a short explanation (1–2 sentences) of a problem or idea. For example, students might explain how to solve a two-digit addition problem, a fraction multiplication problem, or a specific two-step equation. Or they might explain why the sum of any two sides of a triangle has to be greater than the length of the third side, or why $2(5 + 4) = 2 \cdot 5 + 2 \cdot 4$.

Step 1: Students stand up and mingle like they're at a fancy party. Each time they come up to someone or make eye contact, *one* person should say or read their explanation of the problem.

Step 2: After most students have had a chance to say their explanation, add a second step to the mingle: after you hear an explanation, ask one clarifying question. At this point, students *should not answer the questions.* Just have one student explain and another person ask a question.

Step 3: After students have had a chance to ask questions of 2–3 people, start a third round. This time, one student says her explanation, the partner asks a clarifying question, and the explainer answers the question.

Step 4: Debrief the experience. Ask students how it felt to ask for clarification. Ask for clarifying questions that seemed to work well, and ask what made them work well. You might make a class list of great clarifying questions. This can become a resource for groups that are stuck or don't seem to be communicating clearly.

Variation: Another version of Mingle that gets students practicing listening and restating is to have students, on round 2 of the mingle, state back, "What I hear you saying is . . ." and try to repeat their partner's explanation. On round 3 of the mingle, students confirm or correct their partner's version of their explanation.

Variation for large classes: With a larger group, doing a fishbowl version is less chaotic: A group of 6–8 students mingles while the rest of the students listen for questions they especially like. For each round of mingling, switch participants so many students get an opportunity to mingle as well as listen. The first round you might have students simply act out mingling on a topic they are all familiar with (asking about Halloween costumes, for

---

2. This activity was developed by Training for Change, www.trainingforchange.org.

example) and have the role-players and audience focus on good mingling behavior, like walking, using an indoor voice, being brief, looking to see if anyone is free to chat, waiting politely if everyone is engaged, and so on.

Activities for Listening to Compare and Contrast

Following is an activity that we've used to practice getting better at comparing and contrasting different representations or methods for solving the same problem. Suzanne recently used the activity in a fourth-grade classroom to help students think about different ways to visually represent fractions. In a previous session, she had students make an illustration showing how four people could share some pizza if two of them wanted mushrooms, one wanted pepperoni, and one wanted extra cheese. Suzanne then made a handout for each pair of students with two of their classmates' pictures, side by side:

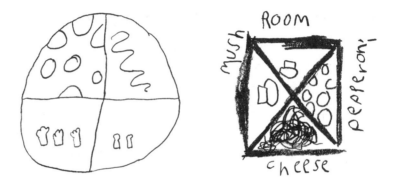

She asked the students what they noticed and wondered about the pictures, specifically asking them to notice things that were *the same* or *different*, and to identify things that they *wondered if they were the same and different*.

She had students look and think first, then turn and talk to their elbow partners, and then had the elbow partners volunteer to share things that were the same, things that were different, and things that they wondered if they were the same or different.

Here are some of the things they noticed and wondered about:

Same

- ▸ Each has pepperoni, extra cheese, and mushrooms.
- ▸ The two pizzas have the same toppings.
- ▸ $\frac{2}{4}$ of the pizza is mushroom, $\frac{1}{4}$ of the pizza is pepperoni, and $\frac{1}{4}$ of the pizza has extra cheese.

Different

- ▸ One is a square and one is a circle.

Suzanne noticed that as the students talked, some were focusing more on the pizza toppings than on the shapes or equal parts. She asked them to put their math hats on, and it was after all the students cheerfully mimed putting a hat on that they started to notice the fractions that were the same in both pictures!

Then, she passed out a sheet with a third picture added and had them look and think, turn and talk, and share out:

Suzanne and the students had a conversation about what was the same and what was different in Pizza Drawing 3. The students noticed that all three drawings had the right toppings for each person (mushrooms for Mom and Dad and extra cheese and pepperoni for Drew and his sister). They also noticed that one thing that was different in Pizza Drawing 3 was that there were two pizzas instead of one. The students seemed to be divided on whether that meant there were four equal parts in that drawing, so Suzanne asked the class, "Are there four equal parts in Pizza Drawing 3?" Some students voted "yes" and some voted "no" and some voted both "yes" and "no." Since the idea of equal parts and different wholes are so important in thinking about fractions, Suzanne decided to have students write something about their thinking. After wrapping up the conversation, Suzanne passed out paper and asked the students to each write their responses.

Are there 4 equal parts is pizza drawing #3

yes because, if you add
2 equal parts plus another you get
4 equal parts

Are there 4 equal parts in pizza drawing
#3?

I said no because there are
two pizza's and they both are cut into 2 equal parts.
I think they would have to intersect for it to become
4 equal. In the story the family made one pizza
not two so if they where to try and split it using
to pizza each pizza would have two equal
parts it would need to be one pizza so it
from be equal.

but they don't intersect
so there not 4 equal parts

Are there 4 equal parts
in drawing 3?

NO	YES
I think NO because there are two pizza's when there are only suppose to be 1 with four equal parts with all the toppings on it.	I think yes because there are 4 equal parts but 2 pizza's.

The students noticed all sorts of mathematically important differences and similarities among the pictures they drew. There was so much in their conversation for Suzanne to learn about their thinking about fractions and wholes as well. The opportunity to talk about similarities and differences gave students a chance to start to question, and eventually deepen, their understanding of fractions: two pizzas divided into two equal parts can also be thought of as one meal divided into fourths. The activity below sums up the comparison activity at the heart of Suzanne's story, the activity in which students worked on comparing and contrasting other students' work.

ACTIVITY What's the Same? What's Different?

In the version of the activity that follows, students produce and compare their own individual drawings or solution methods. However, it also works well to do what Suzanne did, and have all of the groups look at the same pieces of work, shared on the projector or passed out to each elbow pair. A student friendly handout is available on the companion website, http://mathforum.org/pps/.

Format: Students working in small groups.

Step 0: Give students a task, such as solving a problem, making a table, drawing a picture to represent or solve a problem, or making a rule for a pattern. Have students work on the task in such a way that each student creates his or her own individual result.

Step 1: In elbow pairs, instruct students to share their drawings, then work together to answer these prompts:

- ▸ What is the same in both drawings?
- ▸ What is different between the drawings?
- ▸ What are you wondering if it is the same or different?
  - ◆ What is one thing that looks different but could secretly be the same in both drawings?
  - ◆ What is one thing that looks the same but could secretly be different between the drawings?

Step 2: Invite two students from different pairs to the front of the room to share their drawings.

Step 3: The pairs should join with the rest of their groups of four, and answer the same prompts:

- ▸ What is the same in both drawings?
- ▸ What is different between the drawings?
- ▸ What are you wondering if it is the same or different?
  - ◆ What is one thing that looks different but could secretly be the same in both drawings?
  - ◆ What is one thing that looks the same but could secretly be different between the drawings?

The compare-and-contrast routine is an important listening skill! The purpose of listening to other students in math class isn't to be polite (though that's always nice), it's to get valuable information for learning more math. So listening in math class is really about doing something with the information that you hear (or read). One of the most fundamental listening skills for mathematics is being able to compare and contrast different things you are hearing. There are all sorts of deep, philosophical reasons for this, such as:

- Mathematics is the science of patterns, and patterns are about finding out what's always the same and repeating it.
  - *Example*: Find the patterns in this list: (1, 1), (2, 4), (3, 9), (4, 16).
- Mathematics is about resolving ambiguity—finding what's fundamentally the same about two concepts that appear different.
  - *Example*: How can $\frac{2}{9}$ be a single number and a division of two numbers at the same time?
- Mathematics is about equivalence—proving that two ways to say the same thing really are the same.
  - *Example*: How can "The rule is triple the number" and "The rule is add the number to itself and then add it again" both be the answer to the same problem?
- Mathematics is about rigor—finding out that two things that superficially appear the same are really quite different.
  - *Example*: How can $(5 + 3)2 = (5)2 + (3)2$ but $(5 + 3)^2 \neq 5^2 + 3^2$?

But there are all sorts of other reasons to get good at comparing and contrasting, too, like:

- It helps you check your work. How else will you know if your answers are different, and if so, why?
- It helps you check if your understanding of a story or a problem is the same as everyone else's.
- It helps you figure out if another idea is really new or just a new-sounding way of saying the same thing.
- It helps you find and use patterns to generate your own shortcuts.
- It helps you compare two methods to see which is fastest, easiest, most accurate, and so on.
- It helps you connect ideas that are shown in different ways, like connecting a story to a drawing to a math sentence.

Building Independence in Listening

As we described in the beginning of the chapter, one of the most important ways for teachers to support students to become active listeners is to remove themselves from the conversation. Students are forced to listen to their peers when the teacher physically removes herself from the conversation. One teacher we worked with realized that her students were so used to running a group brainstorm activity that they could anticipate the questions she was going to ask. So one day, she announced that they were going to lead the activity and solve the problem, and she'd be in the back of the room grading papers. She made such a show of sitting at her desk, busily sorting through papers, that the students quickly realized they were on their own (even though she was actually listening quite attentively to what they were doing). They led the activity, and when they got stuck, one of them piped up with, "Well, Ms. B's not going to help us. She's busy. We've got to figure this out."

Of course, students don't always know how to work productively and listen to one another whether or not there is a teacher there to rely on. Early on in introducing active listening behaviors and norms, you may want to begin any group work session or time when the whole class will be listening to student thinking with an explicit review of "What should I see and hear when you're being active listeners?" If students have already generated these lists, reviewing them and giving feedback on some good things you've seen lately and some areas that students might give special attention to is a great way to launch small-group work. After bringing students back from groups, in addition to reviewing the math they did, reviewing how they worked together and giving more feedback as well as letting them self-evaluate can support them in continuing to recall the focus on listening.

When you are explicitly focusing on listening skills, the mathematics is taking a back seat to the prerequisite social and cognitive listening skills. But as you notice students reminding each other of good listening behaviors and exhibiting them with less prompting, you will be able to fade out the time spent previewing the listening you want to witness and reviewing the listening that did and didn't happen. You might look for (in rough order of listening development).

- ▸ Students staying on task and not having side conversations while others are talking/working.
- ▸ Students reminding one another to come back from side conversations.
- ▸ Students all paying attention to the one person speaking.
- ▸ Students asking other students, "I don't understand, could you explain that again?"
- ▸ Students indicating agreement and disagreement with each other's ideas.
- ▸ Phrases that indicate connections: "When you said . . ." "That made me think of . . ." "Is that like this?" "I see what you're saying." "Like when _____ said. . . ."
- ▸ Students asking other students, "How did you get that?"
- ▸ Students asking other students, "How did you know?"
- ▸ Students comparing their own and other's work to the given information, problem constraints, background knowledge, or mathematical definitions.
- ▸ Students using polite language to communicate disagreement, like, "I wonder if you thought about . . ." or "I got something different, did you maybe do this. . . ."

When students are getting good at asking for clarification and keeping one another focused in explicitly listening-focused activities, you might try asking them to solve a problem in a small group and simply observe to what extent they continue to use their listening skills. If they do, help them notice and reflect on what they did well. If they did not, remind them of their skills and help them notice and reflect on some specific things they want to do next time. Then try again the next day!

Once you are no longer previewing key listening skills and reviewing them at the end of every lesson, it becomes a matter of reminding students, and helping students remind each other, during the lesson. At first, specifically assigning each group a facilitator whose job is to help the group practice active listening can help students learn to monitor their own group work. As the teacher, you can then focus on the mathematics students are discussing, as long as your facilitators stay on top of their job.

As you observe students needing only occasional, increasingly less obtrusive nudges from their facilitator, the role will start to fade out. After a good group work session, let students know that you saw them doing a great job of facilitating themselves and that next time you'd like everyone to focus on the mathematics and the listening, and see if they can all participate using active listening and contributing their mathematical ideas.

Using Listening to Get Unstuck

Successful groups had real conversations, with students paying attention to one idea at a time, building on it, agreeing or disagreeing, or comparing it to their own thinking.

When students are working in pairs or small groups and get stuck, sometimes it is their listening skills that are getting in the way. In a 2003 study, Brigid Barron observed as forty-eight sixth-grade students worked in groups of three to solve problems about a journey taken by a character in a fifteen-minute video they'd watched in class. What she noticed was that even when the students were individually all of similar mathematics skill levels, some groups were able to solve the problems successfully and others weren't. When members of groups that had not solved the problem were asked to solve similar problems later, they did less well than students whose groups had solved the problem. She reasoned that something about how the groups interacted was affecting their learning. When she carefully observed the video, she noticed that even unsuccessful groups had lots of ideas that could have led to successful problem solving. However, the unsuccessful groups did not take up the good ideas offered by group members. They tended to work in parallel, with each person tackling a different idea. The students in both the successful and unsuccessful groups talked, but only the successful groups had real conversations, with students paying attention to one idea at a time, building on it, agreeing or disagreeing, or comparing it to their own thinking.[3]

Teachers can support groups to get unstuck through modeling and supporting active listening. First of all, teachers can model listening themselves, as they listen to each small group and take time to do some quick assessment before intervening. This way, if group members are already conversing, they avoid interrupting, which would be a way of making the group less successful. And if the group does seem to be unsuccessful, jumping in with advice before observing how the students are interacting wouldn't be very effective—if the group isn't functioning, members won't pick up the tip and work effectively with it.

3. Barron, Brigid. 2003. "When Smart Groups Fail." *The Journal of the Learning Sciences* 12 (3): 307–59.

If you see that the group needs support to work together, you can inquire about whether everyone in the group has been heard from and how members are interpreting one another's ideas, and ask if some different people in the group can summarize what the group is thinking about. Establishing that these listening behaviors are the expected norm, and that everyone is accountable to the group's ideas, can help students learn to be more active listeners over time. But even in the moment, refocusing on what each student is saying can help the group find an idea they can all collaborate around, instead of staying in their own world. Listen as students share their thoughts and ask them to tell you what they heard. You can then prompt them to tell you, "Hearing that, I thought of. . . ." This models a behavior you want students to get better at, while at the same time giving them the start of a getting unstuck conversation.

Conclusion

As we described in the introduction to this section, we believe that a lot of learning, especially in problem-based learning situations, comes from students' ability to make sense of other people's thinking and compare and contrast that thinking with their own.

We want students to become active sense makers, to interrogate the mathematics they encounter and ask, "Why does that work?" or "How does this fit in with what I already know?" Developing their ability to make sense of others' thinking and compare it with their own is at the heart of developing the skills they will need to become active sense makers.

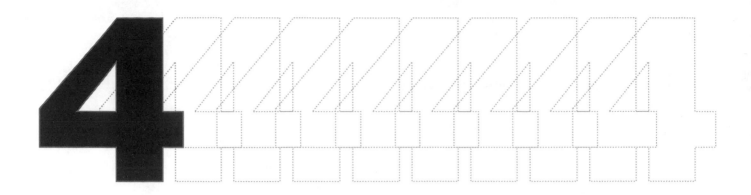

4

Noticing and Wondering

Focal practice:

1. Make sense of problems and persevere in solving them.

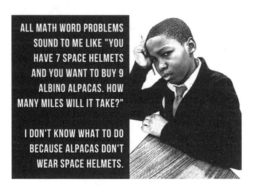

How many of our students feel like the pained-looking student in the illustration above? Too often we hear, "It's never going to make sense to me, so why should I try and understand it?" Lots of students have gotten turned off from trying to make sense of problems when too much of the math they've encountered feels like a set of arbitrary rules to memorize and apply.

Making Sense of Problems and the Common Core Practices

The very first mathematical practice identified in the Common Core is that "mathematically proficient students make sense of problems and persevere in solving them." It is easy to recognize students who aren't yet persistent problem solvers and who fail to make sense of problems: When we hand those students challenging problems, they groan, tell us, "I don't get it!," leave whole problems blank, guess at operations to do, and/or don't know when their answers are unreasonable.

One value of the Common Core State Standards for Mathematical Practice is that they emphasize that solving math problems requires habits of mind, routines that we learn to do and get better at. Although some of our students seem to naturally make sense of problems and persevere, other students seem to flounder. But habits of mind can develop over time and students can move toward becoming mathematically proficient. When our students give up, they aren't being lazy; they are showing us that they still need practice and support making sense of problems.

Even students who have come to expect that problems in math class will make as much sense as "You have 7 space helmets and you want to buy 9 albino alpacas . . ." can practice and get better at making sense of problems. We've often noticed that young elementary students participate much more enthusiastically in math challenges, and their middle school peers seem afraid to even try—the younger students have natural problem-solving instincts that they are engaging, which their middle school peers can be supported to engage, too.

How do we help students reconnect to their own sense making? How do we help them see problems the way mathematicians do, so that they can find the givens, constraints, and relationships?

Notice and Wonder™

Often methods such as asking students to find key words, circle the important information, and cross out unnecessary information rely on students already knowing what is important in a problem—they have to understand the problem in order to use their "understand the problem" strategies! Students who feel disconnected from math often give up before they even try reading the problem, let alone circling key words. Or, they try to guess what we are looking for, blurting out answers that don't make sense.

The wonderful thing that we've found is that students are very capable, with practice, of finding important information in math problems (and stories, images, videos, etc.) and making conjectures about that information. It's a matter of helping them get started, valuing their ideas, and helping them stay connected to their own thinking. We do that using an activity we've developed called I Notice, I Wonder that was introduced by Annie Fetter, a colleague at the Math Forum, in the spring of 2007. The teacher had warned Annie, "This is my lowest-level class. Don't expect too much."

Annie started by drawing the picture in Figure 1 on the board and described to the students what they were about to do.

Figure 1

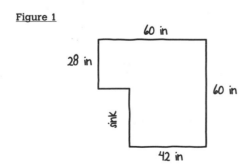

"This is a picture of Teresa's bathroom floor. We're going to list as many things as we can about the picture. I'm going to ask each of you to offer one thing that you *notice*. Anything at all." Here's what they said:

- ▸ Two sides are equal.
- ▸ Two sides are 60 inches.
- ▸ One side is 28 inches.
- ▸ They are longest.
- ▸ One side is 42 inches.
- ▸ It used to be a square.
- ▸ Your lines aren't very straight.
- ▸ The short side of the sink is 18 inches.
- ▸ The sink is a rectangle.
- ▸ The long side of the sink is 32 inches.
- ▸ You can find the area of the whole thing by making it two pieces.

She was excited—that was a great list! She picked out the items she figured were most likely to be both important in eventually solving the problem and potentially confusing and asked for volunteers to explain them to her and the rest of the class. The following responses came from many different students.

Annie: What does it mean to say that it used to be a square?

Student: The floor is like a square, but the sink is in the way.

Annie: How do you know it is a square?

Student: Because all of the sides are 60 inches. That's a square.

Annie: But all the sides in the picture aren't 60 inches long. Could someone show us on the board what you mean?

Student (*drawing Figure 2*): If the sink wasn't there, they would all be 60 inches.

Figure 2

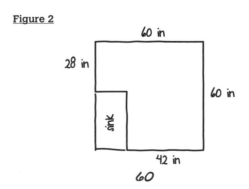

Annie: Okay. How do we know that the short side of the sink is 18 inches?

Student: Because it's 60 take away 42.

Annie: How did you know to do 60 minus 42?

Student: 'Cause 60 is all the way and I only want part of it.

Annie: Would someone like to come up and show us what that means on the board?

Student (*drawing Figure 3*)**:** That part is 42 because it is just like the bottom. So you do 60 take away 42.

Figure 3

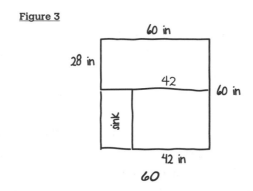

They went through a similar process with the ideas that the long side of the sink is 32 inches and that the area can be found by splitting the floor into two pieces. Then she explained that Teresa was going to put down new tiles, and that the new tiles are squares that are 4 inches by 4 inches. She drew a small tile on the board and labeled it 4 inches on each side. Then she said, "What can we say now?"

- ▸ The tiles are smaller than the floor.
- ▸ Each tile is 16 square inches.
- ▸ It will take a lot of them!
- ▸ Seven tiles will fit across the 28-inch side.
- ▸ Fifteen tiles will fit across the top and the side.
- ▸ Tiles won't fit across the bottom.

At this point, they had reached the end of the class period. Annie gave each student a copy of the full text of the problem and told them that for tomorrow's class, they were to write down everything they remembered from the conversation. She told them that they should not worry about solving the problem. She also told them that they had done an awesome job and that she had had a lot of fun!

Annie told the teacher that she had been really impressed with the students. Turns out the teacher had been too! She was surprised by the number of things they had come up with and by how many of them had participated. A few days later Annie got an email saying that almost all of them had done their homework, and most had remembered more than half of what they talked about in class. A couple of the students had gone on to solve the problem, and when they worked on it in class the next day, many of them were engaged in the process. Annie and the teacher were excited at how well the students did, especially since their teacher said it was their first time solving a problem like this one. Annie went back to share the Notice and Wonder routine with everyone else at the Math Forum and we've been using it ever since!

You may have noticed that when Annie first asked the students to notice and wonder, she started with just a drawing of Teresa's bathroom floor, not a complete math problem with a question to answer. When students see a *question* in math class, they tend to go into "get the answer quick!" mode. Students often feel pressure and anxiety around having to get the answer, whether it's competitiveness to show their smarts or fear that they won't be able to answer that stops them from engaging. We've found that leaving off the question and just sharing an initial story/scenario/image increases participation from struggling students because there are no right or wrong answers to "What do you notice?" and "What are you wondering?" It keeps speedy students engaged in creative brainstorming rather than closed-ended problem solving. It provides a safe, welcoming opening for students who don't often feel like they have anything to say in math class—it starts to unsilence their voices! And often, students generate the very question we would have asked through their wonderings; answering a question *they* generated increases all students' engagement. Through wondering, students see that math problems come from their own thinking and they are no longer encountering problems about which they can exclaim, "I have no idea what this is talking about!"

The I Notice, I Wonder activities in this chapter were developed out of Annie's success with supporting and engaging the supposedly "low-level" math class. The activities are designed to support students to:

When students see a **question** *in math class, they tend to go into "get the answer quick!" mode. We've found that leaving off the question and just sharing an initial story/ scenario/image increases participation from struggling students.*

> ▸ connect their own thinking to the math they are about to do
>
> ▸ attend to details within math problems
>
> ▸ feel safe (there are no right answers or more important things to notice)
>
> ▸ slow down and think about the problem before starting to calculate
>
> ▸ record information that may be useful later
>
> ▸ generate engaging math questions that they are interested in solving
>
> ▸ identify what is confusing or unclear in the problem
>
> ▸ conjecture about possible paths for solving the problem
>
> ▸ find as much math as they can in a scenario, not just the path to the answer.

Notice and Wonder Activities

I Notice, I Wonder Brainstorm

Format: Whole group.

Materials: A student-friendly handout to support students' thinking about this idea is available on the companion website: http://mathforum.org/pps/.

Step 1: Display a problem scenario (without a specific question) at the front of the room. If reading level is a concern, read the scenario to students or have a volunteer read it.

Step 2: Ask students, "What do you notice?" Pause to let as many students as possible raise their hands. Call on students and record their noticings at the front of the room.

Step 3: Ask students, "What are you wondering?" Pause to let as many students as possible raise their hands. Call on students and record their wonderings at the front of the room.

Step 4: Ask students, "Is there anything up here that you are wondering about? Anything you need clarified?" If you or the students have questions about any items, ask the students who shared them to clarify them further.

Step 5: After all students have participated and understand the scenario thoroughly, reveal a question you'd like students to work on. You might ask students to reflect quickly on whether the question clears up any of their wonderings or leads to new noticings or wonderings. Or, ask students, "If this story were the beginning of a math problem, what could the math problem be?" Then solve a problem the *students* come up with.

We often find stories and images for noticing and wondering about in textbooks, whether it's just the diagram from a picture or a story without the question from a word problem. Some texts have good fodder for noticing and wondering in the unit or lesson launch activities, and others have good scenarios in the end-of-unit and end-of-lesson projects and "challenge problems." Additional resources for finding noticing and wondering prompts are available on the companion website for this book (http://mathforum.org/pps/), as are videos of Math Forum staff implementing several different versions of I Notice, I Wonder activities.

Ideas for Differentiating Noticing and Wondering

When noticing and wondering, we've found that it's helpful for students to have the experience both of independently generating as many ideas as they can and of hearing from others what they noticed and wondered. The discipline of careful noticing requires practice and patience, time to think and write on your own. But learning to notice new kinds of things and see math situations through different, useful lenses requires hearing from others. The think-pair-share noticing and wondering activity that follows helps focus students on the individual, written work. The What Do You Hear? noticing and wondering activity (on page 48) helps students quickly hear from others and generate lots of ideas verbally, which can increase engagement and help students, especially younger students or students who have a hard time with writing, stay engaged and active during problem solving.

ACTIVITY: Think-Pair-Share: Increasing Engagement and Accountability

Format: Individual, then pairs, then whole group. Having desks prearranged so students know who their partner is helps make transitions smoother.

Step 1: Think. Give each student a recording sheet. Students brainstorm privately, recording their thinking on the sheet. When the think time is up, students draw a line below their last noticing and last wondering.

Sometimes we set a timer so that students know how long they need to hold their quiet focus.

Step 2: Pair. Students turn to the person next to them and share their list of noticings and wonderings. When one student is reading, the other is recording below the line any noticings and wonderings her partner had that she didn't.

Each pair should choose one favorite noticing or wondering they want to share—it might be something both partners had or one they felt was unique.

Step 3: Share. Quickly go around the room hearing each pair's favorite item. Then ask, "Did anyone have any other noticings or wonderings they wanted to share?" and collect those.

Students should add noticings and wonderings they didn't come up with to their own recording sheets, below the line.

Step 4: Reflect. After hearing from everyone, a chance for students to reflect on the kinds of noticings and wonderings that are easier for them to generate and the kinds they don't see on their own yet can help students set noticing and wondering goals.

Then, the bell rings and the students leave, often still talking about math and wondering about what's going to happen next!

We want to emphasize the idea of calling on all students or groups and asking them for just one thing. It implies that everyone has something to share, and that you want to hear from everyone. Just doing a show of hands and calling on kids can allow some kids to get lost or ignored or feel like someone else took all their good ideas and they didn't get "credit." If everything on a student's list has been shared by the time it's her turn, she can feel heard by telling the person making the public list to write a "Like" or a "+1" next to an idea she had that someone else has already added.

Calling on each group or many groups can feel tedious, though, especially when students have already spent time writing and talking in pairs. An alternative method that works particularly well for younger students, students who struggle with reading or writing, or when you're trying to quickly build engagement is to do the noticing and wondering completely orally at first.

ACTIVITY: What Do You Hear?

Format: Whole-class discussion.

Step 1: Tell the students, "I'm going to read you a story." Wait for students to settle down and then read the scenario from a problem (the entire story minus the question).

Step 2: Ask the students, "What did you hear?" Listen to each student who volunteers to answer. Thank or acknowledge students for participating (we might say "Uh-huh" or "Thanks") but avoid praising or revoicing what the student has said.

Step 3: Read the story again. Ask students "Did what you heard the first time match what you heard this time or do you want to change anything?" Again listen without praising or revoicing.

Suzanne likes to use an I Notice, I Wonder brainstorm or What Do You Hear? activity during the very last five minutes of a lesson. She'll read a story or display a scenario (definitely not using a specific question to solve) and have students notice and wonder. Then, the bell rings and the students leave, often still talking about math and wondering about what's going to happen next! The activity might preview the next day's lesson or be part of a problem-solving task that she will gradually build up over the course of a week or two. Not every noticing and wondering session has to immediately lead into doing math; sometimes it's great to leave them wondering. If you'd like to read more about how Suzanne would build a problem-solving task in five-minute chunks over several lessons, visit the companion website to read her article, "Think You Don't Have Time to Use Problems of the Week?" (http://mathforum.org/pps/).

Noticing and Wondering Tips

Valuing and Unsilencing Students' Voices

If your students don't seem to enjoy noticing and wondering, we've found it's often because the teacher is doing lots of restating. For students to value and own the process, they must recognize that their own ideas in their own words are the beginning of the problem-solving process. As you hear from students about what they notice and wonder, thank or acknowledge each student equally. Record all student suggestions. Avoid praising, restating, clarifying, or asking questions until everyone's noticings have been recorded. Then you might ask, "Is there anything on this list you are wondering about?"

I Notice Versus I Know

Another key to keeping the environment as welcoming as possible and helping students focus on generating as much math as they can rather than getting to one specific conclusion is really just a matter of a single syllable. Asking students "What do you *notice*?" instead of "What do you *know*?" changes how students participate. "What do you know?" can too often tie into students' existing beliefs about whether they know any math—students who feel confident want to rattle off a lot of knowledge, and students who lack confidence already think, "I don't know anything about math, what can I say?" Asking "What do you notice?" focuses students on this specific scenario and welcomes them to start fresh, just saying what they saw or heard. We've had multiple teachers share their observations that they get more students engaged and a better quality of results when they consistently ask "What do you notice?" instead of "What do you know?"

Building Student Independence: Moving from Noticing and Wondering Toward Seeing the World Mathematically

Noticing Mathematically: Finding Quantities and Relationships

Noticing and wondering activities are very open-ended, and at first can lead to noticings and wonderings that are off-topic and even silly. The initial process of writing noticing and wondering lists can take a long time, and students will notice details that they won't end up using as they solve the problem. In short, noticing and wondering is something students get better at over time: more focused, more relevant, more efficient, and more automatic.

How do we support students to move from noticing "The graph is red" to noticing "The graph goes down" to noticing "The graph shows that as time goes by, the car gets closer to home," for example? It is a process that takes time and patience, as the teacher first supports students to notice and wonder at all, and then to be thorough and generate lots of ideas, and finally to begin to think about narrowing down on the kinds of noticing and wondering that mathematicians might do. Once students have become prolific noticers and wonderers, one simple prompt we've found to be very helpful in focusing students is simply asking,

> "Which of these noticings have to do with math?"
> "Which of these wonderings could we use math to help us answer/prove?"

Following is an example from Philadelphia fifth graders who had been noticing and wondering for several weeks. First they listed what they noticed and wondered, and then they used asterisks to mark the entries that they thought answered the question, "Which of these could we use math to prove or did we use math to come up with"?

What do you notice?

Teacher model: I notice that there are 3 different groupings.

Kaya: I notice the middle one weighs the most.

****Kyla:** I notice there are 10 balls all together.**

Safiya: I notice the middle one has more balls.

****Jaquir:** I notice there are 4 soccer balls and 3 baseballs and 3 tennis balls.**

****Omar:** I notice the weight of all 3 adds up to 69 ounces.**

Duwan: I notice each group doesn't weigh the same.

What do you wonder?

Teacher model: I wonder why she grouped them this way.

Kyla: I wonder what the question is.

Sue: I wonder if it is a pattern.**

Safiya: I wonder why the last one weighs more than the first one.**

Michael: I wonder if the soccer balls are 11 pounds [sic].**

Sienna: I wonder why are there balls and what is she doing.

Kaya: I wonder why the middle has too many soccer balls.

Zenaia: I wonder if we have to add or divide.**

Jaquir: I wonder why . . . I don't know, I forgot.

Bria: I wonder why she picked soccer balls, baseballs, and tennis balls.

Students almost always identify as mathematical the same set of noticings and wonderings we would, saying that those items had to do with numbers, math words, measuring, how many, and so on. In middle school, it's appropriate to help students realize that the "mathy" items are (almost always) about *quantities*: things you can count or measure to find the value of. Once students have begun to focus on noticings and wonderings that they feel are mathematical, we start to ask students to challenge themselves to notice as many quantities as they can in a mathematical situation. For example, in the fifth-grade students' noticings and wonderings above, they noticed these quantities:

- ▸ the number of groupings (3)
- ▸ the weight of each grouping
- ▸ the total number of balls (10)
- ▸ the number of balls in each grouping
- ▸ the number of each type of ball
- ▸ the total weight
- ▸ the weight of an individual soccer ball.

Math problems are explored by finding relationships among quantities. Whether the relationship itself is the answer (e.g., problems that ask students to find a formula or to tell how many times bigger something is) or a relationship is used to find a value that satisfies the constraints of the problem, good noticers seek out relationships among quantities. For example, the fifth graders noticed and wondered about these relationships:

- ▸ The middle group weighs the most.
- ▸ The middle one has more balls.
- ▸ The middle group has an extra soccer ball.
- ▸ Each group doesn't weigh the same.

▸ The groupings can be combined to get total weight and total number of balls.

▸ The last one weighs more than the first one.

These relationships involve many of the quantities that students previously noticed. It's interesting that the students haven't yet explicitly connected the different weights to the different types of balls, but perhaps as they explore questions like "Why does the last one weigh more than the first?" they will notice it has a different combination of balls, and even that the baseballs must be heavier than the tennis balls.

Noticing and describing relationships can be challenging for students, but once they are good at noticing all of the quantities in a problem, we push them to try to name any relationships that involve those quantities. As you can see in the example, relationships of comparison (things that are equal, more than, less than) often are easiest to notice, as well as relationships made by doing basic mathematical operations (e.g., how many there are all together). Students have a harder time seeing relationships that are about change or about how two or more quantities are connected (for example, how the type of ball is related to the weight on the scales, how swapping a tennis ball for a baseball changes the weight, etc.). Eventually, students will use relationships based on comparison, mathematical operations, and change/connection relationships to build guess and check tables or mathematical models, identifying constraints, unknowns, and writing relationships mathematically. But just being able to notice and describe relationships in their own language is an important and difficult first step!

Wondering Strategically

What other guidelines might we put on noticing and wondering to help students develop the practice of making sense of problems? In addition to noticing *quantities* and *relationships*, we can look to the standards for more guidance.

The description of "Make sense of problems and persevere in solving them" continues, "They consider analogous problems, and try special cases and simpler forms of the original problem in order to gain insight into its solution. They monitor and evaluate their progress and change course if necessary. Older students might, depending on the context of the problem, transform algebraic expressions or change the viewing window on their graphing calculator to get the information they need. Mathematically proficient students can explain correspondences between equations, verbal descriptions, tables, and graphs or draw diagrams of important features and relationships, graph data, and search for regularity or trends. Younger students might rely on using concrete objects or pictures to help conceptualize and solve a problem."[1]

---

1. © Copyright 2010. National Governors Association Center for Best Practices and Council of Chief State School Officers. All rights reserved.

Some of the strategic behaviors described here bring to mind key problem-solving strategies. The wonderings that follow can help guide students toward strategic behaviors (I've included the related strategies in parentheses after each wondering):

- What does this problem remind me of? Have I ever seen a problem like this before? (Solve a Simpler Problem, Change the Representation)
- What makes this problem hard? What would make it simpler to solve? (Solve a Simpler Problem)
- What must be true? What can't be true? What might be true? (Use Logical Reasoning)
- What am I trying to figure out? (Make a Plan)
- What needs to be organized? (Make a Table)
- What patterns can I see? (Make a Table)
- How is this information displayed (represented)? How else can I represent (display) this information? (Change the Representation)
- What guess can I make? (Guess and Check)
- How would I check if my answer were wrong? (Guess and Check)

Each of the wonderings above can be a launch into the problem-solving strategy listed next to it (we expand more on this idea in Chapter 9). We tend to introduce the questions using a three-phase introduction, releasing responsibility for asking the question from the teacher to the problem solver.

1. The teacher poses the question to the whole group as a noticing and wondering prompt. For example, after noticing and wondering about a problem, the teacher might say, "Now let's sort these into three lists. What *must* be true, what *can't* be true, and what *might* be true? What else can we put in each list?"

2. Once the students have worked as a whole group to address one of these strategy-specific wonderings, the teacher then starts using the questions to support students working in independent groups or individually. The teacher also listens to learn if students working together have begun to ask each other these questions.

3. As students make use of these questions or ways of thinking to solve problems, the teacher supports them to tell other students how these questions are helpful. Students might make a poster listing things they wonder when they solve problems that includes any of the wonderings they find helpful. At this point when students are stuck, the teacher asks, "What can you ask yourself to help you look at the problem strategically?"

Noticing and Wondering to Get Unstuck

Noticing and wondering can be a great way to help students get themselves unstuck. If students have noticed and wondered their way into a problem, those noticings and wonderings can serve as reminders for different ideas that can help students get unstuck. Good ways to use noticing and wondering to get unstuck include:

- ▸ Make a public record of noticings and wonderings and *keep them on display throughout the problem-solving process.* Check back on them when you feel stuck.

- ▸ Use noticing and wondering as a way to step back when you're stuck:
  - ◆ Notice and wonder about the problem text/images again. Look for new things to add to your noticing and wondering list.
  - ◆ Notice and wonder about your own work—read through what you've done so far and let your mind freely come up with noticings and wonderings.
  - ◆ Ask a partner to notice and wonder about your work. Just let them say what jumps out at them and what it makes them wonder.

- ▸ Use wondering as a way to say the things that are in the back of your mind. Try to wonder at least five things like:
  - ◆ I wonder if it would help to . . .
  - ◆ I wonder if it's worth it to try . . .
  - ◆ I wonder what would happen if . . .
  - ◆ I wonder if _____ would work . . .
  - ◆ I wonder why they wrote/drew _____ this way . . .

Using noticing and wondering as a tool for getting unstuck helps students realize that it's more than just an activity—it's a skill that helps them throughout the problem-solving process.

Conclusion

Everyone can notice something, and everyone has something they wonder.

No single other activity in this book has been more popular (or, as far as we know, produced more dramatic changes in math classrooms) than the simple I Notice, I Wonder Brainstorm. The teacher whose fifth-grade students provided the noticing and wondering example discussed earlier credits noticing and wondering about, and then solving, one word problem a week with raising her class' benchmark test scores from 3 percent to 80 percent over their fifth-grade year. Her principal confirmed that during testing, the fifth-grade students had much more "stamina"—they were able to persist on problems that they would have shied away from before.

The magic of noticing and wondering, we think, is that it invites every student to participate mathematically. Everyone can notice something, and everyone has something they wonder. It builds momentum in thinking. It generates content that students record and can then use to generate other ideas. It encourages the process of thinking about math and connecting ideas and wondering. Learning depends on mulling, connecting, wondering, and repeatedly thinking about, and noticing and wondering enables this to take hold and blossom. When we invite everyone to share in math class, and we see how each student's contribution builds toward a complete mathematical understanding of the problem at hand, we invite students to think of themselves as mathematicians. Students' confidence increases, and they have a real tool for beginning the task of making sense of problems and persevering in solving them.

Adding especially mathematical noticing and wondering skills (noticing quantities and relationships, wondering strategically) to students' repertoire increases the usefulness of noticing and wondering. As students get better at targeted, mathematical noticing and wondering, and as they begin to notice and wonder automatically (as mathematicians do), they may find that all of the other problem-solving strategies become easier to learn as well.

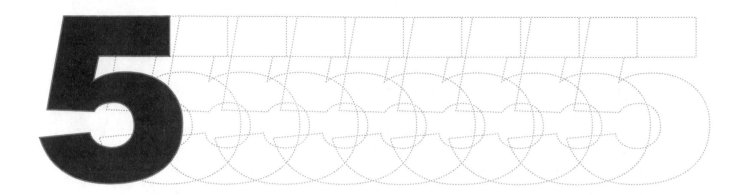

Change the Representation

Seeing the Big Picture

Focal practices:

1. Make sense of problems and persevere in solving them.
2. Reason abstractly and quantitatively.
4. Make a mathematical model.

When students finish solving problems, one of the most common questions their math teachers ask them is, "Does your answer make sense?" or "Is your answer reasonable in the context of the problem?" That is not an easy question for students to answer! How many times have you heard a student confidently announce answers that in fact don't make any sense: "The soccer ball weighs 20 pounds!" "Teresa needs 0.005 tiles!" And then when asked, "Does your answer make sense?" they respond, "No, well, maybe, I don't know. . . . I mean, I divided on the calculator and that's what I got." Why does this happen?

Understanding and Making Use of Problem Context

One reason our students aren't able to tell that obviously wrong answers don't make any sense is that many students have been explicitly instructed in tools for ignoring the context—the very context that tells them whether or not their answer makes sense! This hit home for me one day when I was working with a group of students who had been identified as struggling in math. Their teacher and I had given them a *long* word problem. Our goal with the problem was first to help the students feel that the math they were about to do was relevant and from real life (the teacher did a lot of research for both paragraphs, finding real news articles and talking to a local grocer), and second to help the students learn to weed out numbers given in a problem that aren't relevant to finding the answer. Both of those are useful goals—seeing math in familiar, important contexts can help students connect and stay interested, and modeling tasks require students to sort through information and determine what is needed and what is not (plus lots of standardized tests are designed with "distractors" that students need to be strategic about). But in this case, our two goals got in the way of each other. Here's what happened:

We gave the students a paragraph to read about food waste in the United States. The students learned a lot of sad facts about just how much of the food that we produce ends up in a landfill without anyone eating it. They read facts like:

- Food waste is an increasingly large problem, especially in the United States and Europe.
- Forty percent of food produced is thrown out rather than eaten.
- Every year, 165 billion dollars' worth of food is wasted.

Then in the second paragraph, we presented the problem we wanted them to solve. This problem focused on just one item at a local grocery store, specifically cantaloupe:

At the average grocery store, 11.4% of fresh produce is wasted each week. [The local grocery chain] buys 860 pounds of cantaloupe in a typical week. Estimate how many pounds of cantaloupe their store probably threw away in a week. Then, calculate exactly how many pounds of cantaloupe were thrown away.

We were curious to see how many students would use the numerals from the introductory paragraph, like 165, in trying to answer the question about cantaloupes. And just as we suspected, several of the students did do this, and every single student agreed that they felt "pressure" to use those numbers somewhere. So how do we help students learn to make smart choices about which of the many quantities in the problem will help them find the answer they're looking for?

Our initial reaction was to coach students to ignore the first paragraph, since it didn't have quantities in it that they would ultimately use to solve the problem. The thing is, the adults in the room knew we could "ignore" the numbers in the first paragraph because we had already read and made sense of both paragraphs. The students would have no way to know that those numbers were or weren't important without understanding the two paragraphs and how they were and weren't connected.

When we asked the students if the paragraphs were related to each other, they said, "No, not really." The students just skimmed the problem looking for numbers, without reading and understanding either of the paragraphs. No teacher wants students to avoid understanding what they read. But when we coach the students to *ignore* extra information, that often sounds to them like "Don't bother to make sense of the information, just find the numbers and key words."

What made the teacher and me suspicious was that the students had no emotional reaction to the story at all. They found the two paragraphs to be unconnected and the story to be at best intimidating, at worst boring. When we talked about the math, we learned that the students had come up with completely unreasonable answers like 9,690 pounds of cantaloupe are thrown out (which is more than the total of 860 pounds!). They couldn't tell their answers were unreasonable because they didn't have an understanding of the "big picture" of the story:

- ▸ Americans waste a lot of food.
- ▸ Specifically, grocery stores waste a lot of produce, over 10% on average.
- ▸ There are 860 pounds of cantaloupe total at this store.
- ▸ Some of it (about 10%) is going to be thrown away.

In order to help them understand the story and start to reconsider some of their unreasonable answers, we asked them what they wondered about the story (and even modeled some wonderings). Finally they began sharing things like "My sister used to work at that store and she said they threw out multiple huge trays of cupcakes every day. Like, those *big* trays!" and "I wonder what they do with the food. Do they compost it?" and "Do they have to throw out the food because it rots?" and "Does any of that rotted food end up in my dinner?"

After we discussed the context and students had made a personal connection to the context, the students were able to more effectively estimate with regards to the problem. A student who understands the big picture can tell you that 9,690 pounds is *not* a reasonable estimate for the amount that's going to be thrown away—how could you throw out more that you started with? The students even added their own twist to the question, wondering how many individual cantaloupes, on average, were in the 98 pounds of cantaloupe thrown out. They all agreed on a reasonable range of cantaloupe weights, and estimated that if cantaloupes weighed 1–2 pounds each, there would be 49–98 cantaloupes in 98 pounds. One student was even able to explain why there would be fewer cantaloupes in 98 pounds if each cantaloupe weighed 2 pounds instead of 1, after another student ventured that there would be 196 two-pound cantaloupes in 98 pounds. Overall the students seemed much more confident and able to estimate, round, correct their thinking, and explain their answers after we discussed and understood the context.

Changing the Representation as a Bridge from Notice and Wonder to Solving the Problem

Sometimes, careful noticing and wondering is enough for a student to see a path to a solution. Often, though, we finish noticing and wondering with students and get the sense that they understand and have identified all of the important information in a problem (they found all the quantities and have named the obvious relationships)—but there's still work to do to resolve the question. Students often focus on the details, the numbers given, the units, maybe the main characters, but don't always have a grasp of the overall story. What's happening in the problem? Who cares about what's happening? What are we supposed to figure out?

Rather than teaching students to ignore extra information, we should support them to understand the context of the problem, summarize what the story is about, make predictions about what the next paragraph will say based on the previous paragraph, think of their own wonderings and connections to the problem, and decide what they think is interesting and important about the story. Students who have learned to do those things can decide if answers are reasonable and can make smart choices about which numbers they plan to calculate with.

To see another example of these strategies at work, and how helping students move from noticing and wondering to making connections to acting the problem out with manipulatives can really help their problem solving, you can visit the companion website for this book (http://mathforum.org/pps/) to watch video clips of Suzanne facilitating students to solve the problem Wooden Legs. In the clips, she uses the What Do You Hear? activity (Chapter 4) to get students started noticing and wondering about the following scenario:

WOODEN LEGS

Wendy builds wooden dollhouse furniture. She uses the same kind of legs to make 3-legged stools and 4-legged tables. She has a supply of 31 legs.

In the videos, you hear students saying they heard things like "She had 4-legged tables for every 4 chairs," "She had 31 legs for every table," "She uses the same legs for 3-legged chairs and a 4-legged table." Each of these might represent a misunderstanding of what the problem was trying to express. Suzanne handled that without correcting students or telling them what to think. Instead, she occasionally asked students to clarify their thinking, asking "Do you mean that she makes 1 table with 31 legs?" She also made sure that students had a mental picture of 3-legged stools and 4-legged tables and of dollhouse furniture by asking them to look around their classroom for 3-legged chairs and 4-legged tables, and describe 3-legged chairs when there weren't any in the classroom. She also asked students to think about dollhouses: "How big are they?," "What do you do with them?," "Which table in this room could a dollhouse fit on?"

The main suggestion Suzanne gave students to make sense of the problem was to very gently let them know that there are some different physical objects (straws, toothpicks, and blocks) available they could use to think about the legs. Watching the clips of the students working in groups, we can see that acting out the problem using physical representations helped the students explain their thinking (they use gestures and arrangements of the toothpicks to help them explain how they counted legs), support their number sense (checking to make sure that they added 15 + 4 or counted 5 groups of 3 correctly), and understand the problem scenario (acting out the idea of "using up" some of the 31 legs and having some left to make more furniture out of).

The activities in this chapter help students develop their big-picture comprehension skills. We specifically focus on activities that help students use the Change the Representation strategy to go from written stories to stories they act out or illustrate with physical or visual models. We do this as a bridge from understanding problems to modeling them mathematically. Math problems are often presented in formalized language, language that is almost as different from everyday speech as purely symbolic math is. Changing the representation from formal mathematical language to visual representations, physical representations, or common-language representations helps students to grasp the big picture and often helps to reveal underlying mathematical structure. In later chapters, we'll present other activities in which students use representations like tables and graphs and other models more formally, but the work of this chapter sets students up to be able to begin exploring the underlying concepts in math problems presented in unfamiliar language.[1]

Key Principles for Making Sense of the Big Picture

Changing the representation from formal mathematical language to visual representations, physical representations, or common-language representations helps students to grasp the big picture and often helps to reveal underlying mathematical structure.

In supporting students to make sense of problems and ensuring they understand the context as well as the details of the problem, there are several key principles to keep in mind:

- ▸ Don't encourage students to ignore the context.

- ▸ Support students to connect the context to their own experiences; when students don't have the relevant experiences, preteach the context.

- ▸ Let students make choices about what to represent and how.

Don't Encourage Students to Ignore the Context

As the food waste story illustrated, context is often a helpful hook for getting students emotionally and mentally invested in a problem. After the students started thinking about food waste they had heard about and their own experiences of grocery stores and rotting food, they were able to give more reasonable answers and better estimates. When we coach students to look for numbers and key words, we are taking away a lot of the support that students use to visualize the problem. When students are stuck on solving a problem, my first question to them is usually, "What's the story about?" or "What's going on in the story?" And when students tell me they've solved a problem and want to know if they're right, my first question is not "Did you check your answer?" or "Is your answer reasonable?" but rather "Does your answer make sense *in the story*?" Teaching students to understand the story and only then think about which details are most relevant for their goal makes more sense than trying to anticipate which details are important before you understand the big picture.

---

1. One additional resource for helping students make sense of the big picture of the problem is literacy teachers. They often have ideas and activities for helping students get better at paraphrasing, summarizing, making predictions, relating problems to their own knowledge and experience, and other text comprehension strategies.

Support Students to Connect the Context to Their Own Experiences

I used to tell teachers that it was never okay to "preteach" before problem solving. My experience with preteaching was that teachers would tell the students some mathematical content or have them practice a skill, and then give the students a related word problem. In that situation, instead of making sense of the story, the students tend to apply the math that was previewed no matter what. It takes away the opportunity for sense making from the students. But the last time I told a group of teachers that they should never preteach, one teacher gave an example that stopped me in my tracks.

She asked, "What about preteaching the context?" She explained that she had recently done a problem she wasn't sure her students would be able to solve and she happened to notice that it was about selling tickets to a school dance. Her school didn't have dances and the students weren't charged for school events. She wondered if her students would be confused and so before she shared the problem story with them she asked them about their experiences with profit and break-even points. They talked about events they had bought tickets for and reasonable prices and what happens when ticket prices go up or down. Even though she hadn't previewed any of the specific mathematics of the problem, her students dove into it eagerly, making sense of the complicated story about pricing and demand, and coming up with lots of different unique methods to solve the problem. We all agreed that when a context might be unfamiliar to students, warming up by helping them learn about the context can be a great way to preview an activity without taking away the opportunity for students to be the ones to sleuth out the mathematical connections.

My first question is not "Did you check your answer?" or "Is your answer reasonable?" but rather "Does your answer make sense in the story?"

Let Students Make Choices About What to Represent and How

When Suzanne invited students to solve the Wooden Legs problem with her, I noticed that she did not tell the students, "And then we will use these toothpicks to represent legs. We'll put a group of 3 together for a stool and a group of 4 together for a table." She made sure the students were aware of the manipulatives available, and she mentioned the idea that groups could choose to use them to think about the legs, but she left all of the thinking about how the manipulatives could be used to act out the problem up to the students.

When teachers make decisions for students, we often see that the students don't make connections themselves. If a teacher has always modeled exactly how a manipulative is to be used, when we ask students to use them themselves, they tend to say, "I don't know how," or "We need to wait for the teacher to show us." But when the teacher says, "Well, I have some different things you could use, why don't you see what you can do," the students usually come up with different creative ways of acting out problems or representing what's happening. Even if it takes them a little longer to get started the first time, we often see that time paying off as students get better over the course of a year at independently modeling and making sense of problems. For one thing, if we start this process of sense making young enough, we're harnessing the power of young students' imaginations—I've never met a third-grade student who couldn't use her imagination to turn a pile of blocks into anything she wanted!

A student-friendly handout to support students' thinking about brainstorming representations is available on the companion website (http://mathforum.org/pps/).

Activities for Changing the Representation

Activities for Acting Out the Problem

For me, the value of using the Change the Representation strategy after noticing and wondering came when I was working with a small group of students who had noticed and wondered about the following problem but really didn't understand the action in the story yet:

> **ZOO TRAIN**
>
> The zoo has a train that carries people between exhibits. One morning the first passengers got on at Monkey House. At Alligator Pond the number of people who got on was 3 more than got on at Monkey House.
>
> The train made 4 more stops: Tiger Thicket, Panda Playground, Giraffe Savannah, and Big Cats. At each of these stops, 3 more passengers boarded the train than at the previous stop. At Big Cats 20 people got on the train. How many passengers in all boarded the train?

Most of their noticings had focused on the names of the different zoo stops. They had noticed something about 3 more and they were confident that 20 people got on at Big Cats, but I had a sense that they didn't really see the action in the story, and so they couldn't find any relationships to use to know what to do with the values of 3 or 20. The students recognized it, too, and complained they were stuck and didn't get it. I asked, "What else can you do when you don't understand a problem?" They didn't know of any other strategies besides noticing and wondering, so I said, "Some people like to draw pictures. Others like to act the story out. Some people like to retell the story in their own words."

"Let's act this problem out!" said the student who was most vocal about being stuck. Soon he was directing the other students what to do. They went through the story and I played the role of narrator, helping them see when what they were doing didn't match the words on the paper. Eventually they acted the whole problem out and looked at me like, "Okay, we're done, now what?"

I asked them what they noticed as they acted the story out. The students began to talk about the story with a clearer understanding of what was happening, what they knew, and what they didn't know. Eventually, a student who had been quiet for most of the time mentioned, "Wait, we could just go through the whole story backward and then we could answer it." The rest of her group members agreed that strategy would work. Just noticing and wondering didn't give them an idea of how to solve the problem, and just acting the problem out wasn't enough either, but noticing, acting out, and then noticing again was very useful.

ACTIVITY Act It Out!

Format: Students working in groups of 3–5 with one student in the role of narrator.

Materials: It can be helpful to prepare a basket of manipulatives for each group in advance. If you are using one of the problems available through the companion website (http://mathforum.org/pps/), looking through the teacher packet might give you an idea of some possible manipulatives, such as hundreds charts, plastic counters, base ten blocks, number lines, paper and colored pencils, Unifix cubes, and so on. Or, if your students are already in the habit of getting their own manipulatives from an area of the room, simply reminding them that manipulatives are available is enough.

Before they begin, students should choose who wants to be the *narrator*.

Step 1: The narrator reads the problem as the group listens quietly. Everyone should try to imagine the action in their head as the narrator reads.

Step 2: The narrator asks the group, "What did we hear?" and the students share what they heard in the story.

Step 3: The narrator reads the problem again. This time, the students listen for any details they didn't notice the first time. The narrator asks, "Did you hear anything that made you change what you thought before?"

Step 4: Group members work together to make a plan for how they will act out the story. What roles will they need? What will the steps be?

Step 5: The group carries out the plan. The narrator looks at the problem while the problem is acted out and makes sure that the group's actions match what's on the paper.

Step 6: The group members talk about what they noticed as they acted out the story.

Variation: Steps 1–3 can be done as a whole group with the teacher reading the problem and asking, "What did you hear?" of the whole group. This is especially helpful when the students aren't as strong at reading independently, or if you want to make sure all the groups are ready to work on acting the problem out.

ACTIVITY Variety Show

The role of *narrator* is a challenging role for students. It's not easy to tell when you've changed a detail of a problem, and if that detail is relevant or not. Sometimes students are acting the problem out precisely because their understanding of the problem is shaky. In that case, using the power of the whole group can help students get better at noticing how a problem is being translated "from page to stage." Watching multiple groups act the problem out and talking about what's the same, what's different, and which of those differences are mathematically relevant is a powerful experience we call Variety Show.

Format: Students working in small groups (of about four students) then moving to whole groups.

Step 1: Read the problem aloud to the class. Ask students, "What did you hear?" Acknowledge each contribution without elaboration or comment.

Step 2: Divide the class into groups. Give each group five to seven minutes to reread the problem and plan a one- to two-minute skit acting the problem out. *Note:* If you have more than five groups, we'd limit students to a one-minute skit.

Step 3: Groups take turns acting out their skit. Students who are in the audience are given the job of writing down what was the same in the skits and what was different.

Step 4 (optional): Students turn and tell a partner as many things as they can that were the same in every skit for one minute. Partner then tells as many differences as they can remember for one minute.

Step 5: As a group, list all of the similarities and then all of the differences you can. Ask students which differences, if any, they think change the problem from how it was written.

Step 6: Students work in their small groups to solve the problem. Once the students have some solution paths, return again to the list of similarities and differences. Which were important in solving the problem?

Step 7: Students reflect on what they personally, and as a group, noticed about the problem as they acted it out, and write one thing they are proud of and one thing they want to do differently in the future.

Activities for Drawing a Picture

Another option for using a Change the Representation strategy to make sense of problems is drawing pictures. In general, students (especially younger students) are often comfortable drawing pictures to illustrate math problems. The challenge students face is often in making their drawings mathematically useful. Also, being able to "mathematize" a drawing, to show the details and relationships that are mathematically important while leaving out other visual details that may not be relevant, is really important to feeling like you have a place to get started! (Further discussion of different representations and how students abstract and "mathematize" their representations are in Chapter 8.)

ACTIVITY Picture Gallery

One big advantage to drawing pictures to solve problems is that a lot of math, especially geometry, has a visual basis. Being able to create a good diagram for a problem can help you see the relationships you'll use to think through it. Often, if you can't "see" the relationships, you can't solve the problem. I was working with students who had been studying right triangles and were getting pretty good at identifying them and finding lengths of missing sides. However, when they solved word problems, they struggled to "see" the right triangle relationships and so they didn't even have a chance to use their good finding-missing-sides skills. It was with those students that this next activity, Picture Gallery, was born.

Their teacher wanted his students to work on drawing pictures that would help them see right triangles and identify circumstances in which it would be helpful to use their finding-missing-sides skills in a wide range of real-world scenarios. He observed that many students would struggle to draw a mathematically useful picture. He wasn't sure what he could do other than give students problems to struggle with, and then show them his drawings that he had used to solve the problem. He worried that if he always modeled the drawings, his students would feel that they needed to wait for him to help them every time they had a hard word problem, or that they had to memorize and copy what he did. We had a hunch that the students could come up with at least a good start at a drawing and then work together to figure out how to improve their drawings. Knowing that they could get started on their own and improve would help the students feel more confident and capable visualizing word problems in the future, instead of thinking only a math teacher could come up with a good drawing.

One of his goals for the year was to have students debate and discuss issues in math class, and he was confident that his students could compare drawings, recognize what made a drawing useful, and even critique drawings that didn't match the constraints of the problem, even if they couldn't all individually come up with awesome drawings on their own the first time.

Together we came up with this Picture Gallery activity:

Format: Students working in groups of 3–4, then discussing as a whole group, then moving back into their small groups.

Materials (optional): Big paper or overhead transparencies and markers for students to copy their picture onto. [2]

Step 1: Give each group a problem statement. Instruct them to draw a picture they could use to solve the problem, but let them know they aren't being asked to solve the problem yet.

Step 2: As groups finish, invite one member of each group to draw their picture big enough for the whole class to see it.

Step 3: Display each image or have students turn and look at each image. Students can ask questions of the illustrator to make sure labels and other components are clear to them.

Step 4: Ask students if they were going to solve the problem, which of the diagrams they think would be most helpful. Encourage each group to come to consensus on which they would pick.

Step 5: Hear from each group as to why members chose the image they chose. If there are differences of opinion about the image, encourage the class to come to consensus on the accuracy and usefulness of the images. However, some students may not yet be convinced, or true differences of style may remain unresolved.

Knowing that they could get started on their own and improve would help the students feel more confident and capable visualizing word problems in the future, instead of thinking only a math teacher could come up with a good drawing.

2. If you have multiple whiteboards or chalkboards, students can be stationed around the room. You can also have students transfer their drawing to chart paper or overhead transparencies if you don't have a document camera. Or, students can draw each drawing on a different page of an interactive whiteboard file. Finally, in classrooms with class sets of iPads or other tablets, students can draw on their tablets and send the file or use an app like Air Sketch to share their images on the projector.

Step 6: Students work in their small groups to solve the problem using their diagram. As groups finish, they compare their work and the picture they chose with other groups.

Step 7: Students reflect on what they personally, and as a group, noticed about what makes a drawing useful, and write one thing they are proud of and one thing they want to do differently in the future.

Step 8 (may happen the next class, or as homework): Students apply their reflection to a new problem, coming up with a drawing and then using the drawing in their solution.

In the class that we invented Picture Gallery for, we gave them the following problem:

> You are building a shed. Looking at the shed from the front, the roof forms an isosceles triangle. The shed will be 8 feet wide, and the height from the peak to the top of the shed wall will be 3 feet. How long should you cut the 2-by-4s that will form the front edges (rafters) of the roof?

The students produced a wide range of drawings like the ones below:

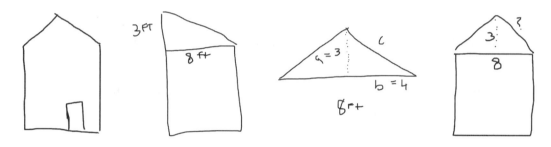

Right away, students began to comment that the diagrams with sides and lengths labeled were easier to use to solve the problem. However, students weren't able to come to a consensus in their initial conversation on which drawings didn't match the constraints of the problem as it was written. In addition, some students, although they recognized the value of labeling diagrams, felt that some groups' very intricately labeled diagrams were "overkill." So we invited students to work in their groups to solve the problem using any drawing they wanted, and then compare their work with a group that had used a different drawing. Some of the differences turned out to be stylistic—the groups with sparser labeling schemes were still successful and seemed to recognize that it was okay not to label things you didn't turn out to need. Other groups noticed that when they compared work, different drawings led to different answers, both of which couldn't be correct.

During the comparison process, the students were able to use the text of the problem and their own experience of houses and building things (we're not sure how many of the kids, who came from a wide socioeconomic spectrum, had experience with sheds, but they all seemed to draw on stereotypical house shapes in making sense of the context) to convince each other that the correct diagram had an isosceles triangle for the shed roof.

Students stayed on task, solving and discussing this problem and the follow-up task they were given, for the entire fifty-minute period (and it was the second portion of a double math block!). This group of students had struggled in the past when asked to stay on task solving challenging word problems, and they had never successfully compared work and come to a consensus across differences (at least, not without throwing pencils). Focusing specifically on the task of creating a picture and having a chance to see and discuss multiple pictures of the same situation before jumping in gave students the scaffolding they needed to persist with the problem and use mathematical reasoning to work through the problem and compare their final results productively.

An additional activity for supporting students to compare representations and exposing them to novel representations is available through the companion website (http://mathforum .org/pps/)

Building Student Independence with Representations

How can these types of Change the Representation activities become part of students' problem-solving strategy repertoire, rather than just activities the teacher recommends? Through trying to draw pictures and act out problems with manipulatives or using their bodies, and through comparing and discussing these representations during activities like Picture Gallery and Variety Show, students will be having discussions about what makes a drawing or way of acting out a problem work well. During these discussions, students might mention things like:

Focusing specifically on the task of creating a picture and having a chance to see and discuss multiple pictures of the same situation before jumping in gave students the scaffolding they needed to persist with the problem and use mathematical reasoning to work through the problem and compare their final results productively.

- ▸ Labels are really helpful for mathematical diagrams.

- ▸ You don't need to be a good artist to make a clear diagram.

- ▸ Good diagrams have just the right amount of detail and information—less than a photograph and more than a scribble.

- ▸ It's important to make sure your diagram or skit matches what the problem says (the constraints of the problem).

- ▸ We can choose different kinds of drawings or different kinds of manipulatives to act out the problem—there can be lots of different ways and sometimes they show different things.

- ▸ Sometimes it's hard in a drawing or using manipulatives to show big numbers or to show quantities that we don't know the value of (students might share different ways to do that like label them with a question mark or write a label to show how many but not draw them all).

- ▸ A good skit or diagram shows what's being counted and measured and how different things in the problem are related.

As you start to hear these comments in student discussions about one another's skits and pictures, you can start to help them internalize these comments into their own criteria for drawing and acting out problems. After students have done activities like Variety Show and Picture Gallery, they might write their reflections on what they're proud of and what they want to do differently in the future in a math journal. Or, as a class, they might come up with their own list of what a good diagram looks like or how to get good at acting a problem out. Displaying these prominently and encouraging students to check them as they solve problems can provide gentle hints to students who need reminders about things like using labels, being organized, including appropriate detail, and so on while at the same time reminding all students what a high standard of creating visual and physical models of problems looks like.

The other piece of supporting students to gain independence with this strategy is to help students think to use it on their own. We want students to get in the habit of using different visualization strategies as they move from initial reading and noticing and wondering about a problem to starting to solve it. One thing teachers can do is to help students recognize that these strategies are in their tool belt. Asking students, "What have you done on other problems that helped you understand the story of the problem better?" can help them recall this strategy when they're stuck. Another way to support students to develop this habit is to do a little training, just like when we try to develop the habit of always putting down our keys in the same place so we don't have to spend time looking for them the next morning. You might work as a class to develop an Understanding Checklist like:

☐ I noticed and wondered about the problem.

☐ I visualized the problem using:

    ☐ a picture

    ☐ manipulatives

    ☐ acting it out

    ☐ in my mind's eye

☐ I can say the problem in my own words.[3]

☐ I have some ideas for getting started.

Then you can help students get in the habit of using the checklist whenever they work to solve a problem. At the Math Forum we often think about the difference between "training" and "facilitating." When there is a classroom routine we want students to learn to use, or a tool (like a spreadsheet) we want them to get good at, we like to use structured, step-by-step instructions (written or oral) that students practice. On the other hand, when we want students to understand a concept or solve a problem, we think it's important for long-term learning for students to have their own ideas and their own process—that way they know the learning came from them and they feel confident and connected to it. So we would *train* students to use an understanding checklist, but we would *facilitate* them in their own process of understanding each problem.

One important note with this strategy is that students are not usually allowed to physically act out problems on high-stakes tests, and so encouraging them to develop the habit of internally visualizing the movie in their own head, and representing it on paper, will become

So we would train *students to use an understanding checklist, but we would* facilitate *them in their own process of understanding each problem.*

---

3. This is another great way to check for understanding of the problem context. Since it's not exactly a different representation, we decided it was outside the scope of this chapter, but we've included some activities for getting good at paraphrasing content in the companion website (http://mathforum.org/pps/).

increasingly important. Eventually, most students will be able to move on their own from a physical, group-based Act It Out strategy to a more internalized, independent Draw a Picture strategy, for example by visualizing how they would act out the problem in their heads. For more kinesthetic learners who always choose a physical model to represent the problem, as they gain confidence and skill in acting out story problems, encourage them to challenge themselves to draw storyboards or pictures for what they would act out. They might close their eyes and quietly move their bodies as they think about the problem, and then draw what they saw or did.

Changing the Representation to Get Unstuck

In addition to making visualization part of the routine for understanding the problem, changing the representation can be a great way to get unstuck. Sometimes, like in the story of acting out the Zoo Train problem, all it takes is the gentle suggestion that sometimes when they're stuck mathematicians draw pictures, act out the story, use manipulatives to model it, and so on. (That's true, by the way—lots of mathematicians are very visual and use pictures and physical models to help them think, even about very abstract concepts!) Even in the upper grades, making sure that students always have access to manipulatives and know how to request them or get up and find some can really help establish that multiple representations are always available.

Changing the representation can also help students get unstuck when they feel frustrated while solving a problem. Sometimes problem solvers have been looking at a problem one way for so long that they just can't make any more headway, and getting a fresh perspective can really help. Choosing *any* alternate representation and just trying it can be enough. In Chapter 8 we introduce the game Representation Speed Dating, which can be useful in this situation. Or having a list of representations to pull from a hat or randomly choose from can help students do something a little fun and off-the-wall when they're stuck. Of course, not every representation works for every problem (for example, I don't think a number line could have helped the students find the length of their shed rafters), but something a little out there can be fun for getting unstuck. For example, what if students who were stuck on the shed problem used popsicle sticks to do a little construction? Or used acting it out to think about what the builder has to measure and calculate? It might help them gain some new insight into the problem and get over the feeling of having "hit a wall."

Conclusion

Mathematicians really value abstraction—removing mathematics from contexts to work with the quantities and relationships in a purely mathematical context. They like to translate word problems into equations and then manipulate the equations using the rules of algebra without regard to the original meanings of the symbols. In math class, we often push students toward that habit of ignoring the context before they have understood it. We imagine that removing the context will help students see the math, because when we as adults read a text we often see what it's about so quickly that we don't even realize how much attention we've paid to it. For an adult, expert reader, used to the language of math problems, we "get" what's going on and the hard work for us is organizing the mathematical relationships to solve the problem. Our students—many of whom aren't the most fluent readers, very few of whom have extensive experience with the way math problems are written, and too many of whom have learned that they can't and aren't supposed to understand math problems—don't have a lot of tools for grasping what the heck a problem is about.

Next time you present a word problem to your students, asking several of them to tell you what the problem is all about in their own words, asking everyone to draw what's going on and hold it up to show you, or asking small groups of students to act the problem out may reveal to your students that their current habits for reading math problems aren't enough to really make sense of them. Explicit work on drawing and acting out problems and comparing different ways to draw and act out the same problem can support students to read for a full understanding of what's going on. We'd love to know that every class that reads word problems about Americans throwing out billions of dollars' worth of food every year first has the reaction not of "Yikes! A word problem! Ew!" but rather "That's crazy! There are too many people who don't have enough to eat and we don't have enough room to put our trash as it is! I wonder how much of an impact I have on food waste." Then we'd know that our students were reading for understanding in math class, and maybe even developing a sense that math can help them solve problems they care about.

Engaging Students' Number Sense Through Guessing

Focal practices:

1. Make sense of problems and persevere in solving them.
2. Reason abstractly and quantitatively.

I was in a fifth-grade classroom recently, working with students on their problem-solving skills, especially noticing and wondering. The students had been studying bar graphs, interpreting them, and answering all sorts of questions about them. We had done a think-pair-share I Notice, I Wonder™ session (see Chapter 4) about this bar graph:

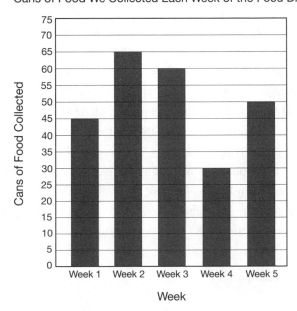

Cans of Food We Collected Each Week of the Food Drive

Then we talked about the problem that was printed on the back of the bar graph:

The bar graph shows the number of cans of food that our grade collected each week of our school's food drive. How many more cans did we collect in week 2 than in week 5?

Students were working in pairs on solving the problem, and most of the pairs looked like they had gotten off to a good start. I noticed a pair that seemed to be stumped so I went over to check in with them. "Should I multiply? Like do 2 times 5?" asked Javi.[1] Wow—at first his question seemed to come out of left field! Then I realized he was thinking about the sentence in the problem, "How many more cans did we collect in week 2 than in week 5?" He was hoping to be able to use the 2 and the 5 he saw in the sentence and his favorite operation to be done. Any sense making he had done about the bar graph went out the window when it was time to calculate—he clearly just wanted to get this problem over and done!

We've found through experience (and heard from other math teachers) that students bring more confidence and more thought to being asked to generate a good guess (or even a bad guess!) than when we ask them to solve the problem right away. Through guessing, they engage in sense making instead of panic.

For a second I didn't know what to do to help. The students had noticed and wondered so much as a class and seemed to have lots of good ideas for thinking about the problem. Why was Javi randomly choosing operations and numbers to try? Part of the explanation was that he had been talking to his partner and struggling to pay attention during the whole-group noticing and wondering. He also didn't seem to realize that the questions on the back of the paper went with the bar graph on the front of the paper. But I suspected something a little deeper was going on as well. The transition from noticing and wondering and making sense of the story to doing actual calculations can be really hard for students—and that made me think of some ideas I could try to help Javi make sense of the calculation part of problem solving, too.

First, I helped Javi and his partner find the bar graph again, and checked that Javi understood it by asking him to tell me more about what he noticed. He noticed all sorts of important things: the labels, that there were five weeks graphed, and the varying heights of the bars. When I asked him, he was even able to read the height of each bar by running his finger along the top of the bar and over to the vertical axis.

After we had looked back at the bar graph, I read the question to Javi and his partner again and, instead of asking them to think right away about how to solve it, I asked them for their *best guess* for how many more cans the students brought in week 2. Specifically, I asked, "Just looking at the bars, how many more cans do you think they might have brought?" Even though Javi was very tentative in his guess, and kept looking to me for affirmation, he was still able to give a pretty sensible guess. He used the bars to estimate how many cans were brought each week and estimated the difference between them—that's a lot farther than he had gotten when he was thinking of multiplying 2 times 5.

Javi's struggles to turn the question into some math he could do weren't about understanding the context, since when I asked him questions about the context, he could answer them. Instead, his struggles were a lot about confidence, and a lot about wanting to find a quick answer and be done with the math that was stressing him out.

---

1. All student names are pseudonyms.

When I gently reminded him of the clues he had, and asked him to make a good guess (something that people usually try to bring a little thought to), Javi was able to do good sense making. When asked to solve a math problem, on the other hand, Javi put his good ideas to the side and tried for dumb luck. Even though most of the other groups had gotten off to a better start than Javi's group and were able to work pretty independently while I talked to Javi, I wish I had thought to have the students do some more estimation and make more best guesses before I asked them to work independently. Maybe Javi would have gotten off to a better start and I could have checked in with more groups.

In this chapter, we'll introduce strategies for gently shifting from noticing, wondering, acting out scenarios, and drawing pictures to getting into actual calculations. We'll focus on making those calculations meaningful and using guessing routines to help students bring their intuition and sense making back into the process, because we've found through experience (and heard from other math teachers) that students bring more confidence and more thought to being asked to generate a good guess (or even a bad guess!) than when we ask them to solve the problem right away. Through guessing, they engage in sense making instead of panic.

The Role of (Good) Guessing and Meaningful Calculation in Good Problem Solving

When we have the sense that students understand a problem's context well enough to tell us what's going on in the story, we're usually confident that they could (if they stopped to think) tell us whether an answer made sense or not. However, when we ask students to do calculations to solve the problem, we've noticed too many students once again abandoning their stop-and-think abilities and going back to a strategy of apply-any-operation-I-can-think-of-to-any-numbers-I-can-see. Students who aren't confident in their mathematical abilities struggle even in contexts they understand.

The trick is to keep the sense making and good thinking they've already done at the forefront of their minds while they begin to do calculations. We've found that asking students to give their best guess, and put out some guesses they are confident are wrong, helps them remember to use clues to make a good guess. We've also found that students tend to have more success when allowed to use Guess and Check as their initial problem-solving strategy, because the process of identifying something to guess for, thinking of what they can figure out based on that guess, and using the story to tell if the guess is right supports them to return to the context and what they've figured out from it.

Students who aren't in the habit of making sense of what's happening in math class, and who try to apply procedures they don't fully understand, are used to ignoring what they think and accepting that math will be confusing. When we ask them if their work makes sense to them, they usually tell us, "How am I supposed to know? I don't get any of this stuff!" On the other hand, when we support those students to start with Guess and Check, they often *can* tell us why they thought their first guess was reasonable, how they know a guess is wrong, and what they can do to improve their next guess. That sense making gives us a platform to build on, to help those students realize that they *can* understand stuff in math class and they have ideas that can lead to problem solutions!

We're the first to admit that Guess and Check can be a tedious process. We've watched students laboriously check every possibility from one into the fifties and beyond! As students learn more sophisticated mathematical techniques, we certainly hope that they will use equations, spreadsheets, graphs, calculators, and logical reasoning in addition to Guess and Check to solve problems. We also try to support students to make Guess and Check an efficient and thoughtful strategy. In this chapter in addition to presenting some guessing routines that help students get started, we've also included an activity to help students learn from one another's Guess and Check work to become more effective at problem-solving skills that are central to Guess and Check, such as:

- ▸ organizing their work
- ▸ spotting patterns and repetition in calculation
- ▸ using previous guesses to make smart next guesses
- ▸ making thoughtful initial guesses
- ▸ using tables and other strategies to reveal patterns.

Guess and Check can serve as a bridge to other strategies like making mathematical models, writing equations, making tables, graphing, working backward, solving a simpler problem, and writing number sentences. If students use Guess and Check in a way that supports them to make sense of problems and then can step back and look for patterns and relationships in their Guess and Check work, other problem-solving strategies that make use of those same relationships can start to make a little more sense.

Key Principles for Teaching Good Guessing and Meaningful Calculation

Guessing activities can be powerful tools for the teacher to assess students' understanding of the problem. If students can't make a guess, or if they guess for the wrong quantities, then they need to do more work to understand the situation. We also want to pay attention to students' number sense—are their guesses within a reasonable margin of the right answer? Because these activities have a formative assessment component and a helping-students-make-sense-of-the-problem component, it's important for the teacher to listen and elicit the students' ideas, rather than giving direct instruction on what or how to guess. We've found that students, once they understand the problem context, are almost always able to come up with at least one guess. Using simple facilitation questions like "How could you check if that was the right answer?" or pointing out another quantity in the problem and saying, "Based on your guess, could you calculate that?" can help students keep persevering with their guess.

Label Everything

One aspect of Guess and Check work that we do tend to be more direct about, though, and try to train students to develop good habits around, is using lots of labels. Occasionally guessing in math class can look more like the kind of wild guessing Javi was doing and less like making a reasonable guess based on all the available data. Javi asked, "Can I just multiply 2 times 5?" completely ignoring the labels on the 2 and the 5. When students are doing their initial calculations and trying to figure out what math they can do to solve a problem, using labels and units helps them keep their calculations more sensible. The Calculate as You Go activity in this chapter explains more about naming what you're calculating, and we want to emphasize that habit in every activity, every time students are guessing or checking, asking about every calculation:

- ▸ What does that measure?
- ▸ How would you label that?
- ▸ What are the units?

Estimation

Finally, when asking students to estimate or use a good guess to start solving problems, we want to help them use the sense-making skills they use in quantitative situations in their non-math-class lives: using benchmark quantities and back-of-the-envelope calculations, noticing clues that can reduce the number of calculations needed, bringing in real-world ramifications, and so on. Sometimes when we ask students to estimate, they try to recall a procedure for estimating that they don't fully understand. In fact, a lot of students, when asked to estimate, will laboriously do an exact calculation and then try to apply a rounding method to the answer. That's not the kind of thinking we're hoping to see here! Asking students for their best guess or their hunch or to take bets on the answer can all disrupt the idea that since this is math class they have to use complicated estimation rules that don't make much sense and can help them use their reasoning skills instead.

Activities

Activity for Estimation

Mathematical-modeling wizard Dan Meyer was one person who helped us see the importance of estimation, and group estimation in particular, for understanding the problem. Estimation is a great way to check for understanding of the problem scenario and begin to move from thinking about the story of the problem to thinking about the answer to the problem—thinking about the problem mathematically.

We'd used a problem-solving activity called Problem of the Week (PoW) IQ—*I* for *information* and *Q* for *question*—that had students working alone and in pairs to write down as much *information* from the problem as they could, and as much as they could about the *question*. What is the question asking? What will the units be for the final answer? Are there any restrictions on the answer? Can it be fractional? Negative? Is the answer a number or range of numbers or rule or explanation or . . . ? Going into problem solving with a goal in mind can be really helpful, and you can find instructions and a student worksheet for PoW IQ on the companion website (http://mathforum.org/pps/). However, we've found that PoW IQ is a pretty advanced activity. Novice problem solvers often struggle to make predictions about answers, and they struggle to make those predictions meaningful.

Meyer developed a routine that helps build these kinds of skills.[2] Once his students have determined the question they're trying to answer (he often uses just an image, video, or scenario as a problem-solving prompt and has students propose the question they'd most like to answer), he asks each student to make their best guess as to an answer. If the problem is a yes-or-no or true-or-false problem, he records how many students predict yes versus no. If the problem will have a numerical solution, he records each student's guess on a number line or list (in numerical order). In addition to a best guess, he also asks for numbers the students think are definitely too high and too low, framing the range of reasonable answers.

From students' best guesses and too-high and too-low answers, teachers can quickly diagnose things like:

- ▸ Are students guessing for the appropriate quantity and using the appropriate units (e.g., in a problem about the cost of bananas, are students' answers in dollars or bananas)?

- ▸ Are students' guesses reasonable (e.g., if students are trying to find the number that 293 is 3% of, are their guesses greater than 293? Are they about 30 times greater?)

- ▸ Are students ruling out negative numbers only when appropriate?

- ▸ Do students recognize the clues in the problem that limit the range of answers?

For example, I was recently leading a problem-solving session with a small group of students who described themselves as not liking math and not being good at problem solving. Overall in their school, most students struggled with reading and math. This problem, which their teacher pulled from *Crossing the River with Dogs*,[3] was on the board:

CHARLIE'S STAMPS

Charlie put postage worth $1.29 on a package he sent to his sister. He used only 16¢ and 7¢ stamps. How many of each kind of stamp did he use?

I was concerned that the students would have trouble making sense of the context, because they may not have had experience with buying postage stamps, and if they had, it was unlikely that they would have used stamps of two different denominations. Not to mention, it's unlikely stamps ever cost a mere 7¢ in these students' lifetimes!

---

2. See http://blog.mrmeyer.com/?p=7604 and http://blog.mrmeyer.com/?p=12141 for more about these ideas.

3. Johnson, Ken, and Ted Herr. 2001. *Problem-Solving Strategies: Crossing the River with Dogs and Other Mathematical Adventures*, 186. Berkeley, CA: Key Curriculum Press.

However, the students had been practicing the Guess and Check strategy, and so I thought that one quick way to get them started thinking about the quantities in the problem, and diagnosing if they understood the calculations that would be needed to solve the problem, would be to have them name some guesses that could work for the problem.

I asked, "If you had to guess an answer to this problem, what would be your best guess?" The responses I got were:

> Six of the 16¢ stamps and four of the 7¢ stamps—Naima
>
> Seven of the 16¢ stamps and four of the 7¢ stamps—Salim
>
> Four of the 16¢ stamps and seven of the 7¢ stamps—Salim
>
> Four of the 16¢ stamps and four of the 7¢ stamps—Zulaikah
>
> There will be more of the 7¢ stamps—Chaneice
>
> I agree with Chaneice—Gladys

From these guesses, I could tell that the students knew which quantities were unknown that could be guessed for and that they were making reasonable guesses. From Chaneice's comment, which Gladys explicitly agreed with and many students nodded at, I got a sense that they were doing some kind of comparison of the prices of the two stamps and noticing that the more stamps used, the more money is spent—likely they could use repeated addition or multiplication to determine how much a given number of stamps would cost.

Then, to help the students narrow their guessing, and to confirm that the students were thinking of multiplying number of stamps times the cost of stamps, I asked them, "What would be a guess that would definitely be too high?" The students suggested multiple possibilities, and there was some disagreement as to whether numbers were too high or not. Several of the students thought Salim had to be wrong in his suggestion of seven 16¢ stamps, but Salim thought it was a good guess. One student settled the debate by confidently declaring, "Seven 16¢ stamps is too high because 7 * 16 = 112." They thought 112 was too close to 129, but Salim thought it was good to have his answer close to $1.29.

I decided not to challenge them further on whether or not seven 16¢ stamps was a good guess, but rather let them continue to think about that as they worked independently. I was confident they would be ready to work independently because they thought to use multiplication to check their guesses and they knew to compare their results to $1.29 (the main constraint in the problem).

Just to have a sense of completion, I also asked for a guess that was definitely too low, and one student quickly said "Four 7¢ stamps." The other students agreed that if you bought only four 7¢ stamps and no 16¢ stamps, you would definitely not have enough postage.

I was confident after getting these guesses on the board that every pair of students understood the problem well enough to generate a guess (at the very least they could copy the guesses from the board) and use multiplication to check the guesses, which turned out to be true—each pair of students was able to get started independently by checking at least one of the guesses on the board and thinking about adjusting from there.

Using the Best Guesses activity helps the teacher diagnose students' current understanding of the problem and helps the teacher confirm that the students can answer, in their own words, the questions "Is your answer reasonable?" and "Does your answer make sense?" If students can't answer those questions, they probably need to do more noticing and wondering, acting out, drawing sketches, and paraphrasing the problem before they continue to calculate or solve the problem (see Chapters 4 and 5).

ACTIVITY Best Guesses[4]

Format: Whole group.

Step 1: Students write down their best guess of the answer to the problem. Then, they write down a number they know is too low, and a number they know is too high.

Step 2: Quickly call on each student to share their best guess. Record each guess on a number line or ordered list, labeling the guess with the students' name and initials (or students can come to the board as they finish and add their own guess to the number line). *Note:* As students give their answers, remind them to use units so we know what they're talking about.

Step 3: Call on multiple students to share their number they know is too low. Record these on the board.

Step 4: Call on multiple students to share their number they know is too high. Record these on the board.

Step 5: Ask if anyone disagrees with any of the too high or too low numbers. For example, the too high and too low numbers may overlap with the range of guesses. Allow students to come to consensus and adjust the range accordingly.

Step 6: Mark the highest "too low" value and lowest "too high" value on the number line or ordered list to provide the range of possible values for the answer.

Guess and Check Activities

In general, we've found that students are pretty comfortable with Guess and Check, at least getting started. Lots of students spontaneously invent the strategy and even get pretty good at it without teacher support (especially if they're already good at making sense of stories and pictures and using manipulatives). But that doesn't mean it's easy or that all students are good at it. The students who were working on Charlie's Stamps had trouble with things like:

▸ Figuring out what headings to put on a table to organize the guesses. The student thought he *had* to use a table and it *had* to be a certain way and couldn't figure out what he was supposed to do, so I had to help him realize I wanted him to guess however he chose.

▸ Choosing a second guess after testing one example that didn't work.

---

4. The Best Guesses activity was inspired and strongly influenced by Dan Meyer's Three-Act Tasks design; see, for example, http://blog.mrmeyer.com/?p=16470.

▸ Keeping track of all of the different numbers in the problem and what to calculate for each guess. I heard things like "What are they supposed to add up to again?" and "Wait, stamps cost 16¢, why was I thinking it was 17¢?"

▸ Persevering: sometimes Guess and Check takes a *lot* of guesses.

▸ Organizing their work to tell what they had guessed before and how it had gone. Some students weren't sure if they were getting any closer or if they had already tried a certain combination of stamps.

▸ Dealing with guessing for two different quantities. Some students kept the number of 16¢ stamps constant and only changed 7¢ stamps. Once they'd tried all the possible 7¢ stamps and none of the combinations added to $1.29, they were stuck.

▸ Deciding if it was okay to be close to $1.29 or if it was possible to get there exactly. This was alleviated by various students shouting, "Ha! I got it!" proving that it was possible.

And those are difficulties that the students had *after* we had done the Best Guess activity and agreed on what we were guessing for and that we were using multiplication and addition to check if the total was exactly $1.29.

Annie (the Math Forum staff member who invented the I Notice, I Wonder activity in Chapter 4) worked with middle school inclusion classes in a small urban district to help them get started with the Guess and Check strategy. Annie and the teachers watched the students attempt to solve a few problems and diagnosed that the students' biggest challenge was understanding the information they were being given and having any idea of how to get started. These students would give up and not even try when faced with any word problem. So Annie worked with their teachers to develop a routine and student worksheet for getting started problem solving using Guess and Check. It was this routine that we later adapted into the Noticing for Guess, Calculate, and Check activity.

Using the Best Guesses activity helps the teacher diagnose students' current understanding of the problem and helps the teacher confirm that the students can answer, in their own words, the questions "Is your answer reasonable?" and "Does your answer make sense?"

ACTIVITY Noticing for Guess, Calculate, and Check

The students had been noticing and wondering together in class but were having trouble getting past that, because as we mentioned, translating noticings and wonderings into unknowns, constraints, and relationships is not easy! The students had a hard time reading a problem and figuring out what to guess for, and they struggled to think of how they would know if their guess was wrong. Annie and their teachers strategized about just what the students needed to do to use Guess and Check independently. They realized that the students needed to focus on noticing the important math: the *quantities* (they defined a quantity as "Something in the problem you can measure") and the *constraints* (they defined a constraint as "Something that is true about the quantities in the problem"). Once they defined these terms they worked with the students to spot quantities and constraints among their noticings.

Then they introduced students to the four basic steps of Guess and Check:

1. Identify the constraints.

2. Make a guess.

3. Check your guess.

4. Repeat as necessary.

With the first problem, many students were writing their guesses all over the paper, or erasing every wrong guess so they saw nothing but the most recent guess. Other students left most of the problem blank, writing down just one guess with no signs that they'd done work to check their answer. A few students systematically checked their guesses, and one student (who rarely worked or spoke during math class!) even recorded whether the guess was too high or too low and adjusted based on that.

After sharing out the work and comparing the different approaches, students had some more ideas for the next problem they tackled with the Guess and Check strategy. Their teachers noticed that most students could identify the constraints and chose a reasonable quantity to guess for. In addition, more students were spontaneously organizing their work in tables and a lot fewer students erased wrong guesses. The teachers emphasized for this problem that they were curious how students would *use their previous guess to decide on their second guess.* Although some students would continue to guess higher numbers even as their results were too high, another student surprised them by reasoning after only one incorrect guess exactly how much to adjust her first guess by to get straight to the correct answer in only two guesses!

As the students solved more and more problems with Guess and Check and shared their work with one another, the teachers started to notice:

- more students getting started independently and confidently
- spontaneous exclamations of "I get it!"
- lots more organization of guesses
- more and more reasonable first guesses and sensible adjustment of guesses
- other strategies that students had not been explicitly supported in or spontaneously used before, such as drawing pictures and using logical reasoning
- students becoming "problem solvers."

The students moved from feeling helpless or that they had to resort to random guessing to believing that they could figure out what the question was asking, how they would know they were right, make reasonable guesses, and figure out if their guess was right.

Format: Whole class.

Step 0: Begin with an I Notice, I Wonder activity (see Chapter 4). Record the noticings and wonderings publicly.

Step 1: Define a quantity as "something you can count or measure." Identify any noticings about *quantities.* Circle the quantities.

Some quantities in Charlie's Stamps include:

- the number of 7¢ stamps
- the number of 16¢ stamps

- ▸ the total number of stamps
- ▸ the amount spent on 7¢ stamps
- ▸ the amount spent on 16¢ stamps
- ▸ the total amount spent on stamps ($1.29).

Note: Students might have named *values*, specific numbers/amounts rather than quantities. When we see that students have noticed the numbers in the problem, we ask, "What does that number measure?" or "What does that number represent?" and we record the quantity as well as the specific value. For example, if the student noticed $1.29, we might ask, "What is 1.29 measuring?" In the stamp problem, $1.29 measures the total amount Charlie spent on stamps so we would record "Total amount spent on stamps ($1.29)."

Step 2: Some of the quantities represent *constraints*, or "something that is true about the quantities in the problem." Put a ★ next to each constraint you noticed.

For example in Charlie's Stamps problem, the main constraint is that the total spent on stamps has to equal $1.29. Another possible constraint is that the number of stamps needs to be a whole number.

Step 3: Choose an unknown quantity or quantities that you can make a guess for. Each student or pair of students should choose a value (or values) to guess and do any calculations that they can with that value. When they reach a quantity that is *constrained*, they should check to see if their guess satisfies the constraint.

Step 4: Invite 2–3 students or pairs of students to share a guess, their calculations, their result, and how they checked their guess. Then ask how they might adjust to find their next guess.

Reflect: Check work and reflect on the process. Did we answer the question by finding the value of the right quantity? Did we identify and satisfy all the constraints? Was the strategy effective? Efficient? Is there anything we want to be sure to do next time we solve a similar problem?

Variation for guided small groups: Small groups that are familiar with the terms *quantities* and *constraints* can work independently to fill out Guess, Calculate, and Check handouts (included on the companion website, http://mathforum.org/pps/). The handouts help them work through and organize the steps above.

The goal with the initial Noticing for Guess, Calculate, and Check activity is independence. To focus on getting good at the Guess and Check strategy, students need to be comfortable with the mechanics. But once students are comfortable, you might hear rumblings of "This takes too long!" or "I don't want to have to do so many guesses," which are signs your students would appreciate exploring how patterns, organization, thoughtful first guesses, and so on can make guessing and checking more efficient. When that happens, talking about different ways to approach and record Guess and Check work gives students a great resource to

The students moved from feeling helpless or that they had to resort to random guessing to believing that they could figure out what the question was asking, how they would know they were right, make reasonable guesses, and figure out if their guess was right.

improve their efficiency and skill. In the class we profiled previously, the students learned a lot from seeing examples of each other's work and talking about what worked well. We like to use class activities like Gallery Walks or presentations with audience questions to help students share and learn from one another's Guess and Check skills and innovations.

When students critique and comment on one another's Guess and Check work, some of the common questions or feedback that they have are:

- How did you know what to guess first?

- It's good to write down your guesses, not just do them on the calculator or erase them. Sometimes you had the right guess or a really close one written down and then you erase it or don't write it down and have to start all over!

- It's easier to read when the calculations go in order instead of being all over the page.

- Making a table helps you read the guesses and see how they came out.

- How did you decide what to guess next?

- When your answer is too high, usually you need to guess a lower number. If your answer is too low, you should probably guess a higher number.

- I could see that each time your guess went up by ____, your answer went up by ____. When your guess went up by 2, your answer went up by 12. You could use that to get to the answer.

- I liked how you changed your guess by the same amount each time so I could see the pattern.

- When you're really far from the answer, sometimes you need to make your guess go up or down by a lot, instead of going one at a time.

- It's a good idea to do your calculations in the same order each time. Maybe you could make a formula so you know what to do for each guess.

If you want your students to incorporate some of these habits and make their Guess and Check work more organized, efficient, and effective, you might try having them comment on one another's work using one of these activities:

ACTIVITY Getting Better at Guess, Calculate, and Check

Format: Gallery Walk

Materials: Poster paper and markers for each group of three, four or five sticky notes in three different colors for each student (12–15 total per student).

Note: On the companion website for this book (http://mathforum.org/pps/), we have some examples of problems that students often solve using Guess and Check, each with a teacher packet. In the Our Solutions section of the packet you'll find one or more Guess and Check strategies. You might consider including one of these examples, perhaps labeled Math Forum Solution, in the Gallery Walk for students to notice and wonder about as well, as a way to bring some new ideas about Guess and Check into the room.

Step 0: Before breaking into small groups, ask students to think about the Guess and Check strategy. What makes it useful? What do they want to get better at? What are some things that different people do differently when they do Guess and Check? Make a list of some categories you want to pay attention to, like choosing what to guess for, adjusting guesses, organizing calculations, showing patterns in results, finding formulas, and so on. Have each group of three students choose one to three categories to focus on.

Step 1: Student groups carry out two or three guesses of a Guess, Calculate, and Check routine. Students should record all their work on the poster paper.

Step 2: Students check over their poster paper work and make sure they showed their guesses, calculations, and checks. Then they hang their poster paper up or set it on their desks for their classmates to read.

Step 3: Give each group one to three different colors of sticky notes, one for each aspect of the Guess and Check strategy the members are thinking about today. Let students know that each color goes with one thing you're paying attention to (e.g., pink is for adjusting guesses, green is for looking for formulas, yellow is for organizing calculations). For younger students, a simpler variation is to give two colors of sticky notes, one for noticing and one for wondering. The students circulate and write one noticing and one wondering on each poster they visit.

Step 4: Group members then circulate to the next poster to their left. For two to three minutes (set a timer!), they read the other group's work and write a noticing or a wondering about each category using the appropriate color sticky note. At the end of the time, they move one poster to the left again, until each group has read all the posters. In a small classroom or if students have trouble moving around the class freely, the students can stay still and pass their papers to the left. In this case, using regular paper works well.

Step 5: Students return to their own poster, read the sticky notes on their poster and discuss them.

Step 6: As a class, students share what they noticed from the Gallery Walk. Address each area you were focused on and think of things you noticed that seemed to work well and things you are wondering about.

Step 7: Each small group answers the question "We can get better at _____ in Guess and Check by _____" for each category.

Variation: Audience participation.

As in the Gallery Walk activity, choose three focal categories for attending to (e.g., picking the next guess, organizing calculations, and picking a good first guess). Have small groups carry out some guesses (make sure each group has at least two guesses recorded, or the correct answer and how they checked it). Before beginning small-group report-backs, count the audience members off by threes. Ones will pay special attention to the first focal category (e.g., picking the next guess); twos to the second; and threes to the third. After each small group presents, give students a chance to jot down thoughts about their focal category. After all presentations, have the ones, twos, and threes get together to discuss what they heard. Each group should answer the question, "We can get better at _____ in Guess and Check by _____" for their category. Ones, twos, and threes can report out to the whole group or make Getting Good at Guess and Check posters to display for the class.

Activities to Build Strategies for Making Initial Calculations

Before we wrap up this chapter, we wanted to share a few more tips and activities for loosening students up and moving gently from open-ended noticing and wondering to (gasp!) actually calculating with numbers. It can be a moment where math-phobic students tune out (and according to recent research, actually feel physical pain) and so helping close the gap between sense-making conversations and calculations is really important. The focus in these activities should be on doing *sensible* calculations, ones that make sense based on the students' current understanding. Focusing on labeling results and asking and answering "What does that calculation tell us?" are really important.

ACTIVITY Calculate as You Go

> **Format:** Students working in pairs.
>
> **Step 0:** Give students these instructions: "Read the problem to yourself. Think about the values in the problem. What do they measure? What are the units? When you've read the problem, find a partner and choose who will be Partner A and who will be Partner B."
>
> **Step 1:** Partner A says, "A calculation I could do is _____" and Partner B fills in the blank.
>
> > Partner A listens for the *values* (aka numbers) in the calculation and says "[Value A] measures _____." Partner B fills in the blank.
> >
> > Partner A: "[Value B] measures _____." Partner B fills in the blank.
> >
> > Partner A: "The label for the answer is _____." Partner B fills in the blank.
>
> **Step 2:** Have students switch roles, trying to do at least four rounds (calculation, each value measures _____, the label for the answer is _____). Each person has two turns to be the asker and two turns to fill in the blanks.
>
> **Step 3:** Have students, working together, write down as many calculations as they can remember. Encourage them to make sure to write the *units* and label the answer! If any of the calculations listed didn't make sense to one or both partners, they can choose to not write them down.
>
> *Variation*: Make this into a friendly competition, awarding points for the most calculations (with measurements and labels), as well as the most calculations that actually make sense.

The idea is to encourage playfulness, acknowledge those calculations that pop into our heads that don't make sense, and begin to internalize some habits for making sure your calculations make sense, like always asking yourself "What does this measure?" whenever you're using "naked numbers" in a calculation.

We like this fill-in-the-blanks format when we want students to learn a routine they can use even without a partner. Learning to ask yourself, "What are the units? How would I label this answer?" is a really important skill! Rehearsing it until you get fluent helps it become automatic. Here is a sample dialogue you could use to model this process for students.

THE PROBLEM: I GET A KICK OUT OF SOCCER

As I watched our high school soccer team practice, I heard the coach instruct the team to do laps and then hit the showers. I got to wondering how many times they would need to run around the field to complete at least one mile.

I walked over to the coach and asked for the dimensions of the field. He said that our soccer field is 75 yards wide and 115 yards long.

How many laps would a team member need to complete to run more than a mile?

The Sample Dialogue

Partner A: A calculation you could do is . . .

Partner B: . . . 75 * 115.

Partner A: Seventy-five measures . . .

Partner B: . . . how many yards wide the field is.

Partner A: One hundred fifteen measures . . .

Partner B: . . . how many yards long the field is.

Partner A: The label for the answer of 75 * 115 is . . .

Partner B: . . . length times width. Area, I guess.

Switch roles!

Partner B: A calculation you could do is . . .

Partner A: . . . 75 + 115.

Partner B: Seventy-five measures . . .

Partner A: . . . how many yards wide the field is.

Partner B: One hundred fifteen measures . . .

Partner A: . . . how many yards long the field is.

Partner B: The label for the answer of 75 + 115 is . . .

Partner A: . . . how far running two sides of the field is.

Switch roles!

Partner A: A calculation you could do is . . .

Partner B: . . . 75 + 115 + 75 + 115.

Partner A: Seventy-five measures . . .

Partner B: . . . how many yards wide the field is.

Partner A: One hundred fifteen measures . . .

Partner B: . . . how many yards long the field is.

Partner A: The label for the answer of 75 + 115 + 75 + 115 is . . .

Partner B: . . . how far one lap is.

Switch roles!

Partner A: A calculation you could do is . . .

Partner B: . . . 1 mile to 5,280 feet.

Partner A: One measures . . .

Partner B: . . . how many miles the team has to run (at least).

Partner A: Five thousand two hundred eighty measures . . .

Partner B: . . . how many feet in a mile.

Partner A: The label for the answer of 1 mile to 5,280 feet . . .

Partner B: . . . how far the team has to run in feet (at least).

Not all of the calculations these partners thought to do are needed to solve the problem. As they reread the problem and begin to use their calculations to actually answer the question, they should see that only calculations about length, not area, are relevant here. However, many students when solving this problem wonder, "Should I multiply the length and width?" Doing that calculation and then noticing what that calculation actually measures makes it easier to rule it out than just trying to think, "Should I multiply or not? Who knows!"

ACTIVITY Do It Wrong!

Format: Whole group.

Step 1: Like in the Best Guess activity, once students have an idea of the question they're answering, ask a volunteer for an answer that they think is probably wrong. It could be too high or too low or just some number they like that's likely to be wrong.

Step 2: Ask students who volunteer, "If, by some miracle, this number were really the right value, what's one other value you could figure out?" Have them explain the calculation they're doing.

Step 3: Continue to ask volunteers, exaggerating that this isn't the right answer but if miraculously it were, what calculations they could do. Listen for the mutterings, "That can't be right because. . . ."

Step 4: Once a calculation has violated some constraint of the problem, mention, "We thought this wouldn't turn out to be the right answer. Can anyone prove it's not the right answer now?"

Step 5: Ask students, "So, we didn't solve the problem. We weren't miraculously right. But did we learn anything about the problem?" Call on as many students as you can to tell one thing they learned from trying the problem, even with an answer they knew was wrong.

Step 6: At this point, some students might be ready to check more guesses, while other students may be able to use their understanding of the problem to find direct methods to solve the problem. They may use logical reasoning, patterns, or encode their calculations into equations or rules for calculating the answer directly. Let students work independently or in groups by strategy to find the right answer to the problem.

The Do It Wrong strategy supports students to find the relationships they will use to solve the problem, without being stuck in the mind-set of "It's not worth calculating if I don't know I'm right." How often do you hear students say, "This probably isn't right but . . ." and then say some brilliant thing? This activity relieves the "This probably isn't right but . . ." pressure—we know we will be wrong, but at least we can think about the problem!

The risk is that, especially as a whole-group activity, students may think, "We're not going to get the right answer, so why should I pay attention?" Too many students who have learned to accept a passive role in math class believe their job is to copy down exactly the steps that get the right answer from the information given.

To avoid some of these pitfalls, playing up the goofiness of what you're doing can help. "We know this answer is wrong, but just, what if. . . ." Also, calling on students randomly (pull their names out of a hat or generate random numbers associated with their desk position or place on the attendance sheet) can make sure everyone's engaged in the "game." But the most important moment is the question of what was learned about the problem from going through these incorrect calculations. What is the advantage of generating and doing calculations based on the answer, even knowing that we aren't using the correct answer? We hope that students might value things like,

> ▸ We could still think about the problem even though we didn't know the right answer.

> ▸ We figured out what made that answer wrong so that helped us narrow down some wrong answers.

How often do you hear students say, "This probably isn't right but . . ." and then say some brilliant thing? This activity relieves the "This probably isn't right but . . ." pressure—we know we will be wrong, but at least we can think about the problem!

▸ At first we didn't understand the problem but when we figured out a guess and why it was wrong, we thought of how we could check other answers and eventually get the right answer.

▸ At first the problem was really confusing but going through one answer helped us see what the problem was about. Now we can have an idea for how to get the right answer!

▸ It was fun doing it wrong because we didn't have to worry about being right, but it was still kind of helpful even though it wasn't going to get us the right answer. It helped us understand the problem.

Analyzing what makes a wrong answer wrong is almost as valuable to solving problems as finding the right answer—for one thing, if you know what made the wrong answer wrong, you might be able to rule out a lot more wrong answers and come up with the right one! Assuming an answer and exploring what properties it does and doesn't have is actually a sophisticated mathematical strategy, and one that students should have some positive experience with as they develop their problem-solving routines.

Building Student Independence: Sensible Guessing

So far, we've explored the sense-making moments at the beginning of solving math problems. We've introduced problem-solving tools like I Notice, I Wonder that support students to slow down and focus on the details of the problem, strategies like Act It Out and Draw a Picture (see Chapter 5) that help students understand the overall story of the problem and what's actually happening. In this chapter, we introduced tools and activities for shifting the focus from making sense of the context and details we've been given (or wish we'd been given) to starting to do calculations based on the numbers and objects in the problem.

The focus has been on keeping those operations sensible and giving students tools to answer the question "Is that reasonable?" or "Does that answer make sense in terms of the story?" As we discussed in Chapter 5, students need to practice making sense of what they read, even in math class. Students who get better at reading the whole story, understanding what it's about and representing it in multiple ways, and noticing and wondering both details and big ideas in math stories can be encouraged to use those skills to really answer the questions "Is this reasonable?" and "Does this make sense?"

As your students do some of the activities in this chapter, from giving problems their best guess before jumping in to purposely working through problems with one wrong answer or several guesses in a thoughtful Guess and Check approach, listen to hear if your students are:

▸ using units and labels to talk about the numbers in the problem (because the numbers are part of a bigger story that they are accountable to)

▸ able to identify one or more unknown values in the problem that they could confidently make a guess for

▸ making guesses that are increasingly accurate (showing they're getting better at number sense or understanding contexts or both)

▸ further restricting the range of reasonable values based on relationships in the problem (e.g., identifying that the answer doesn't just have to be positive but also even and greater than twenty)

▸ able to identify whether possible solutions fit the constraints or "rules" given in the problem

▸ spontaneously developing ways to check their classmates' answers, or mentioning "Hey, that doesn't make sense," or "Are you sure that works?" when they hear something that may not be sensible. Often we hear students learning to check others' reasoning before they internalize the ability to monitor their own reasoning.

Guessing to Get Unstuck

In this chapter we shared several examples of students getting unstuck through guessing, from Javi going from clueless to thoughtful, to the students who worked with Annie to "become problem solvers" as their teachers put it. We also mentioned the idea of using the Guess and Check strategy to diagnose the students' understanding of the problem. Guess and Check can be used to diagnose which "kinds of stuck" students are—can students make a guess? Once they've made the guess, can they figure out any helpful calculations to do? Do they have a way to check if their guess was right? Those are all different kinds of stuck that call for different kinds of getting unstuck. Here are some descriptions students can use to diagnose the kinds of stuck they are:

Guess Stuck

▸ I don't know what to guess. I don't even understand what the problem is asking.

▸ I don't know what is a reasonable guess to make.

Calculation Stuck

▸ I made a guess but I don't know how to use it to see if it works. What calculations can I do, based on my guess?

▸ I could check my guess, but I don't know how to do this calculation.

Check Stuck

▸ I tested my guess and did some calculations, but I don't know what that tells me.

▸ How can I tell if I'm right?

▸ How can I tell if I got closer? How do I figure out if my results make sense?

They can use these diagnoses to

▸ Ask for help.

▸ Reread the problem with a specific goal/question in mind.

Specifically, if students are stuck on the *guess*, they might make a list of all the quantities they can notice and which ones they don't know the value of. Could they make a guess for any of them? What clues tell them whether the number will be big or small?

If students are stuck on the *calculations*, they can try the Calculate as You Go activity in this chapter, or they might try setting up a table and seeing which other quantities in the problem they can figure out the value of. If there's a specific calculation they don't know how to do, they can ask for help.

If students are stuck on the *check*, the first thing to do is make sure they've found all the constraints in the problem. There are the obvious clues, but students might also want to think about hidden assumptions like whether the numbers have to be whole numbers. Students might know the constraints but not know how to get from their guessed value to the constraints. One thing to try is finding a different quantity to guess for. If you're having trouble getting closer guessing the *number* of 7¢ and 16¢ stamps, you could try guessing the *amount spent* on 7¢ and 16¢ stamps, for example.

In summary, not only can making a good guess be a good way to get started when you feel stuck, the Guess and Check strategy can be used on a wide variety of problems to help you say what kind of stuck you feel. Students often struggle to articulate what's going on when they're stuck—beyond "I don't get it!" or "This problem is too hard!" we rarely get to hear a description of what's getting them stuck. Guess and Check gives students a way to ask for help, even if they don't end up using Guess and Check to solve the problem in the end.

Conclusion

As teachers of elementary and middle school students, helping our students get good at the Guess and Check strategy is preparing them to do algebra in important ways. Al Cuoco and Bowen Kerins, from the Center for Mathematics Education and authors of the CME Project high school math books, recommend Guess-Check-Generalize as a powerful *habit of mind* that applies across the high school (and beyond!) math curriculum. In their textbook, they emphasize doing at least one, and probably several, guesses on many algebra problems. Then, by replacing the guess with a variable (an activity that we'll describe in more detail in Chapter 7), the student can make a mathematical equation to solve, graph, or apply to other problems. If students get to high school good at setting up Guess and Check from problem scenarios, by identifying unknown quantities, relationships, and constraints, then think how well positioned they will be in high school to use Guess and Check to generalize equations.

As Kerins and Cuoco point out, Guess-Check-Generalize is a powerful habit of mind because:

- Students have a starting point: try numbers.
- Students learn more about variables.
- Students organize work to see patterns.
- Students look for proportional or linear patterns, and make "nice" guesses.[5]

Approaching problems from a starting point of trying some numbers (which is what research mathematicians and people who use math in their careers tend to do), being comfortable with variables, organizing work to see patterns, and working hard to make "friendly" patterns are all things that mathematicians are good at (and all practices emphasized in the Common Core). Guess and Check is the basis on which these high school textbook authors base those powerful habits of mind!

---

5. See http://cmeproject.edc.org/sites/cmeproject.edc.org/files/2008-04-NCTM-gen-purp-tools.pdf.

7

Getting Organized

Focal practices:

8. Look for and express regularity in repeated reasoning.
2. Reason abstractly and quantitatively.

I n this chapter we'll talk about how guessing and checking, noticing and wondering, and drawing pictures can become part of a process of organizing and recording work very systematically in tables, lists, graphs, and other mathematically powerful ways.

Why Be Organized?

$$(1 \cdot \bigcirc)(2 \cdot \diamondsuit) = 48$$

$$\bigcirc - \diamondsuit = \text{-}5$$

$$\diamondsuit^2 + \bigcirc^2 = 73$$

$$\frac{3 \cdot \diamondsuit}{8 \cdot \bigcirc} = 1$$

Figure 1

I was working with a group of seventh-grade girls on finding values they could plug in for the circle and the diamond (in Figure 1) that would make each of the equations or "clues" true, at the same time. The girls had done a lot of noticing and wondering and had some good ideas about the operations in each equation. They felt very confident that their Guess and Check strategy would get them to an answer. Since they were working so confidently, I left them and went to talk to another group that was having more trouble getting started.

When I came back, the girls looked, well, droopy. They were draped dramatically over their desks, heads in their hands, moaning. It looked like they'd been attacked by a fast-acting flu virus! When I asked what was wrong, they whined, "We're never going to get the answer! We've tried everything! It's impossible!" I commented that when I left, it looked like they'd been close to getting the answer. I asked them what they had tried so far, and they looked at each other, shocked. "We didn't write them down. We don't know what we tried. We just tried everything."

It turns out they'd been thinking of numbers, typing them into their calculators, and when the numbers didn't work, they'd just deleted the calculations and gone onto another set of numbers. One girl had done some calculation by hand, but she had diligently erased each row when it wasn't right.

This was typical behavior in the class. If any numbers ever made it onto paper, they were erased or scratched into oblivion immediately upon being found to be "wrong." What this meant was that, other than maybe adjusting a guess higher if the final answer was too low or lower if a final answer was too high, no one in this class could learn from their Guess and Check work. They were never going to get good at the mathematical practice, "Look for and make use of regularity in repeated reasoning."

The Importance of Organizing Information

Teachers of problem solving often ask, "If I can't tell students the answer, and I can't tell them how to solve the problem, what's my role? What can I tell them? Do I just have to let them struggle for as long as it takes?" I often share the story of the girls who were going to have to guess and check *forever* because they had no good way of organizing their Guess and Check work. It does make sense for teachers to intervene with, and be direct about, strategies and tools for organizing problem-solving work.

A lot of mathematical content, from elementary concepts like arrays and place value, to middle school topics like the Cartesian plane and ratio tables, to high school subjects like algebra, are all about learning the mathematical conventions for organizing and representing information. Place value is just a way of using organization so that the digit 7 can represent seven ones, seven tens, seven hundreds, or even seven tenths, just by where it is placed. The Cartesian plane is a way of representing relationships between two quantities by plotting them on two perpendicular number lines. And algebra is a way of encoding quantities and operations on quantities that is as compact and easily manipulated as possible. As math teachers, one of our main jobs is to expose students to these universal ways of organizing data, because they are such powerful and widely used tools (and waiting around for every generation of students to reinvent them would take more time than we have to wait).

We don't want to teach them rote procedures that they think will work every time, but rather general tools and principles for organizing their thinking.

But remember: We are supporting students to become better problem solvers—to do math that they don't already know how to solve. We don't want to teach them rote procedures that they think will work every time, but rather general tools and principles for organizing their thinking. When showing students techniques for being organized in mathematical problem solving, we like to start with what the student has already thought of, and find an organizational structure that emerges from what they've already tried. We also like to use compare-and-contrast activities that have students looking at multiple pieces of student work and noticing the different ways it can be organized, and the advantages and disadvantages of each. Focusing on organization as the goal and presenting multiple kinds of organizations or organizations that improve bit by bit based on what the student is already doing help students to own and internalize the organization, instead of saying things like "Do we have to?" or "That's too hard!"

Learning to record and organize problem-solving work in a way that reveals patterns, makes repeated reasoning visible, and shows underlying structures is an important skill. Training in certain kinds of organization and representation is important for students, and it is best given (because it is best received) when the student has asked or otherwise indicated that they are ready and willing to learn a new, more powerful way to write their work. Some of the activities in the next chapter, such as Problem-Solving Bids and What Would Happen If . . . ? can provide incentives for students to wish their work was better organized. When students ask, "How can we do this more efficiently?" or tell us, "I don't know how to find a rule/pattern, it doesn't make sense," this is a great time to train them in some of the mathematical habits and skills represented in this chapter.

Different Ways to Organize

The following problem can help us look at different ways students organize information.

CUPCAKES, CUPCAKES!

Andrei's school is having a Science Fair this afternoon and he agreed to bring four dozen cupcakes for the reception afterward. To catch his bus, he needs to be out of the house at 7:50 am. He started icing the cupcakes at 7:40 am at a rate of 3 cupcakes per minute.

He soon realized that he wasn't going to finish in time, so at 7:44 his older sister, Zoe, started icing cupcakes too. She iced them at a rate of 4 cupcakes per minute. As they iced the cupcakes, they placed them directly in the boxes that he would carry on the bus. This way, when they iced the last cupcake, Andrei would be ready to dash out the door.

Question: Did they finish in time for Andrei to catch his bus? Explain.

Extra: When did they finish icing the last cupcake?

Here are three tables that students submitted to the online version of this problem in 2012. What do you notice about the different tables? What do you wonder?

Table 1

At 7:40, in the beginning, the total number of cupcakes frosted = 0.
At 7:41, total cupcakes frosted = 0 + 3 = 3 (3 by Andrei).
At 7:42, total cupcakes frosted = 3 + 3 = 6 (3 by Andrei).
At 7:43, total cupcakes frosted = 6 + 3 = 9 (3 by Andrei).
At 7:44, total cupcakes frosted = 9 + 3 = 12 (3 by Andrei).
Now Zoe also starts frosting 4 cupcakes per minute with Andrei.

At 7:45, total cupcakes frosted = 12 + 3 + 4 = 19 (3 by Andrei, 4 by Zoe).
At 7:46, total cupcakes frosted = 19 + 3 + 4 = 26 (3 by Andrei, 4 by Zoe).
At 7:47, total cupcakes frosted = 26 + 3 + 4 = 33 (3 by Andrei, 4 by Zoe).
At 7:48, total cupcakes frosted = 33 + 3 + 4 = 40 (3 by Andrei, 4 by Zoe).
At 7:49, total cupcakes frosted = 40 + 3 + 4 = 47 (3 by Andrei, 4 by Zoe).
At 7:50, total cupcakes frosted = 47 + 3 + 4 = 54 (3 by Andrei, 4 by Zoe).

Table 2

Andrei		Zoe	
7:40–41	3 cupcakes iced		
7:41–42	3 cupcakes iced		
7:42–43	3 cupcakes iced		
7:43–44	3 cupcakes iced		
7:44–45	3 cupcakes iced	7:44–45	4 cupcakes iced
7:45–46	3 cupcakes iced	7:45–46	4 cupcakes iced
7:46–47	3 cupcakes iced	7:46–47	4 cupcakes Iced
7:47–48	3 cupcakes iced	7:47–48	4 cupcakes iced
7:48–49	3 cupcakes iced	7:48–49	4 cupcakes iced
7:49–50	3 cupcakes iced	7:49–50	4 cupcakes iced

Table 3

Time	Cupcakes Iced
7:40–7:41	3/48
7:41–7:42	6/48
7:42–7:43	9/48
7:43–7:44	12/48
7:44–7:45	19/48
7:45–7:46	26/48
7:46–7:47	33/48
7:47–7:48	40/48
7:48–7:49	47/48
7:49–7:50	48/48

Looking at their work we can see that they saw a lot of things they could count (i.e., a lot of the same *quantities*):

▸ time of day

▸ number of cupcakes iced so far

▸ total number of cupcakes iced per minute

▸ running total of iced cupcakes

▸ number of cupcakes needed to ice (48)

▸ number of cupcakes iced by Andrei per minute (3)

▸ number of cupcakes iced by Zoe per minute (4).

As mathematicians and math teachers we always like to ask more and more questions like "Are there patterns here? Can we make a rule or a prediction? How can we extend the problem? How long would it take them to ice enough cupcakes for our whole school? For our whole city? How many people would need to help if we wanted to ice enough cupcakes for our whole school in just six minutes?"

But interestingly, not every table shows all of the quantities, and they don't represent the relationships in the same ways.

▸ Table 2 doesn't include a running total of iced cupcakes. That might make it tricky to see quickly if Andrei and Zoe will catch the bus.

▸ Table 3 doesn't show the number of cupcakes iced each minute, by Zoe, by Andrei, or by the two together. If some of the numbers in Table 3 were off, it might be hard to check them. Also, if you wanted to write a rule for total number of cupcakes iced in M minutes, it would be hard to see how to write the rule from Table 3.

▸ Table 1 shows us some different patterns in the numbers, for example how each minute after 7:44 is 7 more cupcakes than the previous minute. But even from Table 1, while it would be easy to write a rule to tell how to find the next minute if you know this minute (add 3 if it's before 7:44, add 7 if it's after), it is hard to see how you could write a rule that would help you find how many cupcakes were iced if you didn't know how many cupcakes had been iced in all the previous minutes.

All three of these tables show important ways to organize the quantities and answer the important question: Will Andrei be able to catch the bus and keep his promise of making cupcakes for the science fair? But as mathematicians and math teachers we always like to ask more and more questions like "Are there patterns here? Can we make a rule or a prediction? How can we extend the problem? How long would it take them to ice enough cupcakes for our whole school? For our whole city? How many people would need to help if we wanted to ice enough cupcakes for our whole school in just six minutes?"

Questions that extend patterns and go beyond what's shown in the first few lines of tables often benefit from good organization and thoughtful ways of representing the quantities and relationships in a problem (in Chapter 8 there's a whole activity about extending problems, What Would Happen If?). One of the mathematical practices in the Common Core is "Look for and represent regularity in repeated reasoning." One of the main reasons mathematicians try to be (1) neat and organized and (2) creative and artistic is so that when they do "repeated reasoning" (anything with a pattern!) they can be sure to spot as many patterns as possible and to represent their reasoning in new and interesting ways that make different patterns jump out!

Activities

The activity Getting Better at Guess, Calculate, and Check in Chapter 6 can also be used to focus students' attention on organization and repeated reasoning.

Activity for Moving from Noticing to Organization

My coworkers must have thought I was crazy when I chose to do the following problem (which, despite using arithmetic covered between third and fifth grades, has been known to give undergraduate engineering majors difficulties!) with the parents, siblings, and grandparents of students who had come to Drexel for after-school enrichment. Sure enough, the participants in this Saturday morning workshop ranged from a first-grade sibling to parents and grandparents who hadn't been in a math classroom for decades. After almost an hour of counting games, in which we counted by whole numbers (especially fun ones like nine, ten, and eleven), by fractions, by units of measure, and even by the cost of a subway token, I brought out Cat Walk.

CAT WALK

A dog takes three steps to walk the same distance for which a cat takes four steps. Suppose one step of the dog covers $\frac{1}{2}$ foot. How many feet would the cat cover in taking 24 steps?

It has that classic word problem feel to it, doesn't it? The families at the workshop started to get that look in their eyes, between the confusing wording, the fractions, the hidden ratios. So I quickly said, "Hey, look, another situation to count about! Just like we counted by subway tokens and half cups. What are some things we could count by in this problem? Let's make a table!"

Spending the morning training our brains to see counting, through structured, step-by-step games and activities, made us a little more primed to apply counting in this tougher situation. I continued to lead the group in a more hands-on way because my main goal was to have them feel success that made them aware of the power of counting routines and to learn some good habits for counting in all sorts of problems.

So the families made a list of everything they thought they could count by, and labeled it:

- count by 3s (dog steps)
- count by 4s (cat steps)
- count by $\frac{1}{2}$s (distance of one dog step).

I didn't tell them what to put on the list, though, because I wanted to learn about their thinking and make sure they were connecting their own ideas to the counting routines!

I made a table with columns for Dog Steps, Cat Steps, and Distance (modeling an organization habit). The families started to fill in the table, going down the columns. They stopped when they got to 24 cat steps:

Dog Steps	Cat Steps	Distance
3	4	
6	8	
9	12	
12	16	
15	20	
18	24	
21		
24		

When they went to fill in the distance column, I reminded them that $\frac{1}{2}$ was the length of 1 dog step. No one was comfortable with the idea of counting by $\frac{3}{2}$ for the length of 3 dog steps, so I amended the table (modeling a way to be flexible with tables based on their preference for how to count in this problem):

Dog Steps	Cat Steps	Distance
		$\frac{1}{2}$
		1
3	4	$1\frac{1}{2}$
		2
		$2\frac{1}{2}$
6	8	3
		$3\frac{1}{2}$
		4
9	12	$4\frac{1}{2}$
		5
		$5\frac{1}{2}$
12	16	6
		$6\frac{1}{2}$
		7
15	20	$7\frac{1}{2}$
		8
		$8\frac{1}{2}$
18	24	9

The families were so proud to have come up with a solution to a hard math word problem, one that college students struggled to solve. They were especially proud because the counting method we had practiced gave them a way to not just solve the problem but also to make sense of the answer. That question "What could we count by?" became the seed that germinated into this next activity, Setting Up and Sharing Tables. A student-friendly handout to support students thinking about what to organize is available on the companion website (http://mathforum.org/pps/).

ACTIVITY Setting Up and Sharing Tables

The activity is given in three parts, though you don't need to do all three parts every time. Part 1 helps students who are struggling to transition from open-ended noticing and wondering to mathematical noticing and wondering that helps them make sense of problems: noticing quantities and relationships.

Part 2 is when students actually make the table. If your students have solved problems using Guess and Check, or they are thorough at noticing and wondering, starting with part 2 might make sense.

Part 1

Format: Whole-group brainstorm (or students working in groups of 3–4).

Step 1: Give students a problem in which organizing information is important, such as Cat Walk or Cupcakes, Cupcakes! Give them 2 minutes to write down as much as they can of what they notice and wonder about the problem. Or use the What Do You Hear? oral noticing and wondering method (see Chapter 4) for this portion.

Step 2: As a group, have students generate a list (or organize their noticings based on) all of the quantities that they can find in the problem. You might ask, "What can we *count* in this problem?" and "What can we *measure* in this problem?" Record each quantity using a *specific name* and units for it. For example, if a student says "We can count steps," we wouldn't list *steps* as a quantity. First, we would ask students "Whose steps are you talking about?" As the student clarifies "dog steps" or "cat steps," we would record that more specific name for the quantity.

For older students, we sometimes ask them to use three columns to organize their thinking: Quantities, Values, and Units. These help establish their good habits of labeling the numbers they use with descriptive quantity names and units. For example:

Quantities	Values	Units
Length of dog step	1.5	feet
Length of cat step	?	feet
Number of cat steps	24	steps
Number of dog steps	?	steps

Step 3: As a group, have students make a list of (or continue to organize their notic-ings based on) relationships. We often follow up the question, "What relationships did you notice?" with "What calculations can you think of to do?" as well as asking students about things that have to be equal, greater than, or less than other things. Record re-lationships using the names of quantities, for example rather than writing 0.5 * 3, write Length of 3 dog steps = 3 * Length of 1 dog step. The Calculate as You Go activity in Chapter 6 is a good way to practice finding relationships and using quantity names and units.

Make sure the list is displayed publicly so that students have it available for part 2.

Part 2

Format: Students working in pairs.

Note: Since students will be reflecting on ordering rows and columns, working on a com-puter using spreadsheet software will make it easier for them to reorder and add or sub-tract rows and columns. If that is an option in your classroom, you might make computers available to each partnership.

Step 1: Each pair of students works together to set up a table. Let students know that you'd like to see them *label* their rows and columns, and it might be helpful to use the names of *quantities* that they've already written to label each column.

Step 2: Then have each pair fill out the table by adding rows and filling out each row. They can use the *relationships* they identified to help figure out what goes in each cell of the table.

Step 3: Encourage them, if they notice ways to reorder the table or columns to add or combine, to make those changes. Ask them to take note of what they changed and why so they can share with the group.

Step 4: If students finish early, suggest they use their tables to look for patterns and generate some new wonderings:

- Look for patterns within each column.
- Look for patterns in the calculations you are doing.
- Look for patterns across the rows of the table.
- Can you think of any ways to make patterns more visible in your table?
- Can you think of any ways to write the patterns as rules, formulas, equations, or in other mathematical ways?
- What do you wonder, looking at your table?
- Is there another way someone could make a table for this same problem? What might be different?

<u>**Part 3**</u> Table Gallery Walk

Format: Gallery Walk (for more ideas for structuring Gallery Walks for students of different ages and abilities, see the Guess and Check Gallery Walk in Chapter 6).

Materials: Poster paper, two different colors of sticky notes.

Step 1: Partners post their table in a spot on the wall. If they have questions about their table, they include them on the poster.

Step 2: Students rotate around the room to look at each different table. For each table other than their own, students write one thing they notice that was similar to their own table, and on the other color sticky note, one thing that was different from their own table. You might want to set a timer to help the students circulate efficiently.

Step 3: As a group, discuss some of the similarities and differences among the tables. For each, make a list of the pros and cons of the different ways. For example, a table that shows results but not calculations might be easier to spot numerical patterns in, but harder to see repeated calculations that lead to formulas.

A teacher friend of ours, Christine Yeannakis, recently started working with second-grade students at a private school. The students were using a Singapore math–based curriculum and their teacher decided to supplement it with some "juicy" problems—problems that would get students developing reasoning and sense making. The students got to use a version of Setting Up Tables when they worked on one of their first "juicy" problems, Marble Mayhem:

MARBLE MAYHEM

Fred, Ginger, Julio, and Dawn decided to play marbles. Fred emptied his bag of marbles and divided them equally among the four players. Everyone got at least one marble. There was one marble left over.

At that moment Jake arrived and asked to play. They gathered up all Fred's marbles and divided them equally among the five kids. There was still one marble left over.

Just then Maria joined them, so they gathered all the marbles again and divided them equally six ways. There was still one marble left over.

What is the fewest number of marbles that Fred could have had in his bag?

Here's how their teacher described it: "I modeled the noticing process. I helped them make notes on big paper. Two girls are working together, one alone. (The other kids were doing other work.). I helped them make a big guess and check chart. The girls told me the other columns that were needed."

The teacher had divided the paper into two columns, "Guess" and "Check." Her young students, even though they were new to juicy problems, realized from their noticing and wondering that there was more to be organized than just making a guess and checking it in one step. They were able to suggest additional columns called "÷ 4" "left over" "÷5" "left over" "÷6" "left over." These columns provided enough organization for the students to work through the problem. Their teacher continued, "The girls immediately grabbed stuff to act out the problem. They used wooden figures to stand for each of the players and centimeter cubes to stand for the different number of marbles they were guessing. They guessed numbers, acted the problem out, and recorded the results in the tables they had set up and organized themselves. The girls were so engaged and thoughtful I grabbed another teacher to come in and have a look."

Even for young students, using noticing and wondering to think about what you could write in a table or organized list is an accessible and powerful strategy! It's worth mentioning, when thinking about young students' tables, that a table can be as simple as just a few rows, like these two tables that helped elementary students think about some patterns in calendars (mistakes or deletions are the student's):

Years between 1923 and 1934	1923	1924	1925	1926	1927	1928	1930	1931	1932	1933	1934
Multiple of 7	No	No	Yes	No	No	No	No	No	Yes	No	No
Multiple of 4 (leap year)	No	Yes	No	No	No	Yes	No	No	Yes	No	No

Boar Years
1. 2007
2. 1995
3. 1983
4. 1971
5. 1959
6. 1947
7. 1935

Although these tables are just a few rows or columns, they helped the students organize their thinking and supported them to see patterns, such as the twelve-year difference between successive Boar Years or when a year would be both a multiple of four and seven. The students thought of important quantities, and labeled their tables with them (e.g., "Years between 1923 and 1934" and "Boar Years"). The labels helped the students communicate their thinking, and the tables helped them keep track of their work and systematically keep track of different values.

Activities for Finding Structure and Patterns

The reason mathematicians value organization so much is because mathematics can be thought of as *the science of patterns*. Organizing information in different ways can make different patterns pop out. For example, can you spot the pattern here? 1, 1, 1, 2, 2, 4, 3, 3, 9, 4, 4, 16, 5, 5, 25? It's possible, but it really pops out here:

1	1	1
2	2	4
3	3	9
4	4	16
5	5	25

And even more so if you put the operations in:

1	× 1	= 1
2	× 2	= 4
3	× 3	= 9
4	× 4	= 16
5	× 5	= 25

Seeing patterns in tables, especially more complicated patterns, is not easy. Sometimes students need explicit support in looking for patterns, whether it's writing out calculations to show repeated reasoning, or looking for patterns of change across a row or down a column.

The Write It Out activity helps prealgebra and algebra students recognize repeated calculations they do in a Guess and Check strategy or when making a table and supports them to turn those repeated calculations into a formula.

ACTIVITY Write It Out

Format: Students working in pairs.

Step 1 (calculations): Give students a problem to work on. After they've noticed and wondered, have them set up a table to record their information. Have them label the columns and do the calculations to fill out one row of the table, and check that their calculations are correct. Then have them repeat with one more row and this time, write out the calculations that they did, just numbers and symbols for operations, without any words or explanation. Each step should go in the appropriate column.

Step 2 (description): Each member of the pair now takes a turn reading the calculations row to his partner. The partner should listen and write down a description of what the first student did in words. The label of the first column and the word *result* will be useful in this summary. (As students do this process, they will often catch corrections that they need to make in their calculations or in the order of the steps.)

Step 3 (algebra): Students then go back to their calculations and write them again, but this time, they replace the number that they used from the first column with a variable. Because they are using a variable, they won't be able to completely simplify their expressions and will just use the whole expression with the variable in the next step.

Example:

Calculations (no words; each step on a new line):

Jon's Age	Mai's Age	Ty's Age	Mom's Age	Check
20	40	$\frac{100}{3}$	$63\frac{1}{3}$	$63\frac{1}{3} \neq 40$
10	10 * 2 = 20	$20 * \frac{5}{6} = \frac{50}{3}$	$\frac{50}{3} + 30 = 46\frac{2}{3}$	$46\frac{2}{3} \neq 40$

Description (only words):

You picked "Jon's Age." You doubled it. You took $\frac{5}{6}$ of that to get a result. You added that result to 30 and checked to see if it was equal to 40. If it was not, then you made a new number for "Jon's Age."

Algebra (use a variable for your guess):

Jon's Age	Mai's Age	Ty's Age	Mom's Age	Check
20	40	$\frac{100}{3}$	$63\frac{1}{3}$	$63\frac{1}{3} \neq 40$
10	10 * 2 = 20	$20 * \frac{5}{6} = \frac{50}{3}$	$\frac{50}{3} + 30 = 46\frac{2}{3}$	$46\frac{2}{3} \neq 40$
A	A * 2	$A * 2 * \frac{5}{6}$	$A * 2 * \frac{5}{6} + 30$	$A * 2 * \frac{5}{6} + 30 = 40?$

You might have noticed that when we wrote out the algebra for our calculation, we ended up leaving a lot of the multiplication unsimplified at first. Part of what makes transitioning from numerical calculations to an expression in terms of a variable tricky is that when we calculate we simplify as we go, which can make it harder to see all the calculations that were done to the original number. An *extreme* variation on Write It Out, in which we don't simplify any calculations until the very end, and focus on substituting whole expressions for numbers, is included on the companion website (http://mathforum.org/pps/).

The Write It Out activity can be seen as a way to look for patterns horizontally within rows of a table: "Within this row, can I see how to get this number from the column before? Can I calculate this number based on the number in the very first column?" The next activity, Patterns of Change, supports students to look for patterns vertically in a table. "Can I predict the next row based on this row? Can I predict the tenth row based on this row? Can I predict which row will have the answer?"

ACTIVITY Patterns of Change

Format: Students working in pairs.

Step 1: After students have noticed and wondered about a problem, have them make a table, label the columns of the table, and fill out at least three rows in the table by changing the number in the first column and calculating the rest of the columns.

Step 2: Have pairs answer the following questions:

  ▸ How much did you change the number in the first column by?

  ▸ When you changed your first number by that much, how much did the result change by [in this column]? You can fill in the blanks of this sentence: When I changed the number by _____ units, the outcome went (up/down) by _____ units.

  ▸ How far away are you from the result you want?

  ▸ Repeat for the change from the second row to the third row.

Step 3: Based on the results from step 2, have students predict or figure out how much they would have to change the number in the first column by in order to get the result they want. Then have them try their idea and write down the calculations and the results in the same table they used for step 1 so that they can compare this trial with the first three.

Step 4: Have students check their predictions. If their predictions didn't work out, here are some questions that might help them adjust their guesses:

  ▸ Did your result change in the same direction as your guess (e.g., both got bigger or both got smaller)?

  ▸ Did the result change by the same amount as you changed your guess or by several times that amount?

  ▸ What did you notice as you calculated with the first few guesses? For example, did you realize that the guess has to be even, or be a multiple of a certain number?

Step 5: If students' prediction did work out, or they were able to adjust it and make a rule that works for the table, have them find a way to represent that rule in the table. What could they add to the table to show the rule or pattern that lets them predict how each column changes when they change the first column?

Tip: If students find it hard to figure out from the first two trials how to "jump" to the right answer, it might be that they need to change their guess by an amount that is easier to analyze. Here are some suggestions you can offer:

  ▸ It might be easier to see the effect of changing your guess if you change it by easy numbers, such as 1 or 10. These are easy numbers to compare with the changes you get in the results.

▸ Sometimes, because of the calculations you do, you don't get a nice whole number to work with unless you pick certain types of numbers for your guesses. You might discover that only even numbers come out well, or only certain multiples, for example.

Building Student Independence in Structuring Information

This chapter focused explicitly on making tables and organized lists to explore calculations and to look for and represent regularity in repeated reasoning. Making organized tables, in addition to being a mathematical skill that will come in handy in all sorts of real-life situations (like planning a party, a household budget, or even a fantasy football draft), is a huge component of the transition from arithmetic to algebra. One way to describe algebra is that it's systematizing the rules of arithmetic. Tables let you write and represent patterns in arithmetic and generalize them into input-output rules or algorithms.

The activities in this chapter present some very concrete strategies for making tables and organizing the information in the tables. We encourage students to write out their calculations within the table to look for repeated patterns. We also encourage students to look down the rows of the table to fill in the blanks in "When I changed the number by _____ units, the outcome went (up/down) by _____ units." Within the Table Gallery Walk (part 3 of Setting Up and Sharing Tables), we hope that students will see table-making strategies that they want to get better at and use—strategies that are worth repeated practice and modeling until the student gets good at them.

Because this chapter involves more specific, concrete skills we want students to master, as well as general habits of mind about noticing and organizing quantities and looking for patterns by representing in ways that reveal patterns, we wanted to pause here to give some more tips on how you can help build students' independence in the context of teaching a specific strategy.

The organization of this chapter is not accidental. We begin with an extended first activity, Setting Up and Sharing Tables, that invites students to think about quantities and relationships and organize them into tables, but gives very little instruction beyond the initial support for noticing. We would use this initial activity as a kind of formative assessment, as well as an opportunity for students to see possibilities beyond what they have thought of. The idea is that students will make the best table they can, and the teacher will get to notice things like:

▸ Who is struggling to understand what needs to be organized in a table?

▸ Who likes to put just the bare minimum into a table?

▸ Whose rows and columns are organized in a logical order? Whose rows and columns leap from one thing to another?

▸ Who has some ideas about representing calculations or formulas in the table, in addition to numbers?

One way to describe algebra is that it's systematizing the rules of arithmetic. Tables let you write and represent patterns in arithmetic and generalize them into input-output rules or algorithms.

> ▸ Who is making smart choices about intervals to use for the independent variable of the table?

> ▸ Who insists on "going by ones" no matter what size numbers the scenario asks them to explore—which can make patterns easy to spot but can make the table *enormous*?

> ▸ Who makes tables in ways no one else has thought of, for example, by picking an unusual quantity for the independent variable, or using row operations (like adding whole rows together), or using color-coding to show patterns?

The Table Gallery Walk gives students an opportunity to notice those same things and set goals for themselves, such as "I want my tables to be as neat as his" or "I want to get better at finding formulas in my table" or "I'm not sure how she thought to do her columns in that order. I want to get better at choosing the order for my columns." As the teacher, you can also help set goals for the class. You might make a table that you add to the gallery to help move the whole group forward in looking for and representing patterns across rows or down columns.[1] Or you might notice a table in the gallery that does an especially nice job with something like representing the differences between successive rows. Pointing out that table and giving students the task of making a table (for the same problem, an extension of the same problem, or a new problem) using that skill helps students to practice and own that kind of table.

When training in a specific skill, students, like athletes, need models and feedback.

We particularly like Write It Out and Patterns of Change activities for helping students with the fundamental table skills of looking for and representing patterns across the table and patterns moving down the table. These activities ask students to perform very specific skills—we think of them as training or drills, rather than problem solving. When training in a specific skill, students, like athletes, need models and feedback. For these activities, an I Do–We Do–You Do model can support students to understand the drill or skill they're being asked to learn and practice it until they get good at it.

You will know that students not only have the table-making skills they need, but value those skills and see their utility when students are faced with a novel problem and they can think, "A table might help me here. I can make a table that shows patterns across and down using my new table skills!" If you are confident in your students' table skills, but find that they aren't using tables in situations where they could be helpful, you may want to look at Chapter 10, "The Problem-Solving Process and Metacognition," for some planning and strategy selecting activities. But you can also go back to the Table Gallery Walk, and the facilitation questions throughout the Setting Up and Sharing Tables activity may help. When you use the I Notice, I Wonder strategy with students or first introduce a problem, ask them, "What needs to be organized?" or "What can we count by in this problem?" Let those questions percolate for a while and see if you start to get more tables.

If not, explicitly remind students that making a table is a problem-solving strategy you want them to remember to use, and for several rounds of problem solving, ask students to

---

1. Each PoW mentioned in this chapter is included on the book's companion website at http://mathforum.org/pps/. You can look in the associated Teacher Packets for sample tables (made by both students and adults) that you could incorporate.

think of all the ways a table could be used to solve the problem. Each time students make tables, post them around the room and ask students, "How did these tables help you solve the problem?" Having student-made models of many different kinds of tables will help students reflect on and value the idea that tables can help them when there are things that need to be organized in the problem. As tables become something that students think to do for themselves, you can fade out the scaffolding and reminders of the value of tables, and see if students continue to include them in their repertoire now that they've been reminded of their value.

Finally, sometimes students will get stuck and not think to use a table when it could be helpful—if we always thought of just the right problem-solving strategy the first time, problems wouldn't be that problematic! The facilitation question of "What's making this problem hard?" can lead to some answers that just cry out for a table:

- There are too many things to keep track of.
- They want us to figure out what will happen after 100 times. That's so far!
- I've guessed and guessed and I'm not getting anywhere.
- We're supposed to make a rule and I tried adding, subtracting, multiplying, and dividing and it's not working.

Conclusion

Some of the themes that we've explored in this chapter, specifically using tables and organization (representing repeated reasoning, as the Common Core says) to move students toward increasingly algebraic reasoning and using tables to generalize patterns into formulas will be continued themes throughout the rest of the book. However, it's worth taking time to recall that mathematical problem solving involves many representations and strategies in addition to algebraic representation, and for younger students, algebraic representations aren't an option. We'll look more at some of these alternative ways to organize, represent, and make sense of problems in the next chapter, but for now we wanted to remind all of us to be on the lookout for those students who see the world visually, who make use of color, line sketches, connected notes, and other equally mathematical representations, and for whom ordered lists of numbers in grids might not be the most natural way to represent a problem. Encourage those students to add their alternate representations to your table galleries and discuss the similarities and differences among representations. Encourage students who are comfortable with tables to step out of their comfort zone by adding some color-coding or representing the situation with visuals or manipulatives.

8

Generalizing, Abstracting, and Modeling

Focal practices:

2. Reason abstractly and quantitatively.
4. Model with mathematics.

In this chapter we focus on the problem-solving habits of mind students use when they use different mathematical representations, like tables, number sentences, equations, diagrams, and so on to reason about situations. We focus both on using the concrete story or situation students are given to support their "mathematization" and the ways that more abstract representations can help students make their mathematics more "sharable, transportable, and reusable."[1] In particular, we offer activities that create a need for students to communicate their math (sharable); apply their work to other, related contexts (transportable); and solve many iterations of the same problem (reusable). We believe that students are capable of making many different abstract models of mathematizable situations, but that they need to be in the driver's seat regarding when and how to make their representations and models more mathematical and abstract.

---

1. Lesh, Richard, and Helen M. Doerr. 2003. "Foundations of a Models and Modeling Perspective on Mathematics Teaching, Learning, and Problem Solving." In *Beyond Constructivism: Models and Modeling Perspectives on Mathematics Problem Solving, Learning, and Teaching*, ed. Richard Lesh and Helen M. Doerr, 16. Mahwah, NJ: Lawrence Erlbaum Associates.

Concrete and Abstract

I was working with fifth-grade students on the topics of area and perimeter using this scenario:

FROG FARMING

Farmer Mead would like to raise frogs. She wants to build a rectangular pen for them and has found 36 meters of fencing in her barn that she'd like to use.

1. Design at least four different rectangular pens that she could build. Each pen must use all 36 meters of fence. Give the length and width for each of the pens.
2. If each frog needs one square meter of area (1 m^2), how many frogs will each of your four pens hold?

Be sure to explain your strategy and your reasons for your steps.

One traditional theory suggests that what's hard for students when solving word problems is getting rid of the "fluff" and decoding the underlying abstract mathematics hidden in the context, and that if the teacher can restate the problem in mathematical language, it will support the students to solve successfully. Here's what I observed when the classroom teacher and I used that model:

Students' Concrete Action	Teachers' Abstract Response	Students' Concrete Response
Mention 36 meters of fence.	Restate the idea as "the perimeter is 36 meters."	Ignore the word *perimeter*, not use any of the teachers' taught strategies for finding side lengths of a given perimeter.
Make guesses and draw pictures to find different-shaped rectangles that would use 36 feet of fencing; it's taking a while.	Remind the student of the "hint" that the first step is to divide the perimeter in half. "What is half of 36? Can you find two numbers that add to 18?"	The students can, but as soon as the teacher leaves, they start looking for 4 numbers that add to 18 because they look at the picture and remember that rectangles have 4 sides.
Mention that each frog needs 1 square meter.	Ask, "Great, what do square meters measure? Area? Yes! Now you need to find the area of each pen you came up with in part 1."	Ignore the suggestion to find area; give up on the problem; raise their hand to ask for more help. One student tells me, "I know how to find area, but I don't get what that has to do with how many frogs can fit."

The next period we tried an alternate theory of supporting students to solve word problems, in which the context was used to elicit the students' concrete ideas and the concrete ideas were valued. We helped the students organize their ideas and look for patterns.

In short, we avoided abstraction that the students didn't suggest, while supporting organization and pattern recognition: some abstract generalization and plenty of referring back to the concrete.

Once we established that when frog farmers say *pen* they mean fenced-in-space-for-keeping-animals-safe, not ink-based-tool-for-writing, there was enough going on in the context that the students had some ideas about how to draw different pens, check if they fit the farmer's specifications, and try to fit the frogs into the pens.

Students' Concrete Action	Teachers' Organizing Response	Students' Concrete Response
Mention 36 meters of fence.	"Great, that's one of the requirements the farmer has."	Check their guesses against the 36 meters of fence constraint.
Make guesses and draw pictures to try to find different-shaped rectangles that would use 36 feet of fencing; it's taking a while.	Organize a few of the guesses that worked into a chart with the columns for length and width: L $\quad$ W 10 $\quad$ 8 9 $\quad$ 9 8 $\quad$ 10 7 $\quad$ 11	Immediately generate all of the other missing fence shapes that work, and confirm they had them all. No one explicitly mentioned that $L + W = 18$, but it was clear from the speed of their mental math they were using some version of that pattern.
Mention that each frog needs 1 square meter.	Diagnose student understanding by asking, "How many frogs do you think will fit in one of your pens?"	Make guesses using reasoning that shows they aren't making sense of the area the frogs take up: guessing 36 frogs or 9 frogs (each square meter uses 4 of the meters of perimeter).
Assume that 36 meters of fencing means 36 frogs will fit in each pen.	Invite students to use a drawing to show how many frogs will fit in a pen.	Suddenly blurt out, "I can just multiply these! Six rows and 12 columns of frogs is 72 frogs!" and even "That's just the area!" One student who filled her 3 × 15 pen with lots of small squares (over 100) suddenly said, "I did it this way but I wasn't supposed to. It should be 45 frogs but I drew the boxes too small. All I had to do was multiply."

One thing that's particularly notable in this example is that students in the second class, where they were supported to use the frog farming context and multiple, concrete representations and weren't pushed to use mathematical terms like *perimeter* and *area* that were more abstract to them, started to make the connections to area and perimeter anyway. The students had been studying procedures for finding the area and perimeter of quadrilaterals, and once they had a firm grasp of this context, they found that area and perimeter were the most useful ways to describe and make sense of what was going on, but only after they had explored the problem concretely and made connections among fencing, measuring length, and measuring perimeter, and among measuring the room a frog needs, counting square meters, and measuring area.

Mathematical Models and Abstraction

Mathematical modeling is both a skill for solving problems and the goal of problem solving. We use mathematical models to answer questions about the world around us, and we explore the world around us (including the world of math) in order to build better mathematical models— better understandings and descriptions of the world.

When students solve interesting math problems, and especially when they need to consider and compare multiple solution approaches (both correct and incorrect), they are getting the opportunity to do abstraction and model building. A mathematical model is a representation of a mathematical idea. Often, among mathematicians (and physicists and engineers and biologists and social scientists) a mathematical model is an equation (or system of equations), a set of mathematical relationships written in symbols that describes the numerical aspects of something, whether it's dark matter, the forces on a joint in a bridge, the changes in an ecosystem when an invasive species is introduced, or if rewards motivate us or unmotivate us. But there are lots of other types of mathematical models: anything that "encodes" or describes a situation in a way that is "sharable, transportable, or reusable."[2] Tables, graphs, drawings, physical models, spreadsheets, even descriptions and metaphors can model a situation for a student.

Mathematical modeling is both a skill for solving problems and the goal of problem solving. We use mathematical models to answer questions about the world around us, and we explore the world around us (including the world of math) in order to build better mathematical models—better understandings and descriptions of the world.

These models are, by definition, abstract. When we make a model, we leave information out. If we didn't leave information out, we wouldn't be making a model, we would be recreating the whole situation. For example, when we translate "Three bananas cost the same as four oranges" as $3b = 4o$, we are getting rid of all sorts of information about the story. The story is no longer explicitly about money, or fruit. We don't have the sense of barter or trade, let alone the visuals of yellow bananas and orange oranges. What is left is just the information about the numerical relationship, which we happen to care about.

For example, consider this story from researchers Dick Lehrer and Leona Schauble as they studied young children's mathematical modeling and use of abstraction and representations:

> First graders recorded the heights of growing amaryllis bulbs by cutting green strips that matched the heights of the plants at successive days of measure. . . . At first, the children insisted that all the strips be green (like stems), and that each be adorned with a large flower. Soon, however, the first-graders began to ask questions about the changes in height over time, an orientation that shifted their attention to successive differences in the heights of the strips at different days of measure. With this new focus, the need to distinguish among small differences in height made it important to be able to mount strips side by side so that they were

---

2. Lesh and Doerr, p. 16.

contiguous, and when the flowers interfered with this goal, they were deemed no longer essential and were eliminated. When children decided they wanted to compare the growth of one plant to that of another, they found it important to be able to inspect several strips mounted on a timeline, which in turn, made it difficult to tell at a glance which strips represented which plants. Someone suggested that it might be easier to see a pattern in the clutter of strips if they used different-colored strips to represent different plants. Shortly thereafter, the records for the Red Lion bulb were represented by strips of red, not green. As questions like "Which grew bigger?" evolved into questions like "How much faster did Red Lion grow than Hercules?," quantification and precision became central concerns. Increasingly, the strips themselves, rather than the plants, became the focus of investigation. With each shift in these directions, the strips progressively lost the properties of similarity that originally supported their generation and relied increasingly on conventions, like height = quantity.[3]

It was important for the children at first to represent the heights of their flowers with images that looked like flowers—green stems with flowers on top. Their teachers let their representations evolve naturally. As the children's questions shifted, their representations had to shift to keep up. As their questions became more sophisticated, they removed more and more concrete, resembling-real-flowers details. Again, their teachers helped them stay grounded and organized, and the students chose to use more and more abstract representations as they grew more comfortable with, and more interested in, the questions that *needed* such abstract representations.

But too often, as math teachers who are comfortable ourselves with abstract representations and who are pressured to teach students many of these representations in a short time span, we rush students to use representations they don't fully understand.

Key Ideas for Supporting Students to Use Abstraction

Learning to use abstract representations is a key component of solving mathematical problems (and on the flip side, learning to solve specific mathematical problems helps students get better at creating, using, and understanding abstract representations). But too often, as math teachers who are comfortable ourselves with abstract representations and who are pressured to teach students many of these representations in a short time span, we rush students to use representations they don't fully understand. Imagine if the first-grade teachers in the earlier example had insisted that the students use different-colored strips of paper arranged chronologically from the very first. The students would not have connected those strips with their flowers, and they would not have been interested in asking questions about their flowers' growth, nor would they have made good use of the information displayed. Instead the students would have been stuck wondering, "What do those pretty strips have to do with my

---

3. Lehrer, Richard, and Leona Schauble. 2003. "Origins and Evolutions of Model-Based Reasoning in Mathematics and Science." In *Beyond Constructivism: Models and Modeling Perspectives on Mathematics Problem Solving, Learning, and Teaching*, ed. Richard Lesh and Helen M. Doerr, 64–65. Mahwah, NJ: Lawrence Erlbaum Associates.

pretty flower?" In supporting students to use representations and models in their math work, it is important that teachers:

- ▸ Wait to see what models students come up with on their own.
- ▸ Use situations and questions to support students to improve their own models—*generate the need* for more abstraction, rather than *telling* students to use more abstract models.
- ▸ Provide opportunities for students to discuss, compare, and use multiple models for the same kinds of situations (because comparing and critiquing creates more need for generalizing, abstracting, and improving).
- ▸ Encourage students to refer back to more concrete representations, and the problem situation, to ground their models in their most concrete understanding.

Activities

In this chapter, we'll introduce some activities for making the acts of "abstracting" and "concretizing" more visible, and some tips for facilitating students to use generalizations and abstractions without pushing them to a place where the mathematics becomes too abstract for them to make sense of.

The Basics of Mathematical Models: Quantities and Relationships

This chapter closely relies on and extends the initial work on understanding and representing situations and making sense of quantities in Chapters 4 through 7. This is, in large part, because we've noticed so many examples in our work with students in classrooms where students' struggle to make sense of the problem situation kept them from being able to apply mathematical tools meaningfully. Understanding scenarios and representing them mathematically is a looping process—the student forms an initial understanding, tries to represent it, gains new understanding from the representation, refines the representation, and so on. To help students gain an initial foothold, we must help them come to an initial understanding of the problem scenario, one that will help them to focus on the *mathematics*. This is why we emphasize having students make an oral or written inventory of the *quantities* (in words!) or *shapes/figures* in a mathematical scenario and try to name any relationships they can *in terms of those quantities or shapes* before jumping into symbolic or numerical representations.

A simple example of supporting students to use the names of quantities and talk about their relationships before writing number sentences, equations, or other models comes from a classroom of students who were practicing applying a new skill in the context of word problems. Two girls working together seemed off task, and I went over to ask them what was going on. They said they didn't get the problem and nothing made sense. They asked, "Are we just supposed to do this?" and showed me a procedure that didn't make sense in the context of the problem.

"What is that number counting? And what does the *x* stand for?" I asked.

"We don't know."

"Well, what does it say in the problem?"

"Oh, we didn't read the problem yet."

"Aha! Why don't you read the problem to me, and just tell me what's being counted in the problem."

The girls read the problem and decided that it was about the cost of ordering supplies for a party, and that they were ordering small and large tables, for two different prices. They pretty quickly said, "We could just do this times this plus this times this." When I asked them to say again what they were multiplying in terms of the problem, it was easy for them to give, essentially, a model for the problem: "The cost of the small tables times the number of small tables plus the cost of the large tables times the number of large tables equals the total cost." They still had several steps to go, such as writing their insight down in words and then symbols, and then finding the additional constraints, but I was nonetheless impressed with how relatively easy it was to direct their attention back to the problem with the simple questions of "What is this number counting?" and "What else is being counted?" My hunch is that part of the reason they hadn't read the problem in the first place is because they didn't have a strategy for making sense of the story—they wanted an answer to jump out at them, or some rule for translating directly from words to equations. In addition to helping them do basic sense making (à la Chapter 4), the questions helped them to have a guide for reading mathematically—looking for what was being counted. If they had had more exposure to formal math language, I would have asked them to look for all the *quantities* in the problem, instead of using the more informal, "What is being counted in the problem?"

ACTIVITY Quantities and Relationships

Format: Students work individually or in pairs on the following activities for just a few minutes, then share ideas with the larger group of four students.

Step 1: Have students work alone or with their elbow partner to notice and wonder as much as they can about the problem, focusing on quantities (things that can be counted or measured) and relationships between quantities (e.g., calculations using operations such as addition, subtraction, multiplication, division; statements about equality, inequality, etc.).

Step 2: Encourage students to use specific names for the quantities (not just the number), and then, if they haven't already, write the values that they know next to the names or descriptions of the quantities, and be sure to include units; for example, cost of an apple (50 cents).

Step 3: Have students write mathematical sentences or equations for the relationships that they understand already, using the names or descriptions of quantities (but without plugging in the values yet).

Step 4: Have students share their lists and sentences with their group of four students. Encourage them to focus on these questions:

Do I have all the quantities whose values I know?

+ Do I have specific names for them?

+ Do I know the units?

Do I have all the quantities whose values I don't know?

+ Do I have specific names for them?

+ Do I know the units?

Are there relationships that I don't know how to write as a mathematical sentence yet?

Generating and Comparing Multiple Models

Making mathematical models can draw on multiple representations. Modeling and abstracting can be an iterative process, as students represent a situation in one way (for example, making a verbal model by putting the problem in their own words), then reflect on the representation and refine it (for example, by making a drawing to go with their verbal models, or by putting their verbal model into a more abbreviated, symbolic form). In addition, the very act of comparing multiple models invites abstraction.

In 1960, a math educator named Zoltan Dienes wrote about how students use concrete manipulatives to learn abstract mathematical ideas (the base ten blocks with unit cubes, ten sticks, hundreds squares, and thousands cubes are sometimes called *Dienes blocks* after him). One principle that he put forth was the Multiple Embodiment Principle. Basically, he was saying that at first manipulatives and representations are tools for thinking *with*. Eventually, we also want students to think *about* them. Why does this manipulative work well for this problem? Why do I use it this way? How is it similar/different from other tools I could have used? These questions, he said, come up when students use multiple representations for the same problem. Comparing these different representations helps students learn about the underlying math. For example, a student who can talk about how base ten blocks and an abacus both show place value has a very clear understanding of a tricky idea.[4] An additional activity to support students to think about about representations, Representation Reflection, is available on the companion website (http://mathforum.org/pps/).

ACTIVITY Representation Speed Dating

We've found that students, when they have an initial understanding of a problem, are often quite creative "representers," and so our job is mostly to suggest that they try to show what is happening in the problem and then stand back and see what develops. This Speed Dating activity is a fun way to try to tap into that creativity.

---

4. Dienes, Z. 1960. *Building Up Mathematics*. London: Hutchinson Educational Ltd.

Format: Students working in groups of three to five.

Materials: Strips of paper, pens or pencils, loose-leaf paper, various manipulatives.

Step 0: Read the problem to be solved to the students.

Step 1: Each person writes a representation on a strip of paper. The activity will be more fun if each person chooses a different representation. Some good examples: drawings, tables, arrows, flowcharts, spreadsheets, graphs, vertex-edge representations. If students write the name of a specific manipulative on their paper, they should also go get some of that manipulative to pass around, using your classroom routine for borrowing manipulatives.

Step 2: Pass out copies of the problem to be solved. When everyone is ready, have each member of a group pass his or her strip of paper (and needed manipulatives) to the left. Each person has three minutes to try to represent the problem and work toward a solution using the representation received. Students should record their work and what they notice and wonder on their own sheets of loose-leaf paper (that way, at the end, they will have ideas from a few different representations to look back at as they work on finishing the problem).

Step 3: After three minutes, tell students to stop wherever they are, draw a line or a box around their work, and write the name of the representation used.

Step 4: Students pass the representation strip they were working on to the left, and receive a new one on the right. They have three minutes to work using the new representation to represent the problem and then work toward solving it. Students should keep working on their own paper with each new representation, labeling as they go. Remind students that the goal is to represent the problem lots of different ways, whether or not they come to a solution within the three minutes.

Step 5: Students pass papers every three minutes until they receive the representation strip that they originally wrote. They finish by working to represent the problem using their original suggested representation for three minutes.

Step 6: Students in each group discuss any new relationships, patterns, quantities, interesting ideas, or things they are wondering about, and add to their list of noticings and wonderings.

As an example, here are some different ways that students in elementary, middle, and high school have chosen to represent or model a Math Forum scenario called Ostrich Llama Count.

OSTRICH LLAMA COUNT

Raul and Esteban just started working at their uncle's farm on the weekends. Their first task was to count the ostriches and llamas.

When they reported to their uncle, Raul said, "I counted 47 heads."

Esteban added, "I counted 122 legs."

Note that all spellings and descriptions in these examples are the students' own.

Table/Chart:

47 o, 0 l = 47 × 2 (legs) = 94 legs; 94 legs is less than 122 legs so its not correct.

46 o, 1 l = 46 × 2 = 92, 1 × 4 = 4; 92 + 4 = 96 legs

45 o, 2 l = 45 × 2 = 90, 2 × 4 = 8; 90 + 8 = 98 legs

44 o, 3 l = 44 × 2 = 88, 3 × 4 = 12; 88 + 12 = 100 legs

43 o, 4 l = 43 × 2 = 86, 4 × 4 = 16; 86 + 16 = 102 legs

42 o, 5 l = 42 × 2 = 84, 5 × 4 = 20; 84 + 20 = 104 legs

41 o, 6 l = 41 × 2 = 82, 6 × 4 = 24; 82 × 24 = 106 legs

A table or chart is a model of a problem because it organizes the quantities and relationships in a systematic way that can be shared with others, tweaked, and reused to find other results.

Algebra:

Let x = ostriches

y = llamas

$x + y = 47$

$2x + 4y = 122$

An equation is a model of a problem because it organizes the quantities and relationships using compact, symbolic notation. An equation can be shared with others (if they "speak math"), tweaked, and reused to find other results.

Picture:

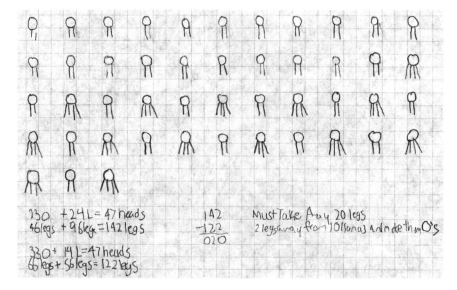

A picture, especially one that has been pared down to the bare essentials like this one, can be a model of a problem. We can see the 47 heads represented with circles and the 122 legs represented with lines. Ostriches are represented by circles with 2 legs; the llamas by circles with 4 legs. The picture could be tweaked or reused if the quantities in the problem changed, and it can be shared with others (especially if there were a key).

Line Diagram:

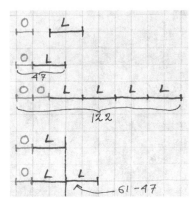

This picture, which the student referred to as a "line diagram," can be another kind of visual model of the problem—and there is no visual reference to animals, heads, or legs. Instead, the number of ostriches and the number of llamas are represented by lengths, and the lengths are used to show different relationships. The picture could be tweaked or reused if the quantities in the problem changed, and it can be shared with others (especially if there were a key).

And here's another example of a very different Math Forum scenario:

TRICK-OR-TREAT ROUTES

Mrs. Anderson told her son Todd that he was going to have to take his little sister, Grace, trick-or-treating around their neighborhood on Halloween night. His mother agreed that he only had to take her to 4 houses, and then he could go out with his friends.

Todd wants to plan ahead, so today his friend Joe helped him create a map of the neighborhood with all the houses he must visit with Grace. When Grace saw what Todd was doing, she decided to plan her own route to maximize the time she will be out trick-or-treating.

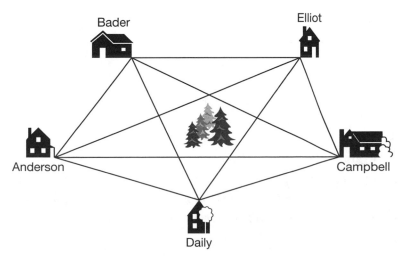

Tree Diagram:

```
          B
        / | \
       C  E  D
      /\ /\ /\
     E D C D C E
     | | | | | |
     D E D C E C
```

This diagram models the relationship of the number of different possible paths at each decision point. The picture could be tweaked or reused if the quantities in the problem changed (e.g., for more or fewer houses, or if there were no paths between some houses), and it can be shared with others (especially if there were a key).

Table with key:

A	B	C	D	E	A
A	B	C	E	D	A
A	B	D	C	E	A
A	B	D	E	C	A
A	B	E	C	D	A
A	B	E	D	C	A

Key:
A: Anderson
B: Bader
C: Campbell
D: Daily
E: Elliot

This table (or organized list) shows all the possible paths after traveling from house A to house B. It can be used to find patterns, but it can also be replicated to show all the possible paths after traveling from house A to house C, or house D, or house E. It also has a key, which makes it more shareable. An organized list can be a model of a problem situation.

Drawings:

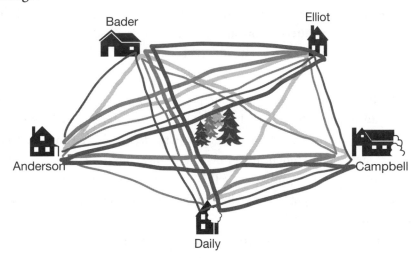

This drawing is an incomplete model of the problem. It is difficult to share with others since the paths overlap and are difficult to follow. It's also not clear if there was a systematic effort to show all the paths. However, there are ways that the model could be made easier to share, which might also make the effort more systematic.

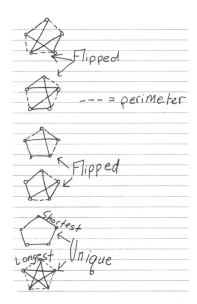

Here's what the student said about his model:

This is the way that I came up with my answer to the first question. I made a little chart (see attached) that showed all the possible ways that the children could have gone around the neighborhood. I made several maps of the houses and drew all the ways that I could see, and studied them. I came up with the ways by looking at the little map and seeing in my head how the lines fitted in. I am not sure if there any other ways to do this problem other than trial and error.

I saw four unique patterns. Two of the patterns could be flipped. Two paths couldn't be flipped and were unique. The last two shapes were the star and the pentagon. This equals six patterns. For each pattern the kids could go one way or the other. So all together there are twelve different routes the kids could take.

Much like the systematic table of all the possibilities after traveling from house A to house B, this student's systematic, pared-down visual representation of all the traveling patterns he sees can be shared with others, and could, perhaps, be adapted and reused in similar problems. For example, the student might be able to turn another story about the order to do six options into a mapping problem like this one, by making a hexagon with each vertex labeled with an option. It might be difficult to apply this exact model to a problem with more or fewer houses though.

Examples like these, that draw on so many unique ways of seeing problems and organizing and representing information, also provide opportunities for students to compare models and consider what is the same about each model and what is different. Using some of the comparing and listening activities from Chapter 3 can help support students to further refine their models.

ACTIVITY Gallery Walk

Facilitating conversations that support students to improve, refine, and make their models more useful is not easy. One great resource, of course, is that students like to be right and they like to know where they stand in relation to one another. So activities that just ask students to compare models and determine which are *effective* and which are *efficient* are really useful. Using the Gallery Walk activity featured in Chapters 5 and 6 and having students begin their comparison with positive noticings and helpful wonderings is a good way to start having these conversations. The goal is to work toward conversations in which students with differing models can figure out:

- What's different.
- What's the same.
- What, if anything, is definitely right.
- If any of the differences are unresolvable, and if so, if any represent a misunderstanding.
- Ways in which either model could be made more efficient, more effective, easier to read, and so on.

"Abstracting" Concrete Models

Here is a sample activity that supports students who are drawn to concrete, literal representations, to help them make their representations more mathematically useful, and to abstract away some of the data they don't need. Students who would represent an amaryllis the way the first graders in the vignette at the beginning of the chapter started out, green with flowers on the top, would benefit from an activity like this. And although this activity focuses on sketches, the facilitation questions and activity structure could be applied to students' other representations of the problem: skits, flowcharts, algorithms, or even tables, if students are including extraneous details that distract from rather than help them focus on key quantities, shapes, or relationships.

ACTIVITY Rough Sketches

Format: Students working in groups of four.

Step 1: Give students a problem to solve. Ask them to imagine a movie or photograph in their head of the problem. They can imagine the story of the problem or the perfect illustration for it. Then have them, to the best of their ability, draw an illustration of the story or a cartoon showing the different important parts of the movie. *Note:* If you have serious artists you may need to put a time limit on this!

Step 2: Have students look at their drawings with a partner. Did they include the same things? What was in both sketches? What were the most important things to include? Are all of the quantities they could count or measure included? Are all of the shapes included? Do the pictures show relationships? What else is in the drawings that doesn't show quantities, shapes, or relationships between them? Encourage them to imagine removing from each drawing all of the "extra" nonmathematical stuff. What's left?

Step 3: Have each pair work together to draw a rough sketch of what was left. Suggest that they represent shapes and/or quantities they can count or measure, and leave out as much of the "extra" information as they can. Remind them to label their sketches with numbers, letters, or words if they can.

Step 4: Have students share both their original drawings and their rough sketch with their group. As they compare their sketches with the other drawings, encourage them to consider: What are the similarities? What are the differences? What countable things do you see? What measurable things do you see? What would you label? Do all the drawings include all the shapes, quantities, and relationships? Did you make different decisions about what to keep in and what to leave out?

Step 5: Ask each group to try to make the simplest, clearest sketch possible, that includes the most information, or decide on one of the sketches they already made. What makes it the most useful? Then have them use it as they try to solve the problem.

For example, elementary students worked on representing the Math Forum scenario Mr. Lincoln's Line:

MR. LINCOLN'S LINE

Mr. Lincoln's fifth-grade students are standing in line to go to lunch.
The 3rd child, and every 3rd child after, is a boy.
The 5th child, and every 5th child after, is wearing glasses.
The 4th child, and every 4th child after, is carrying a lunch box.

Here are some illustrations that re-create pictures elementary students described using to solve this scenario.

"I drew 32 circles and used the clues to solve the problem."

"I drew a picture."

"I drew a number line and labeled *B* for boy, *G* for glasses, and *L* for lunchbox."

It's interesting that all of the pictures represent some kind of abstraction of Mr. Lincoln's real line. They leave out some details that exist in real life. We have to leave out some details when we represent problems, and the question is which details do we keep for mathematical representations? What makes a mathematical diagram as useful as possible? Which of the diagrams would you find easiest to use to solve the problem? Which are most sharable? Transportable? Reusable?

Making Models That Are Sharable, Transportable, and Reusable

One huge motivator for representing problems in streamlined ways that make patterns visible is to be able to apply patterns and tools to harder versions of the same problem. One way to encourage students to develop better and better models is to require them to reuse their models.

The following activities and facilitation strategies provide a structure for extending problems that help students engage with the task of creating reusable, efficient models.

ACTIVITY Problem-Solving Bids

Format: Students working in groups of 3–4.

Note: This activity is used after students have created a model that works for small numbers, such as a table, a guess and check algorithm, or a drawing.

Materials: Four additional problems that are very similar to the original problem but with different (larger, non-whole, etc.) numbers.

Step 1: After students have created models that allowed them to solve a given problem, let them know that their expertise has been recognized and will be required to solve some similar problems. Make them feel like problem-solving superheroes being called on by the residents of Gotham City!

Step 2: Give students a second problem, and let them know that this problem has just come to your attention and you have a hunch several more just like it are to follow. Ask students to use their answer and work on the first problem to help them solve the second.

Step 3: Inform students that you are looking for a group that feels they can solve all the incoming problems accurately and efficiently. Tell them they have ten minutes to study this problem and their previous problem and make a bid to you for why they should get to be the ones to get the problem-solving contract. Their bid should include:

- ▸ the method they plan to use
- ▸ how long they think it will take them to solve three more problems like this
- ▸ why they think their method will be accurate and/or efficient
- ▸ what patterns or repeated reasoning they have noticed that they are using to speed up their thinking.

Step 4: Each group presents their bids and the other students should consider if each method will be accurate and efficient. Let students know that you will give each group a copy of the problems since they all impressed you, and that you would like to see how many of them can come in under their projected time. Explain that there will be a small bonus for groups that can come in under bid.

Step 5: Allow the groups to work, checking in and supporting those groups that struggled to see patterns or find efficiencies. Help them to organize their work, tell you what they did the same each time, ask them what calculations they are doing over and over, and so on. Computer spreadsheet software or, for older students, graphing calculators can be used to support struggling groups. Using a spreadsheet can help students do the work more efficiently, and the idea of creating a formula or telling the computer/calculator what calculations to do can help students understand and make use of patterns in their own calculations.

Some good examples of problem types to use with this prompt are:

▸ Problems that ask students what will happen on the fifth or tenth iteration of a pattern. The additional problems can ask students what will happen on the 20th, 43rd, 100th, and 2013th iteration, for example.

▸ Guess and Check problems in which the constraints can be varied. For example, the Ostrich Llama Count problem featured in this chapter can be adjusted to have more heads and feet to account for.

▸ Guess and Check problems in which it is reasonable to have non-whole-number answers, which are deliberately designed to come out with fractional solutions, such as problems involving measurements, dimensions, cooking, and so on.

▸ Counting problems, such as "How many different ways are there to arrange these?" or "How many different combinations are there?" like the Trick-or-Treat Routes problem in this chapter. Just use increasing numbers of items to raise the difficulty level and encourage students to find patterns and rules.

▸ Problems that encourage students to invent methods for doing arithmetic calculations, such as "How many of these are in that?" problems related to division ("How many sticks of butter ($\frac{1}{2}$ cup each) are needed for a recipe that calls for $4\frac{1}{3}$ cups of butter?").

The inspiration for the Problem-Solving Bids activity comes from noticing how often teachers assign problems to students hoping that the students will come up with the efficient method the teacher expects them to use to solve the problem (finding a pattern, using logical reasoning, writing an equation, using an efficient procedure like division rather than repeated subtraction, etc.). When students don't come up with the efficient method, we often hear teachers say, "You need to learn to do it this way, because it is quicker." Or they ask, "What would you have done if the numbers hadn't come out so neatly?" Or they tell students, "Please find a formula or pattern to solve this problem, so that you could solve it for any number I give you." Despite having a clear sense of some of the many situations that have motivated mathematicians to come up with more efficient methods, we've seen very few teachers actually give their students the opportunity to *be* in those situations. Often, the "real-world" or "challenge" problems we assign to students are designed to be solvable without calculators, and so we rely on small numbers that come out "nicely." The Problem-Solving Bids activity gives teachers a chance to explicitly put students in situations of needing to solve multiple problems of the same type with increasingly challenging constraints—the very situations that encourage applied mathematicians to come up with models they can apply over and over to changing constraints.

In addition, given the challenge that understanding problem contexts and mathematizing situations present to novice problem solvers, the opportunity to solve multiple problems within the same context frees up students' brainpower to focus on the mathematical structures. Once they understand the way Raul and Esteban are counting animals, when asked to solve another strange-ways-to-count-animals problem they might be more able to focus on setting up an organized table and quicker to spot repeated reasoning, since they aren't constantly worrying, "Is this even what the problem is asking me to do?"

ACTIVITY What Would Happen If?

The next activity, What Would Happen If?, gives another, somewhat less complex/structured, way to put students in situations that require them to refine and improve their initial (less efficient) models.

Format: Whole group, then moving to students working in pairs.

Step 1: Begin with a whole-group I Notice, I Wonder brainstorming session (see Chapter 4) using the scenario only. As students generate their wonderings listen for wonderings that might extend beyond the question associated with this scenario.

Step 2: Present the full question to students and have them add any new noticings and wonderings based on the question. Again, listen for wonderings that extend the given question.

Step 3: Let students work on solving the problem with any strategy they can. They might even do some of this part for homework.

Step 4: When students have solved the problem and have shared multiple methods for solving, refer back to the list of wonderings. Highlight any wonderings that extend the problem in some way.

Step 5: Have students turn and talk to the person next to them, brainstorming a list of more wonderings that will take this scenario and extend it. Welcome outside-the-box wonderings!

Step 6: Encourage partners to share out one wondering that they particularly liked. As you hear students' thoughts, avoid generic praise or revoicing their thinking, but you might try to thank each pair for something specific in their work.

Step 7: Look at the collective list of extension problems. You might casually add one that you had thought of that didn't come up, but we wouldn't add more than one. Ask if anyone needs any of the wonderings further clarified. At this point, either pick one task that the whole class will work on as an extension (by vote or, since classrooms are rarely democracies, by executive decree), or allow pairs to choose their favorite and welcome a variety of extensions to the problem.

Step 8: Ask each partnership to prepare a short (two-minute) presentation about:

- how they solved the original problem
- what they noticed in their work on the original problem that helped them answer the harder extension
- what they had to change, if anything, in their method to solve the new problem
- what patterns they noticed that they used to work on the extended version.

You might sequence the presentations from most concrete to most abstract methods as you circulate and observe what each partnership is doing.

Step 9: After hearing the presentations, reflect as a class on:

- why what-if questions and wonderings are useful for mathematicians
- how extending problems can help you learn more about the original problem, and what you learned from this one
- techniques that helped solve the harder extension that you didn't need for the easier original problem
- techniques you could "borrow" from your work on the original problem so you didn't have reinvent the wheel to solve the extension problem.

Both of the these activities focus on turning students' initial problem-solving methods into tools that are "sharable, transportable, and reusable"—aka, turning them into mathematical models. This might involve students inventing their own mathematical models, or learning to apply models they have already been taught, such as learning to apply algebraic equations to situations they previously have solved with Guess and Check, or learning to use multiplication in problems they previously acted out with repeated counting of groups.

Building Student Independence in Modeling

In order to build student skill and facility with model building, whether it's moving students from arithmetic to algebra, helping students make diagrams and physical models that are as effective and efficient as possible, or helping students make use of a wider range of models, there are four themes that we've found support students to get good at creating mathematical models for solving problems:

- not pushing too hard or too fast
- welcoming multiple representations
- encouraging student-to-student talk to compare, contrast, and check models
- putting students in situations that *require* abstractions.

Not Pushing Too Hard or Too Fast for Abstraction

As the Frog Farming example at the beginning of this chapter illustrates, students aren't always supported by removing context from problems. Sometimes they use the context clues to help them make sense of what's going on and make reasonable guesses. Often, what pushes students to "abstract away" information in the problem is a desire to be more efficient, to communicate more clearly, or to apply similar reasoning repeatedly. For example, in the Frog Farming example, students abstracted from guessing and checking different dimensions for the frog pens using drawings, to using the relationship Length + Width = 18, only after they had (1) organized their initial work to see patterns and (2) wanted to quickly generate *all* the possible pen dimensions. They came up with the connection between area and number of frogs penned only after drawing pictures of filling their different pens with small boxes, and then they wanted a method to quickly apply to each pen they had to fit frogs into.

Follow students' lead on when to remove information from a drawing, table, or number sentence. Students should almost always be the ones to say things like, "Do we have to write out their names? Selena, Forrest, and Araceli are too long to write down! Can't we just use S, F, and A?" Or, "Since Selena, Forrest, and Araceli all earned the same amount, can't we just use S for all of them?" Or, "You don't need to make it look like a llama. Just draw a head with four legs." Students can also take the lead on signaling when they're ready to try a more abstract representation, for example, by complaining about the inefficiency of a drawing or Guess and Check strategy, or by using a very organized Guess and Check strategy that clearly shows repeated calculations to write in a math sentence or equation, or by wondering about the clearest way to communicate their ideas.

Welcoming Multiple Representations

When math teachers encourage students to solve problems using their own representations and methods, it can be very challenging to support so many students using multiple methods all at once. Most math teachers have one or two methods they are most comfortable with, whether it's the former math major who always reverts to algebra, the visual thinker who always reasons things out using pictures, or the teacher who's adopted her students' favorite method and always begins with Guess and Check. Every teacher we've worked with on preparing for and working with students on open-ended problem solving has noted that it's much, much easier to quickly support and extend the work of students who solved the problem the same way we did. When the student is using the method we used, we can quickly spot miscalculations, ask brilliant questions that help the student take that next step, and even support a student who's gotten hopelessly tangled to persevere and work through her difficulties independently. But when we encounter a student who's using a unique method, it's often hard to even notice that it's right, let alone tell whether an incorrect result is due to an arithmetic error or a fatal flaw in the logic. When helping those students, our best efforts to help them untangle their thinking often end up pushing them toward our methods, rather than helping them develop the skills of monitoring and fixing their own thinking.

A first step, then, in supporting students who are using a wide range of models and representations is to solve the problem before doing it with students, using as many representations as possible. Sometimes I will get a list of problem-solving strategies (there are lists in Chapters 4 and 9 of this book) and make myself spend at least three minutes for each strategy, brainstorming how it could be used with this problem. I love pushing myself to try crazy, new strategies. At the Math Forum we sometimes get to have "Math Monday," where we bring the Problems of the Week we plan to run in the upcoming weeks. We all solve one another's problems and try to anticipate as many different student responses as possible. When I first arrived at the Math Forum, my main strategy was to avoid using pencil and paper, so I did as much as I could with logical reasoning and almost never drew pictures. But watching other staff members, like Annie and Suzanne, come up with amazing visual representations using virtual manipulatives and The Geometer's Sketchpad® made me jealous—their work looked really cool and stimulated an entirely different part of my brain. So from then on, I decided to try to use a visual method for every problem.

A first step, then, in supporting students who are using a wide range of models and representations is to solve the problem before doing it with students, using as many representations as possible.

Another resource for preparing to work with multiple representations is to find colleagues (and spouses and children and neighbors) willing to do math problems with you. Sometimes math teachers will solve one anothers' problems to make sure they all have a range of solutions to study, or English teachers will solve problems for the math teachers in exchange for the math teacher's opinion on a piece of student writing. Also, many math teachers these days share problems they'd like other opinions on with other math teachers on Twitter, using the hashtag #mathchat to bring their tweet to the attention of others (or you can tweet to @maxmathforum and I'll direct some attention toward your math problem!).

However you do it, solving the problem with many strategies is one of the best ways to support your students to solve the problem using multiple representations. Multiple representations help students bridge from their current thinking about a problem, at their comfort level, to gradually extending their thinking to more sophisticated versions of their own representation, and through comparing their representation with others, to a more nuanced understanding of the problem as a whole.

Encouraging Student-to-Student Talk to Compare, Contrast, and Check Models

Many of the activities in this chapter (and previous chapters) are designed to help students discuss and compare their mathematical models. That is because good models are sharable, reusable, and transportable. The act of communicating an idea can turn it from a half-fledged idea to a genuine representation of a situation. In addition, comparing one model to another forces students to figure out if one model is right, if both are, or if neither is. These conversations can take place within small groups, as students bring work that they did in pairs to a group of four to compare, or they can occur at the whole group level when one or more groups presents their ideas and the rest of the class notices, wonders, and compares. A student-friendly handout to support students' thinking about these ideas is available online on our companion website (http://mathforum.org/pps/).

One thing that we've noticed through reading thousands of students' written submissions to the Problems of the Week is that the more students communicate their thinking, get feedback, and read and compare their work to others' (for example, by reading the Highlighted Solutions at the end of every Problem of the Week cycle), the more they start to anticipate the questions that others will have and answer them in their work. Experienced students who have been solving Problems of the Week for months or years often write both sides of a dialogue, writing their thoughts and then following up with justifications, or explaining how they knew other alternatives could not be correct. The impulse to justify your thinking and provide counterarguments comes in part from having conversations with others in which they asked for reasoning or offered their own counterarguments that you had to think about and respond to.

Putting Students in Situations That *Require* Abstraction

The Problem-Solving Bids and What Would Happen If? activities are examples of activities that put students in situations that encourage, or even require, abstraction. Math education researchers Evan Fuller, Jeffery Rabin, and Guershon Harel make a distinction between tasks students are motivated to do due to *social need* (e.g., "Could you please use a number sentence to show us the math you just did?") and tasks students are motivated to do due to *intellectual need* (e.g., "I got a different answer then you. How can we figure out who was right?").[5]

Here are some examples of situations that create an intellectual need for abstraction:

- ▸ Extending a pattern. What would happen if you did this a million times? Students sometimes like to think of what will happen with big numbers, and to choose the big numbers themselves!

- ▸ Winning an argument. When you're faced with an alternate opinion, sometimes you have to quantify your position more precisely, which can lead to more sophisticated representations, focusing on more relationships, and so on. Plus, winning an argument often means attending to counterexamples and making sure that the rules or explanations you've come up with work in all the cases your opponent can throw at you.

- ▸ Applying the same thinking to a slightly new situation. If the problem asks for the students to answer a question for one set of constraints, extend the problem so they need to find the answer for five different sets. For example, in the Ostrich Llama Count problem, have the students solve a problem for ostriches and llamas, alpacas and emus, cows and chickens, and maybe even spiders and pigeons or lions and snakes. That's pretty much why mathematicians come up with formulas.

- ▸ Communicating in writing/orally (without drawing or pointing). Students often come up with the need for labels and precise vocabulary on their own, just from the tedium of talking about "the dark-green triangle with two long

5. Fuller, Evan, Jeffery Rabin, and Guershon Harel. 2011. "Intellectual Need and Problem-Free Activity in the Mathematics Classroom." *International Journal for Studies in Mathematics Education* 4 (1): 80–114.

sides and one short side." Things like using coordinates to pinpoint a location can be motivated by trying to communicate about points on a grid, or using two points or a point and slope to describe lines can be motivated by having students give each other instructions for drawing lines without being able to point or draw.

▶ Answering curiosity questions. The first graders graphing their amaryllis flowers were motivated to make their graph more and more abstract as they became more and more interested in the flowers and what would happen to them. Listening to what students wonder often provides the perfect "hook" to introduce a new tool for organizing and displaying math thinking.

Conclusion

As math teachers, we make abstractions all the time. When we read a problem about fencing and think "perimeter," we're abstracting. When we read a problem that says, "Sean bought at least five copies" and write down "copies ≥ 5," we're abstracting. Sometimes when we support and scaffold our students to solve problems, we're making decisions about abstraction, and we don't always think to clue them in. Any time we choose to leave out information or use a different representation, we are choosing what's important to show or focus on. Sometimes as the teacher we need to model a certain way to write or show something, or we're teaching a unit that's all about a certain, more abstract way to do things. In that case, one thing we need to do is help our students be really aware of the choices we're making. Here's an example from a fourth-grade math text:

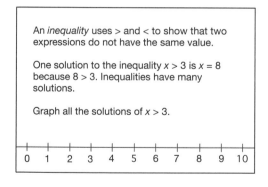

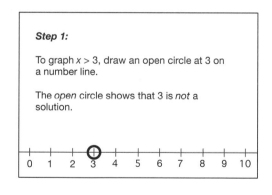

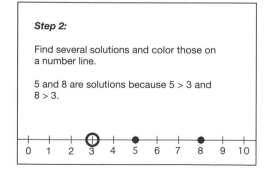

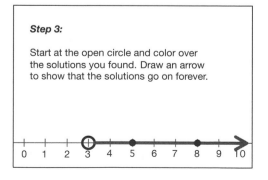

What decisions have been made about how best to show $x > 3$?

▸ We need to use a number line as a way to show all the numbers.

▸ We need to make the number line go from 0 to 10.

▸ We need to show that 3 is not a solution, and we need to do it in a special way.

▸ We will use shading/coloring to show something is a solution.

▸ We need to shade between integers, not just make dots on the integers.

▸ We need to put an arrow when we run out of represented number line to show that the solutions go on forever.

Each of these decisions is a kind of abstraction, a way of encoding information about the world using only symbols. A lot of these abstractions make intuitive sense, but they can be confusing and seem arbitrary, too. For example, students might wonder if some of the numbers really close to 3, like 3.001, are inside the open circle and therefore aren't included in the solution, because the open circle goes around them too!

A simple way to motivate the need for this abstraction, and make the choices clear, is to ask, "Who can show me all of the numbers that are greater than 3?" You'll probably get many volunteers, most of whom will say, "Four, 5, 6, 7, 8, 9, 10, 11. . . ." They'll either run out of breath or say "and so on" or someone might even say, "To infinity . . . and beyond!" if they're a fan of Disney's *Toy Story*. Noticing that the answer will go on and on and on to infinity motivates using an arrow when visualizing the answer.

You can ask, "Are there any other numbers greater than 3 that wouldn't be in that list?" Depending on everyone's comfort with fractions and decimals, you may or may not hear about 3.1 or $3\frac{1}{2}$. If you don't, mentioning them will likely get students started naming all sorts of other numbers greater than 3.

"How could we show all those many numbers? Can anyone think of any tools we've used to show how the numbers go on and on?" At that point, introducing the number line and asking, "How could you show all the numbers greater than 3 on the number line?" would be quite natural. Methods from pointing at 3 and then sliding to the right, putting an arrow above 3 pointing to the right, and coloring the numbers above 3 might all come up, and again would all seem natural to introduce. Reminding students, "Does that show all the numbers, even 3.5 and 3.1?" and "Does that show how the numbers go on and on to infinity?" will help them appreciate the shading between the integers and the arrow to the right.

Finally, asking students, "What about the 3? Is 3 > 3?" and hearing their thoughts on that will make it natural to introduce the convention of the open circle. At the end, we would ask students what they notice and wonder about the final result and how it relates to their thoughts about finding all the numbers greater than 3:

As we help students learn about tools to represent information symbolically, we can train ourselves to spot these abstractions—the ways we're encoding information into symbols, or

Sometimes when we support and scaffold our students to solve problems, we're making decisions about abstraction, and we don't always think to clue them in. Any time we choose to leave out information or use a different representation, we are choosing what's important to show or focus on.

removing distracting information—and tell students about what we're doing and why we're doing it. Or even asking students about what they think is important to represent and how we could encode it.[6]

In the subsequent chapters we'll present some problem-solving tools for specific types of problems, and we will try our best to be explicit about our decisions about different representations and times we may be making abstractions.

6. I am indebted to Dan Meyer's "ladder of abstraction" blog posts for helping me think about the importance of making abstraction explicit. You can find them at http://blog.mrmeyer.com/?cat=98.

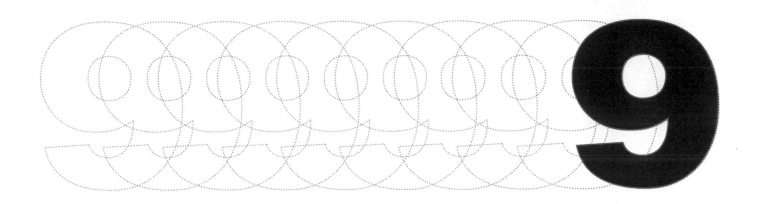

Looking for Structure

Focal practices:

1. Make sense of problems and persevere in solving them.

7. Look for and make use of structure.

In previous chapters, we've focused mainly on general problem-solving habits of mind that help students get better at solving almost any math problem. Another component of mathematical problem solving is learning to recognize and use specific problem-solving strategies like Work Backward, Look at Cases, or Solve a Simpler Problem, which, while they might apply to many problems, don't apply to every problem. How do we help students learn these new strategies and build up their repertoire so they feel they can say, "I have lots of things I can try!"?

Helping Students Say, "I have lots of things I can try!"

The first step of getting good at choosing a problem-solving strategy is having a sense that you have strategies you can try, in general, on math problems. Maybe it's sad that it took me this long in life to reach the point of feeling like the Chuck Norris of math problems, but I remember in one of my first years working at the Math Forum, Steve handed me a ridiculously intricate math problem (one that barely required middle school *concepts* but that required some professional perseverance, willingness to change tactics, record keeping and organization, and awareness of multiple strategies I could try). I was excited, because even though I worried the problem would take a long time or be tedious to solve, I was never worried that I would run out of things to try. I knew I could try Guess and Check, I could make several different Simpler Problems, I could Change the Representation in at least three different ways, I could use Logical Reasoning, I could even ask Steve for the answer and Work Backward to prove it. Sitting there staring that problem in the face was my Chuck Norris moment. I was confident that I could handle anything this problem threw at me.

Eventually, I ended up solving the problem using a Get Unstuck technique, which was getting a partner (Steve) and telling him all the things I would like to try but thought sounded too hard. I asked Steve if they sounded worth trying and he agreed they did and so he helped me. After about ten minutes we saw a new fact we'd never seen before and used that to unravel the rest of the problem. If you'd like to experience the problem that stumped me for yourself, you can find The World's Hardest Simple Math Problem on the companion website (http://mathforum.org/pps/).

The Strategy Speed Dating and Sticky Note Strategies activities in this chapter support students to start recognizing that they have a tool belt of things they can try, general strategies that they can use on almost any math problem (from word problems to "naked numbers"). In this chapter we focus on generating that feeling of "I have some different things I can try," as well as helping students learn new problem-solving strategies to add to their toolbox. In Chapter 10 we'll focus on students monitoring their problem-solving process, making plans, and being aware of when they need to try something else.

When and How to Introduce New Strategies

For students to feel like they have something to try, they need to experience lots of problem-solving strategies. What are good ways to introduce new strategies to students? As we've worked with problem solvers and observed small groups engaged in problem solving, we've identified two moments that people are most receptive to input on their problem solving. The first is as they move from understanding the problem to getting ready to think about how to work on it, and the second is after they've worked on the problem and want to check and compare their work to others'. In the first moment, solvers often want to check their interpretation of the problem as well as hear if anyone had any insights that might lead to a particularly elegant or efficient solution. In the second moment, solvers want to see if their solution matches others' as well as to learn if anyone did the problem a different way than they did. The activities in this chapter capitalize on the moments in problem solving when students are most interested in hearing, "What are elegant or efficient ways to solve this problem?"

Introducing Problem-Solving Strategies During the "Understand the Problem" Phase

A good way to introduce new strategies during students' Understand the Problem work is through introducing additional noticing and wondering prompts that guide students' thinking toward problem-solving strategies:

Question	Related Problem-Solving Strategy
"Could you draw a picture to show what's happening?" or "Could you use any of the manipulatives we have to model/act out the problem?"	Change the Representation
"What's your best guess for the answer?" and "What's a number that would definitely be wrong?"	Guess and Check
"What could we count?" and "What has to be organized?"	Make a Table
"What *must* be true? What *can't* be true? What *might* be true?"	Use Logical Reasoning
"What makes this problem hard?" (additionally: "What can I do to make it simpler?" and "Is my simplification valid or does it change the problem?") or "I could solve this problem if only. . . ."	Solve a Simpler Problem
"What are the different possibilities for this situation? Have you found all the kinds? What different kinds of _____ could there be?"	Look at Cases
"In order for this to happen, what had to happen before?" or "If this story was a movie, what would you see if you played it backward?"	Work Backward
"Does this problem remind you of any problems you've solved before? What worked in those problems?"	Any strategy

We've had success with using these questions in check-in conversations with small groups, pairs, or individual students, as well as using them as organizing questions for a whole-group brainstorm, to get lots of different ideas visible. In Chapter 4 we described a three-phase process for helping students use and then own these questions:

1. The teacher poses the question to the whole group as a noticing and wondering prompt. For example, after noticing and wondering about a problem, the teacher might say, "Now let's sort these into three lists. What *must* be true, what *can't* be true, and what *might* be true? What else can we put in each list?"

2. Once the students have worked as a whole group to address one of these strategy-specific wonderings, the teacher then starts using the questions to support students while they are working in independent groups or individually. The teacher also listens to learn if students working together have begun to ask each other these questions.

3. As students make use of these questions or ways of thinking to solve problems, the teacher supports them to tell other students how these questions are helpful. Students might make a poster listing things they wonder when they solve problems that includes any of the wonderings they find helpful. At this point when students are stuck, the teacher asks, "What can you ask yourself to help you look at the problem strategically?"

EXAMPLE: What Must Be True?

Here's an example of introducing one of these facilitation questions during a teacher-guided group in a third-grade class. Here is the prompt the students were working on:

COUNTING SHELLS

Jack has a lot of shells. He has more than 40 but less than 60. When he counts them by twos, he has one left over. When he counts them by fives, he has none left over.

The number of shells is more than half of 100.

How many shells does Jack have?

The teacher described the activity as follows.

I decided to focus on doing this problem/strategy with four students. I selected students who regularly struggle with math problem solving and understanding written communication. We used paper copies and I started by reading the problem to them and having them write down everything that must be true, can't be true, might be true. . . . Only one student even understood what I meant by this direction. So I backtracked to explain the strategy and what it means.

I told them logical thinking is when you think about the possibilities and then narrow possibilities down by eliminating what isn't true and figuring out what is actually true. We talked about what the definition of true is. Then I asked, "How do you know when something is definitely true?" They gave examples and said things such as you can see it or prove it without any doubt. Then, I said, "What is one thing that must be true in this situation (problem)?" We wrote one example on our papers and agreed because it was clearly stated.

Then I said, "How do you know when something is definitely not true?" We discussed that it's not real or didn't happen. When I asked, "What can't be true in this situation?" the first example given was something that was just obviously not true. Then I asked why and students were able to explain with support from a clue in the problem: it can't be true that [the number of shells is] greater than 60 because it said between 40 and 60. I pointed out how important it is to use the clues and information we are given to support when something is true or isn't true. Then I asked if someone could think of something that might be true and why. We discussed that when something might be true it means I have some information but not enough to prove it's definitely true. After the discussion they understood what these phrases meant.

One student did very well making sense of the logic and inferred that "the number must be odd." This brought up a very good conversation about even and odd numbers, which I know for certain one student in this group previously misunderstood . . . So we used counters to look at small number examples of even and odd. Then we discussed what other clues would be helpful as you try to think of the solution. All four students were very engaged by this point, so I let them solve the problem.

Everyone was pictorial in their solving. One student solved it in less than a minute with just pictures. Another was pretty quick too and used pictures with multiplication and skip-counting representations. The remaining two were both struggling with what to do. They understood counting by 5s, but they were ignoring the other clues. I kept redirecting them to the other clues (it's between 50 and 60). They still weren't sure, so together we listed every possibility of numbers between 50 and 60 and then from there put an x over ones it couldn't be. Then one of them realized it was 55. The other student wasn't sure why 55 was right. I reviewed the clues again to prove why 55 was correct.

The teacher in this story used the "What must be true, what can't be true, what might be true?" prompts to help her third-grade students uncover the clues in this problem—there are a lot of details that students might miss, or clues that are challenging to interpret, such as "more than half of 100," "When he counts by twos there is one left over," and so on. She figured out that if her students were going to be successful, they needed to know how to think of possible numbers of shells and eliminate incorrect ones. Using this activity, one student was even able to make an inference based on the clue "When he counts by twos there is one left over" to be able to say confidently, "The number of shells is odd."

The teacher first supported the whole group to use and understand the key questions, "What must be true, what can't be true, what might be true?" and then as she diagnosed individuals continuing to struggle, she offered other components of the logical reasoning strategy, such as using a process of elimination or reviewing the clues about what must, can't, and might be true. In the future, the teacher can listen to see if these students use logical reasoning on their own, as well as enlisting these students to share how "What must be true, what can't be true, what might be true?" can be used to solve problems.

A student-friendly handout to support students thinking about what must or can't or might be true is available on the companion website (http://mathforum.org/pps/).

Activities

Learning Problem-Solving Strategies Through Solving Problems

Essentially, problem-solving strategies are methods invented to solve one problem that turn out to be useful for solving a whole set of problems. A key to problem solving, then, is making sure to remember to use the methods that have worked in the past (that you or others came up with) on future problems. One way to help methods stick is to give them names—once students know the name of a problem-solving strategy, they may be more likely to remember it, to include it in their problem-solving planning, to make it part of the Strategy Speed Dating game we'll describe in Chapter 10, and so on. In addition to naming the strategies, it's also helpful to use key phrases or hints that remind students of the problem structures that go with each strategy. We've tried to incorporate those into the tables in this chapter.

A great way to start students thinking about named, general problem-solving strategies is to train yourself to listen for students using different strategies. As you hear, for example, students saying, "Well we could try this number and then if it's not right we'd have to try again" or "This problem looked really hard so I just thought about what would happen if I just looked at this part," then you can either play the Name That Strategy game or even just mention the common name of the strategies: "It sounds like you're using a process mathematicians call Guess and Check" or "That sounds like the Solve a Simpler Problem strategy." Then you can write that strategy name on a slip of paper (perhaps with a hint as to how to get started with the strategy on the back—see the strategy tables in this chapter for ideas) and stick it into a jar or container of strategy strips that you can use to play Strategy Speed Dating.

> *One way to help methods stick is to give them names—once students know the name of a problem-solving strategy, they may be more likely to remember it, to include it in their problem-solving planning.*

ACTIVITY Name That Strategy

Format: Students working in pairs or small groups, then moving to larger groups.

Step 1: Students work in pairs or small groups to solve a problem together, using any problem-solving strategies and activities they are familiar with. As students work on the problem, listen to their conversations to determine the method/strategy they are using. Focus on how to combine the small groups into larger groups that are using similar strategies to approach the problem.

Step 2: As students reach a stopping point (each group doesn't have to be done, but they should all have settled in to a particular method), join them into bigger groups that all used similar approaches.

Step 3: In their larger groups, students share the problem solving they did and figure out what their work has in common. They try to identify the reason you grouped them together and the name of the problem-solving strategy they were all using.

Step 4: Each large group shares out why they thought you grouped them together and the name they gave their strategy. Listeners see if they agree based on the students' descriptions of what they did. You indicate whether their reasoning matches yours.

Step 5: Each large group makes a poster of their strategy using their work on some different examples. The poster should have the name of the strategy, at least two examples, and some reasons *why* or *how* the groups chose that strategy.

Note: If any group is using a new or unique strategy, meet with them during the large-group phase to check in and see if they can name their strategy, or make some suggestions for names.

ACTIVITY Strategy Speed Dating

This next activity, Strategy Speed Dating, is one of my favorites—it's really helpful for forcing me to look at a vexing problem in novel ways. Plus, it's fun, and having to try each strategy for only a few minutes takes off the pressure to get the answer and refocuses me on finding patterns, untangling relationships, and enjoying math.

Format: Students working in groups of 3–5.

Materials: Strips of paper, pens or pencils, loose-leaf paper, or strategies from a class "strategy jar."

Step 0: Read the problem to be solved to the students.

Step 1: Each person writes a strategy or short description of something to try on a strip of paper (or pulls from the class strategy jar). The activity will be more fun if each person in a small group chooses a different strategy. Some good examples: Guess and Check, Change the Representation, Make a Table, and Solve a Simpler Problem.

Step 2: Pass out copies of the problem to be solved. When everyone is ready, each group member should pass his strip of paper listing a strategy to the left. Students have three minutes to do what they can with the strategy or idea that they receive. Tell students to write their work and what they notice and wonder on their own sheet of loose-leaf paper (this way, at the end, they will have ideas from a few different strategies that they can look back at as they work on the problem).

Step 3: After three minutes, tell students to stop wherever they are and draw a line or a box around their work, and write the name of the strategy used.

Step 4: Have students pass the strategy strip they were working on to their left, and receive a new one from the right. Give them three minutes to work on the new strategy. Tell them to keep working on their own paper with a new section for each strategy that they do.

Step 5: Pass papers every three minutes until students receive the strategy strip that they originally wrote. Finish by working on that strategy for three minutes.

Step 6: As a group, have students add any new relationships, patterns, quantities, interesting ideas, or things they are wondering about to their list of noticings and wonderings.

ACTIVITY Sticky Notes Strategies

While teachers are often all too familiar with the blank looks their students give them when they're asked to come up with strategies or get started on a difficult problem, our students do actually know lots of problem-solving strategies, and even have ideas about how to use them. In Chapter 10 you'll meet a class of second-grade students who noticed and wondered about a scenario involving sharing gumballs. When their teacher asked them what strategies they could think of to solve the problem, they thought of subtraction, adding, Guess and Check,

Having to try each strategy for only a few minutes takes off the pressure to get the answer and refocuses me on finding patterns, untangling relationships, and enjoying math.

While teachers are often all too familiar with the blank looks their students give them when they're asked to come up with strategies or get started on a difficult problem, our students do actually know lots of problem-solving strategies, and even have ideas about how to use them.

Counting Off, Tens and Ones, and Work Backward. They then went on to spontaneously use at least four more strategies, including acting the problem out with cubes and counting on their fingers! The following activity draws out the strategies students can already think of, and helps students make the connection between what they notice and wonder in a problem and what they think to do to solve it.

> **Format:** Older students might do part 1 on their own, and then go on to do part 2 in their small groups, learning how to compare strategy ideas and think about choosing an efficient, effective, or elegant strategy. Younger students might do part 1 together as a group, noticing and wondering, brainstorming strategies, and then using sticky notes to group what they noticed with what they thought to try.

Part 1

Step 1: Students notice and wonder about the problem, and record their noticings and wonderings on sticky notes.

Note: Reorganizing and sorting noticings and wonderings can help students choose a strategy they have enough information to use and that fits this problem well. For more ideas of how to sort noticings and wonderings, see the table after this activity.

Step 2: Have students choose a strategy or starting approach that they think they have enough information for and that fits the problem well.

Step 3: Have students gather up all the sticky notes that helped them think of this strategy and stick them on a copy of the handout (available on the companion website, http://mathforum.org/pps/).

Step 4: Ask students to write any problems they think they might encounter as they carry out this strategy. Encourage them to play out the strategy a little to help figure out what could go wrong.

Step 5: If students can think of any other strategies that might work too, have them record those as well, and be sure to include the sticky notes that show how they thought of it!

Part 2

Step 6: Students choose someone to be the organizer for the group. That person will collect what members wrote about their strategy after they present it.

Step 7: Students present the strategy they thought of to the group, along with what led them to choose it and why they think it would be a good strategy.

Step 8: After hearing all the presentations, the organizer reminds everyone what the strategies are. Groups discuss each one and whether it could be used to solve this problem. If students think it could work, the organizer should put it in a "candidates" pile.

Step 9: The organizer reminds everyone which strategies are candidates, then group members can vote on the candidates and choose the strategy they want to use to solve the problem. The organizer should put the other candidates in the "parking lot" so that if the group gets stuck students have other strategies to consider.

Note: After each time you do this activity, you can save the sticky notes (one way is to snap a photo using a camera phone). Build up a library of things students noticed that went with each strategy. One day, bring them all out, mix them up, and have students characterize what kinds of noticings go with, say, Make a Table, Guess and Check, and other strategies. Answering questions like that could help students make a chart or a poster like this:

If you noticed or wondered about . . .	Then try . . .
Noticed: • an unknown quantity you could guess for • some calculations and relationships • some constraints (things that have to be true)	• Guess and Check • Mathematical Model
Noticed: • things that made the problem hard • things that remind you of problems you had solved before Wondered: • why they made the problem so hard • what would happen if you used different numbers • what would happen if the situation were different	• Solve a Simpler Problem
Wondered: • what the relationship is between two quantities • what the maximum or minimum values are • if there is a pattern	• Make a Table
Wondered: • if this is always true, no matter what • if you've found all the possibilities • if the relationship would change with different kinds of quantities or objects	• Look at Cases
Noticed: • things that must, can't, and might be true Wondered: • if this is always true	• Use Logical Reasoning
Noticed: • that you don't know either how the problem started • how the problem got from the beginning to the end	• Work Backward
Noticed: • reminded you of a picture, story, scenario, graph, and so on Wondered: • if a different way of writing or showing things would help	• Change the Representation

Teaching New Strategies: Modeling the Thinking Process

A key moment when students are ready to learn a new problem-solving strategy is after they've had a chance to struggle with a new problem, when they're wondering, "How else could this problem be solved?" Manu Kapur, a researcher in Singapore, has coined the term *productive failure* (also called *productive struggle*) to describe a structure in which students begin by exploring ill-defined problems or problems in which students don't know a clear way to get to an answer they're confident in. After working on the problem and inventing some strategies and representations on their own, students were eager to hear instruction on a more efficient or widely accepted method to solve the problem. Researchers have used productive failure successfully with students from second grade to ninth grade. Other researchers have pointed out, though, that productive struggle only works if students know they're struggling—if they have a sense that there is a better way than they have come up with so far.[1]

This activity gives students an opportunity to understand a problem, get a feel for it, and generate some questions about it before learning an efficient strategy to solve it. Understanding the problem is especially important so they can make sense of the process you will model, and so they can check if your answer makes sense.

ACTIVITY Strategy Modeling—Productive Struggle

Format: Whole-group instruction, or instruction of a small group during a station or pullout activity.

Step 1: Present students with a problem using your favorite I Notice, I Wonder variation. It should be a problem that can be efficiently solved using the strategy you want to model that you think is new to the students.

Step 2: Determine if students understand the context and could check their work on the problem using an Estimation, Act It Out, Draw a Picture, or Paraphrasing activity/routine.

Step 3: Give students a short amount of time (5–10 minutes depending on their attention span and how quickly they settle down to work) to try solving the problem in groups of three. Some students may use a strategy like Guess and Check and get to a solution, in which case, use the optional Step 3.1

Step 3.1 (optional): Invite students who have a worked out a solution to the problem to present their work to the class. Encourage them to "tell the story of their thinking," even some of the ideas that might not have worked. If a student used the strategy you hoped to model, you can invite them to be the ones to do steps 4 and 5.

Step 4: Tell the students that you would like to show them your problem-solving process as you solved the problem. Let them know you solved the problem in a different way

1. Kapur, Manu. 2012. "Productive Failure." ICLS 2012. Available at www.isls.org/icls2012/downloads/K2Kapur.pdf.

that you think they might like learning about, because it will let them solve problems like this efficiently.

Step 5: Do a think-aloud, modeling your problem-solving process with lots of visuals. Model using the question prompts for your strategy such as, "I noticed this problem was really hard! One thing that made it hard was there were so many bricks to count and I could lose track. I thought it would be a simpler problem if I only had to count some of the bricks." Or "I noticed that they never told us how many fish he had at the beginning of the problem, but they did tell us exactly how many he had at the end. I wondered if I thought of the problem as a movie and ran it backward, if I could 'see' how many fish he had at the beginning." *Note*: You might include some ideas that didn't work as well!

Step 6: Ask students to quickly tell you one thing they heard as you modeled the problem. Listen to students' responses to hear what stood out to them in your think-aloud. This can give you a diagnosis of how ready they were to hear it and what they might take away.

Step 7: Ask students what they would name your approach.

Step 8: Summarize your approach again for students, or ask them to summarize for you, hitting key parts of the problem-solving strategy you used such as:

First, I noticed how hard the problem was! I thought of what changes would make a simpler problem to solve. I thought about if the methods were valid. Then I chose one of my simplification ideas and applied it to the problem. I looked for patterns and ways to use my simpler problem to answer the bigger problem.

or

First, I noticed that I knew a lot about the end of the story but nothing about the beginning. So I thought of what happened in the problem and then I played a movie of it backward in my head. I thought of the math steps that I saw in the movie and wrote them in forward order and then "undid" them in backward order. Then I went through with the answer I got and checked that it made sense in the original story.

Step 9: Give students another problem that makes use of the same strategy in a similar way. Ask them, "How is this problem like the one we worked on before?" Let them know they can use any method they want to solve it, but that you encourage them to try the ideas in your example and see how they work for them.

On the following page is a table with some different strategies, a quick definition, and an outline version of key steps/questions for each. Visit the companion website (http://mathforum.org/pps/) for example problems for each problem-solving strategy, with sample solutions, as well as a video of me modeling solving one of my favorite Solve a Simpler Problem tasks, Where's Juanita Walking?

Related Problem-Solving Strategy	Summary
Change the Representation: Show the relationships in a visual or physical way.	I noticed this problem was about _____. That reminded me of a picture/manipulative I have seen. I thought of that picture/manipulative and drew/modeled the problem. I used the picture/model to find the answer/find a pattern/write a rule. Then I checked my answer and made sure it made sense (e.g., graph on the coordinate plane, model with counters, model with fraction bars, draw a tree diagram, etc.).
Guess and Check: Think of a possible answer, apply it to the problem, check if the possible answer was right, adjust if necessary.	I noticed that we didn't know the value of _____. I thought of a good guess for that value. I noticed we could use the value to calculate _____ and _____. I did the calculations and got an answer. I noticed a *constraint* in the problem that said the answer had to be _____. I checked if my result matched. It didn't but I used the result to adjust my guess to be _____. After some guesses, checks, and adjustments I got the answer!
Make a Table: Look for the quantities (what's being counted or calculated), organize them in a table, and look for patterns or the solution in the table.	I noticed in the problem that we could count _____, _____, _____. I thought to organize them in a table to show how the different counts are related and to see patterns. I labeled the columns with the different quantities, and then filled out the rows trying different values in increasing or decreasing order. (I showed the calculations at the top of each column.) I used my table to see patterns/to find the answer to the problem.
Use Logical Reasoning: List what must, can't, and might be true; then try to move things from the "might" category to the "must" or "can't" categories.	I read the problem and asked myself, "From the clues in the problem, what *must* be true no matter what? What definitely *can't* be true? What *might* be true?" I wrote a list. I looked at the things on the "might" list and tried to move them to the "must" or "can't" list. I used the questions, "If this is true, then what?" to see if I could come up with more things that had to be true or couldn't be true. (I used a list/logic table to organize my thinking.)
Solve a Simpler Problem, version 1, build up from smaller examples: When the problem asks for what will happen after many steps, start with the first step and work up one by one. Keep organized and look for patterns to skip ahead.	This problem felt really hard! They were asking me to think about what would happen after using so many things (e.g., on the 43rd iteration, using 10 circles, etc.). It was so hard to draw out and count and come up with what would happen. I thought, "How could I make this simpler? What if it was just one time or just two times?" I started with just one thing. Then I added another to make two things. Then three. I organized a list of the results and I saw a pattern! Each thing I added _____. Then I saw a way to get to the step they were asking for! I used a rule, finished my table, and found the answer!
Solve a Simpler Problem, version 2, break into smaller/easier problems: When the problem seems too hard, look for ways to answer, "I could solve this problem if" or ways to break down a big job into smaller jobs.	This problem looked really hard. There were so many things to find. It felt like a lot of work. I thought, "What would be one simple thing I could try?" I noticed that I could start with a small section/try the problem with friendlier numbers/use a simpler shape at first. I tried my simpler problem and realized that now I understood the big problem better. I could use what I did in my simple problem to solve the hard problem!
Look at Cases: What are the different situations we have to think about with this problem? Can I break this problem into parts where I focus on one situation or type of number, line, shape, etc.?	I noticed this problem was about finding *all* the kinds or situations or finding what would happen depending on the situation. I thought, "How will I know I've found all the ways/tried all the situations?" I thought, one way to find them all is to find all the kinds ("flavors") _____ comes in. I started making a list and playing around with some different examples. I thought of these cases: _____. Then I thought "What would happen in this case?" for each one. After I went through the cases I thought, "Am I sure I found them all? How do I know?" When I was sure, I compared with a friend. We found all the same possibilities and found an answer that worked for each one so we were pretty confident in our answer!

Related Problem-Solving Strategy	Summary
Work Backward, version 1: We know the steps but don't know how it starts. Think about the end of the problem and play the problem backward in your head, thinking about undoing.	When I read the problem, I noticed I knew a lot about what happened at the end (the final result), and I needed to know what happened at the beginning. I thought to myself "What are the steps of the story in order? What math happens at each step?" Then, I played the story backward in my head like a movie! I saw the steps happen backward and I thought of what would happen when we undid each math step. I took the end result and undid each math step in backward order. Then I knew what must have happened at the beginning! I went through the problem forward just to check to make sure I was right.
Work Backward, version 2: We know the end state (and maybe the beginning state) but don't know what happened to get there. Ask yourself, "In order for this to happen, what must have happened right before?"	When I read the problem, I noticed I knew what the final result had to be, and I needed to figure out the steps to get there. I thought since I know what the last step looked like, it might be easier to figure out the second-to-last step, then the step before that, and then the step before that. At each step I asked, "In order for this to happen, what must have happened right before?" It wasn't easy, but I figured out each step. Then I went through the steps forward and got to the goal, so I'm sure my answer is right!

Practicing Strategies Using Peer Expert Groups

A nice follow-up activity to Strategy Modeling is Expert Groups. Expert Groups works best when students have tried and had some success with a new strategy but everyone could still use practice getting fluent. The teacher works with a selected group to coach them to be experts on a particular problem-solving strategy (everyone else starts making sense of the problem and working on it using whatever method they can figure out). Once the experts are ready, all students form small groups with at least one expert in the new strategy who coaches them in solving a problem using the target strategy (either the problem they were working on, or, if many were already successful, a new, related problem). It's a nice way to support students to learn from their peers, give everyone a chance to practice, and differentiate instruction to spend time with students who are struggling or are on the cusp of mastering a new problem-solving strategy.

ACTIVITY Expert Groups

> **Format:** Students working as a whole group, then moving to small groups.

> **Step 1:** Present a problem to students (including the question). Ask each student to write on a small piece of paper their first thought about one thing they might do to solve the problem. Collect students' papers.

> **Step 2:** Have the students do their favorite I Notice, I Wonder activity with a student leading the session. In the meantime, use students' initial ideas to group them in pairs and threesomes that might have similar approaches to solving the problem. Gather a group of students who you'd like to coach to be the experts (ideally, enough so that you can later put the students in groups of three to four with an expert in each group). You might choose some struggling students who need a little help or recognition, or students who are on the cusp of mastering the new strategy.

Step 3: Let students know what groups they're in and that they'll work on solving the problem in those groups.

Step 3.1 (optional): Give each group four minutes to plan a one-minute skit that acts the problem out, if you're concerned that students don't have a firm understanding of the problem.

Step 3.2 (optional): Have each group come up with an initial best guess for the problem and tell why they thought it was a good guess, to check if students have a firm understanding of the problem.

Step 4: Have groups solve the problem using whatever strategy they choose, while you work with and coach one expert group with a particular strategy in mind.

Step 5: Arrange the students back into different groups so that there's at least one expert in the focal strategy in each new group. New groups solve a second, similar problem using the focal strategy, with the peer expert there to coach them.

Step 5.1 (optional): Students who solved the initial problem a different way then share their strategies for the second problem and students listen for similarities and differences.

Step 6 (optional additional practice): Students go back into their expert groups and solve a third, similar problem together using what they've learned from the activity, and write a reflection on the method they learned, when they might use it, and why.

Building Student Independence: Making Strategies "Sticky"

To help make a new problem-solving strategy a little "stickier," after students use any new strategy, take some time with their small groups or as a class to:

- summarize what was done
- reflect on what worked and what could be improved on
- make connections between the problem and the strategy
- recall other problems that remind them of the one just solved, and
- predict/write an example of a problem that could be solved with a similar strategy.

Once students have some practice with, and a name for, a particular problem-solving strategy, they need practice to bring it into their problem-solving repertoire at the right moment. You can facilitate that by: (1) having students make posters for the strategies they know and hanging them around the room, (2) using them as part of Strategy Speed Dating, and (3) asking students, "What other problems does this problem remind you of?" when students are noticing and wondering or ask for help getting unstuck.

Making Thinking Visible

One of the problem-solving techniques that expert solvers refer to often is "Turn this into a problem I've solved before." The strategy is often lumped in with Solve a Simpler Problem, since it makes a problem simpler if you can make an analogy to a problem you recognize. Getting good at recognizing problem situations in different scenarios is tricky, and it was tricky to think of how to include it in this book. We can't exactly say, "Relate it to a problem you've solved before," because we don't know what problems our audiences have solved before. After much thought, we decided that making strategy structures visible, suggesting ways to change representations and organize information, and offering lots of activities for comparing different approaches would help build up the underlying skills students use to recognize problem structures in different situations.

One thing that the teacher can do to support this habit of mind is to become more aware of when they are recognizing problem structures and making decisions about how to represent problems based on what they already know or remember. It can be very challenging as a teacher to remember why you first realized it was a good idea to "draw a picture for this *type* of problem," for example, but making that thinking visible is really powerful for students. If you recognize that "this is just that other kind of problem in a new situation," look for ways to ask students,

> ▸ Does this remind you of anything you have solved before?
>
> ▸ Could you imagine this same diagram or list or table going with another story? What kind of story?
>
> ▸ Can you think of any other ways to represent the same thing?

Once students have had a chance to do some productive struggling and really have a feel for a particular problem situation, using the Expert Groups with an analogous problem or using Strategy Modeling to make visible the analogies you saw can help students learn about the idea of "Relate this to a problem I've solved before." Looking at some old collections of Strategy Sticky Notes can also help students begin to see some different common problem types.

That said, relating to a problem you've solved before is an advanced strategy, and one that requires students to have a library of problems they've solved before in their head, and then to be able to think flexibly to imagine the same math in different contexts. If this is something you'd like to practice more with your students, you might try the Same Math Idea, Different Math Story activity that's available through the companion website (http://mathforum.org/pps/).

After much thought, we decided that making strategy structures visible, suggesting ways to change representations and organize information, and offering lots of activities for comparing different approaches would help build up the underlying skills students use to recognize problem structures in different situations.

Conclusion

Helping students to identify and name the strategies they already use, introducing new strategies using personal stories and brief conceptual introductions right before or right after independent problem solving, and supporting students to reflect on why and how new strategies work are all powerful tools for expanding students' repertoire of specific problem-solving strategies that work for specific types of problems.

A great way to get really good at the ideas in this chapter is looking for others who are interested in exploring different problem-solving strategies, solving problems together that you'll then do with your students, and then finding more challenging problems using the same problem-solving strategies. You might see if there is a Math Teachers' Circle (or a Math Circle open to students and adults) in your area, use and follow the #mathchat hashtag on Twitter to share your favorite problems and read good problems from others, or recruit a group of teacher friends to solve some tough problems. The recommended readings and links that follow can provide some great sources. If you remind potential participants that failure and struggle are expected when solving hard problems and won't be seen as a sign of not being good at math (plus they help build empathy with your students!), and you offer to bring really good snacks, you'll probably find some takers.

Related Links and Books for Finding Rich Problems and Problem-Solving Strategies

Books on Problem Solving and Related Problems

For the Teacher

Pólya, George. 1957. *How to Solve It*. Garden City, NY: Doubleday.

Elementary

Burns, Marilyn. 1996. *50 Problem-Solving Lessons: Grades 1–6*. Sausalito, CA: Math Solutions.

Lester, Frank, and Randall Charles. 2003. *Teaching Mathematics Through Problem Solving: Prekindergarten–Grade 6*. Reston, VA: NCTM.

O'Connell, Sue. 2007. *Introduction to Problem Solving, Grades 3–5*, 2d ed. Portsmouth, NH: Heinemann.

Wedekind, Kassia Omohundro. 2011. *Math Exchanges*. Portland, ME: Stenhouse.

Middle School

Herr, Ted, and Ken Johnson. 2001. *Problem-Solving Strategies: Crossing the River with Dogs and Other Mathematical Adventures*, 2d ed. Emeryville, CA: Key Curriculum Press.

Hyde, Arthur. 2009. *Understanding Middle School Math*. Portsmouth, NH: Heinemann.

Schackow, Joy, and Sue O'Connell. 2008. *Introduction to Problem Solving, Grades 6–8*. Portsmouth, NH: Heinemann.

Schoen, Harold, and Randall Charles. 2003. *Teaching Mathematics Through Problem Solving: Grades 6–12*. Reston, VA: NCTM.

Links

All Grade Levels

The Math Forum Problems of the Week (requires a subscription): http://mathforum.org/pows/

Free Math Forum Problems (requires a free login):

Technology Problems of the Week: http://mathforum.org/tpow/

Financial Literacy Problems of the Week: http://mathforum.org/fe/

Free Math Forum Scenarios: http://mathforum.org/blogs/pows/

Short articles on problem-solving from the Math Forum: http://mathforum.org/pow/teacher/articles.html

Doing Mathematics: Habits of Mathematicians: www.doingmathematics.com/2/category/habits%20of%20a%20mathematician/1.html

Math teacher Bryan Meyer blogs about his action research project to support students to become aware of and use ten mathematical habits (similar to the ones this book is organized around).

Estimation 180: www.estimation180.com

Math teacher Andrew Stadel provides visual estimation challenges to build students' number sense.

Illuminations: http://illuminations.nctm.org

NCTM (National Council of Teachers of Mathematics) provides lessons and virtual manipulatives for many topics across many grade levels.

Illustrative Mathematics: www.illustrativemathematics.org

The Institute for Mathematics & Education solicits, writes, and catalogues rich tasks aligned to the Common Core.

Math Pickle: http://mathpickle.com

Mathematician Gordon Hamilton poses math puzzles, games, and challenges that are "hard fun!" including several problems accessible to K–12 students that lead to unsolved problems in mathematics.

NRICH Maths Weekly Challenges: http://nrich.maths.org/public/viewer.php?weekly=true

From the University of Cambridge, this website poses mathematical challenges for elementary and middle school grades.

Visual Patterns Project: http://visualpatterns.org

Math teacher Fawn Nguyen provides pattern puzzles, asking, "Can you find what will happen on the 43rd iteration?" to build students' skill at organizing and representing patterns.

Yummy Math: www.yummymath.com

Former math teachers Brian Marks and Leslie Lewis provide topical math activities that relate to happenings in our world. PDFs, Microsoft Word documents, and Excel spreadsheets offer prompts and tables on topics ranging from the oil spill in the Gulf of Mexico to the Academy Awards; from the Super Bowl to the Chilean mine rescue; from March Madness to American Idol.

Middle School Focused

Dan Meyer's Three-Act Tasks: http://threeacts.mrmeyer.com

Former math teacher and current graduate student Dan Meyer offers problem-solving challenges launched and explored using video and images.

Graphing Stories: http://graphingstories.com

Dan Meyer creates and curates video of quantitative relationships that students are challenged to graph.

MATHCOUNTS: http://mathcounts.org

The MATHCOUNTS program provides challenging problems for middle school students, designed for their competitive math team challenges.

Mathalicious: www.mathalicious.com

Former math teachers Karim Kai Ani, E. A. Jackson, Matt Lane, Chris Lusto, and Kate Nowak craft lessons that help middle school teachers teach math in a way that engages their students and helps students understand how the world works. (Note: Free samples are available, after which a sliding-scale subscription is required.)

Mathematics Assessment Project: http://map.mathshell.org/materials/index.php

The Shell Center provides middle school tasks and challenges aligned to the Common Core.

Beyond Middle School Math

Park Mathematics: http://parkmath.org/curriculum

An independent school in Baltimore has developed their own secondary curriculum based around habits of mind. They'll send you PDFs on request.

PCMI (Park City Mathematics Institute): http://mathforum.org/pcmi/hstp/problemsets .html

The Park City Mathematics Institute shares the problem sets used in the Secondary School Teachers Program Developing Mathematics courses since 2001. These problems challenge the math teacher!

Phillips Exeter Academy Problems: www.exeter.edu/academics/72_6539.aspx

Phillips Exeter Academy in Exeter, New Hampshire, shares the problem sets they've developed for their high school mathematics curriculum.

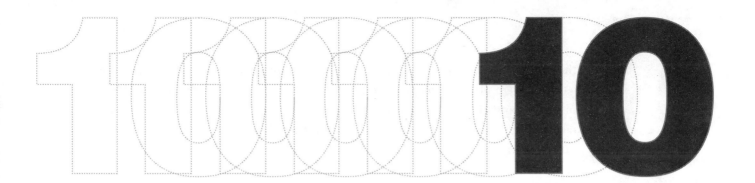

The Problem-Solving Process and Metacognition

Focal practices:

1. Make sense of problems and persevere in solving them.
5. Use appropriate tools strategically.

The Problem-Solving Process and Metacognition

In this chapter we focus on activities and teacher facilitation moves that can help students learn about problem solving as a *process*—not something to be over and done with, but something that involves pausing, analyzing, and reflecting. We will focus on metacognition and reflection as well as problem-solving steps like making a plan and getting unstuck.

Metacognition

I was working with a group of middle school students who were solving the Wooden Legs problem described in Chapter 5, in which the students are asked to figure out all the different ways Wendy could use exactly 31 wooden legs to make 3-legged dollhouse stools and 4-legged dollhouse tables. We had made Unifix cubes available as manipulatives (since we didn't have anything small and table-leg-shaped in this classroom), and the students also had multiplication tables available on their desks. I noticed a group of students spending a lot of time putting together groups of 3 Unifix cubes to get up to nearly 31 cubes used, and then putting together groups of 4 Unifix cubes to get up to nearly 31 cubes used. Another group was spending lots of time writing out the 3s and 4s multiplication tables. Both of

*We focus on activities and teacher facilitation moves that can help students learn about problem solving as a **process**—not something to be over and done with, but something that involves pausing, analyzing, and reflecting.*

these ideas could be used to help think about the problem, and so I wondered how the students were planning to use their ideas. Might the students with Unifix cubes plan to make as many stools as possible and then figure out how to systematically swap stools into tables to find all the combinations? Might the multiplication table group look for pairs of numbers, one from each table, which added to 31? Nope—when I asked the groups, "Why are you doing that?" they could tell me things like, "She makes 3-legged stools and these are stools," or "We noticed the stool legs go by 3s and the table legs go by 4s so we are writing down the 3s and 4s times tables." When I asked, "Then what will you do?" or "How is that helping you solve the problem?" they weren't really sure. Part of me was just excited to see them persevering in math class, but I was also concerned that something was missing from their problem-solving process.

Dr. Alan Schoenfeld, a professor of math and math education at the University of California, Berkeley, teaches an introductory course on problem solving for undergraduates. He noticed his undergraduate students behaving like these young students, and he wondered what was going on. One day he thought to observe, during twenty-minute problem-solving sessions, how his students used their time and compare it to how his colleagues used the same amount of time to solve a problem that was proportionately difficult.

The students were unsuccessful in solving their problem (even though they had earned A grades in the course and had solved a similar problem on their calculus final a few weeks before), while the professional mathematician solved his problem successfully even though it was in an area of math he hadn't studied in many years. Dr. Schoenfeld graphed how the undergraduates spent their time during problem solving (trust a mathematician to find a way to use graphs to answer any question!):

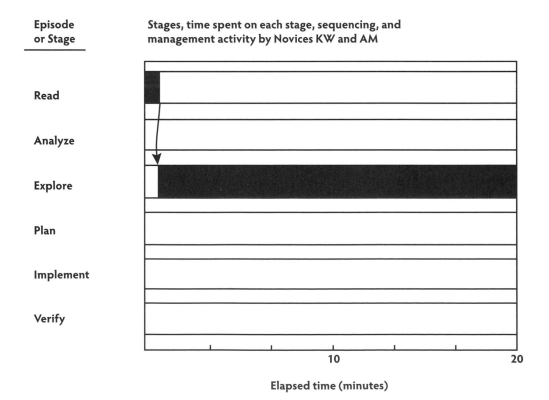

And here's how Dr. Schoenfeld's mathematician friend spent his time solving the problem:

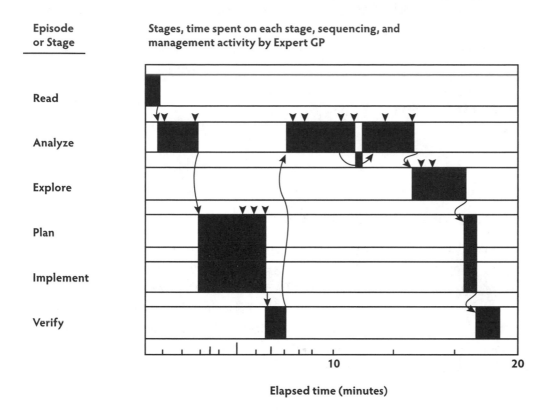

| Episode or Stage | Stages, time spent on each stage, sequencing, and management activity by Expert GP |

Elapsed time (minutes)

One thing that jumped out about the mathematician's graph was that he spent much more time thinking about the problem than actually doing any calculating. He worked hard to make sure he understood the problem and what it was asking, he generated several ways he might be able to solve the problem (plenty of which were wrong and could have led him on a wild goose chase), and he evaluated each of those strategies as he worked to make sure he was getting somewhere. On the mathematician's graph, you see little triangles above many of the black bars. Each of those triangles marks a time point when he stopped to ask himself, "How am I doing?" and/or to comment on where he was in his *problem-solving process*.[1]

The undergraduate students, on the other hand, like the young students working on Wooden Legs, thought of a calculation they could do and immediately started doing it. They used almost all of their time bogged down in arduous calculations. But when their professor asked them, like I asked the young students, "How will these calculations help you solve the problem?" the students had no idea.

Many teachers who have taught problem solving as part of their math classes will recognize the same behaviors in their K–12 students as Professor Schoenfeld saw in his undergraduates, and I saw with the younger students solving Wooden Legs. When confronted with a problem, students often latch onto one idea, whether it's the most recent strategy they learned or a procedure or formula they feel comfortable with. They immediately start

1. Schoenfeld, A. H. 1987. "What's All the Fuss About Metacognition?" In *Cognitive Science and Mathematics*, ed. A. H. Schoenfeld, 189–215. Hillsdale, NJ: Lawrence Erlbaum Associates.

calculating without ever seeming to stop and reflect. He called what they are missing *meta-cognition* (thinking about thinking). Metacognition is what prevents students from going on wild goose chases, pursuing dead-end ideas come hell or high water. Solvers who are engaged in high-quality metacognition can answer questions like "What are you doing?" "Why are you doing it?" "How will it help you?" throughout their problem solving. The Facilitated Problem Solving, Group Roles, and Roll the Tape activities work toward building students' metacognitive skills as they solve problems.

Activities

Activities for Building Metacognition

The difficult balance for the teacher in facilitating students' metacognition is that he must transition from being the voice in the student's ear to letting the student hear her own internal voice. Sometimes our students tell us, "The problems are so easy when you're there, but when you're not there I don't know what to do." The students add, "It's not even like you help us, you just ask questions!" They don't always realize that the questions we ask are metacognitive questions, and that without these questions, problem solving is much more difficult. *The key principle for the teacher to remember is that students must be given ample opportunities not just to be facilitated, but also to facilitate themselves, to monitor their* own *thinking.*

> *The difficult balance for the teacher in facilitating students' metacognition is that he must transition from being the voice in the student's ear to letting the student hear her own internal voice.*

Developing a metacognitive voice inside your head, the questioner who asks things like "How am I doing?" and "How does that information help me?" can be a lot like developing a conscience. At first, it is other people who stop us from doing bad things, and praise us when we do good things—"No, Max! Put that cookie back!" After a while, we start to anticipate their judgments and act based on what we think they would say—"Mom will be mad if I take a cookie before dinner." Finally, we come to have a voice in our head that sounds more like our own voice, helping us decide right from wrong on our own—"If I eat a cookie now, I won't be hungry for dinner, which would be rude and not very healthy."

In fact, the Russian social scientist Lev Vygotsky theorized that this is how all learning occurs: as learners attempt tasks that they can only do with others' assistance (tasks in their zone of proximal development), they gradually internalize the conversations and scaffolding their parents, peers, and teachers provide, until they can do the tasks on their own.[2]

In the Facilitated Problem Solving activity, the teacher and eventually a student volunteer serve as the "conscience"—the metacognitive questioner that monitors progress, checks for understanding, seeks multiple proposals, weighs the options, and so on. As students get used to solving problems with an external facilitator, and even take on the role of facilitator themselves, they begin the process of developing their own internal problem-solving conscience.

---

2. Vygotsky, L. S. 1978. *Mind in Society*. Cambridge, MA: Harvard. "An interpersonal process is transformed into an intrapersonal one. Every function in the child's cultural development appears twice: first, on the social level, and later, on the individual level; first, between people . . . , and then inside the child. This applies equally to voluntary attention, to logical memory, and to the formation of concepts. All the higher [mental] functions originate as actual relations between human individuals" (57).

ACTIVITY Facilitated Problem Solving

Format: Whole group.

Step 1: Put a problem on the board for the students to solve. Lead an I Notice, I Wonder brainstorm about the problem, recording the noticing and wondering on the board next to the problem statement.

Step 2: Ask, "Do we understand what the problem is asking well enough to say it in our own words?" Ask multiple people to say the problem in their own words. (Ask as many as will volunteer. Use a long wait time to encourage more volunteers). Ask, "Do all these different ways of asking the problem say the same thing?"

Step 3: Ask, "Do we have any ideas about what the answer will be like?" You might follow up with questions like, "Do we know what the units will be?" or "Do we know a number that's definitely too high or too low?" or "Will the answer be a single number or something else (a range, an explanation, a proof, a formula)?"

Step 4: Ask, "Does anyone have any ideas of how we might solve the problem?" Listen to as many ideas as possible. At first, students will think you are just listening for the right idea, or that you'll stop after the first suggestion and start working. Tell them and show them that you want to hear all the ideas! Make a note of all the ideas you can gather. *Note*: Hearing from many students before seizing on a strategy is not what many students are used to in math class. They may think the initial strategies aren't good enough, so you might want to say something like, "Thanks for sharing that! I'm curious to hear other ideas, too!"

Step 5: Ask, "How can we choose a method to try?" Listen to students' thoughts about the methods. They may admit that they're not really sure how to try a certain strategy, or that they know a certain approach will be inefficient, for example. Let them come to a consensus on a method to try.

Step 6: Scribe as the students tell you the steps to carry out the strategy. Your job is to record the work publicly, but also to stop every 2–5 minutes to ask, "What are we trying to do? Why? How is this helping us?"

If students get stuck, ask, "Is there anything we *noticed* or *wondered* that could help us now?" or "Is it time to try another one of our strategy ideas?"

If students solve the problem, ask, "Did the answer match what we thought it would be?" or "Is there anything we noticed or wondered that we didn't address?" or "What helped us solve the problem?" or "Could we have solved it another way?"

Variation: Use student leaders. After facilitating this activity several times, ask, "Do you think you can remember all the questions I ask?" Help the students to make a list, and then ask students to sign up to take turns leading the group, with your help.

Variation: We call this variation "1-2-4-8." After facilitating this activity several times, ask, "Do you think you can remember all the questions I ask?" Help the students to make a list.

Then split the class in half and ask for your two bravest volunteers to each lead half the class. Next time, get four volunteers to each lead one-quarter of the class. Each time, have more volunteers lead smaller groups, until students are able to work through a problem in groups of four, with each student having had a turn to serve as the leader.

Some questions that might come to mind reading through the Facilitated Problem Solving activity are "How is this different from any other example of leading the class through a problem at the board?" or "My class does problems together and I take suggestions from them all the time, but I don't notice them getting better at independent problem solving. What can I do to make this activity more effective?"

Consider this story, from a second-grade teacher who used this problem (from our Problems of the Week) in her classroom:

CHARLIE'S GUMBALLS

Charlie has a giant bag of gumballs and wants to share them with his friends.

He gives half of what he has to his buddy, Jaysen. He gives half of what's left after that to Marinda. Then he gives half of what's left now to Zack. His mom makes him give 5 gumballs to his sister. Now he has 10 gumballs left.

How many gumballs did Charlie have to begin with?

I worked on the Problem of the Week Charlie's Gumballs with my second graders. I chose it because I wanted something where there would be a lot of opportunity for discourse. I wasn't sure how this would go since I have not worked yet on fractional parts with the students.

To start the lesson I placed the problem in the center of a piece of chart paper and divided the paper into fourths. Every group of 4 students worked together on the problem in the section that was divided off for them. I also placed another copy of the problem on the board that I used for myself. I introduced the problem to the students by reading it to them and then asking them what they noticed. I wrote their responses in the first section.

- Charlie cuts the amount into $\frac{1}{2}$ each time.
- He had some left over for himself.
- Giant bag of gumballs can be split evenly.
- We need to figure out how many he started with.

In the next section I had them tell me what they wondered. I recorded:

- How many gumballs he gave to his friends?
- How many he started with?
- How big was the bag?
- How big are the gumballs?

By recording the students' noticings and wonderings exactly as they say them, the teacher is helping the students see the value of their own ideas and first thoughts about the problem. In terms of "coaching" them as problem solvers and serving as a "mental voice" that the students can learn to use, she is helping them ask, "What do I notice? What do I wonder?" and then *value what they come up with*. When we constantly rephrase students' thoughts, we can be sending the message, "What you come up with isn't enough to help you solve the problem."

> Next we talked about their noticings and wonderings and I told them they would need to find out how many gumballs Charlie started with. As a group I had them discuss what strategies they would use to solve the problem and why. After the discussion they shared out that they would use subtraction, adding, Guess and Check (a child explained the method and I told her what the strategy was named), Counting Off, Tens and Ones, and Work Backward.

As their metacognitive coach, the teacher is modeling double-checking understanding and assumptions by discussing students' noticings and wonderings. We often ask, "Are there any of these noticings that you're wondering about?" which gives students a chance to voice different understandings and come to consensus. The teacher is modeling the process of checking that we understand a problem and what we're trying to figure out before thinking of what we might do. Then she is helping the students realize that they have ideas about the problem based on what they saw by asking them to generate strategies, and then waiting to hear and acknowledge *all* strategies students come up with, not just the ones she expected to hear. By discussing the strategies, the teacher is supporting students to consider different strategies for the same problem and think about why someone might choose a particular strategy. This is moving toward metacognitive questions like "How do we think this strategy will help us?" and "What are some good reasons for trying this strategy?" Helping a student name a strategy she describes is also helping students remember and make use of their ideas in the future.

> After we discussed the strategies the students were then given the task of solving the problem. Many students right away said they already knew the answer. I handed out cubes that they could use and I saw students also using the hundreds chart on their desk. One child right away told his group that the answer had to be over 100 because of the number of times Charlie gave away half. As I walked around the room I saw students drawing a picture model to solve the problem, using the cubes, chart, and even their fingers. This problem took us the entire math block to complete and two students were able to successfully get the answer. They were also able to explain that to their groups and the whole class. I was impressed with my students' ability to work backward and to do fractional parts. *Even the students who were not able to come up with a solution were able to communicate a method in which to go about figuring out the problem.*

Lots more metacognitive coaching is happening in this paragraph. For example, the teacher supported students who right away had an answer to keep working and think about if they were sure that was the answer and what math they could do to confirm (or disconfirm) their thinking. It sounds from the story as though the teacher stepped back as long as students were working, but that the students supported each other or the teacher supported them to sometimes change their strategies, as students spontaneously began using cubes or the hundreds chart, or counting on their fingers, in addition to their planned strategy. The teacher might have helped facilitate this by checking in with students and asking questions like "How's it going?" or "What are you trying right now?" or "What are you hoping to figure out?" or "How is this helping you?" If students were feeling stuck (which it doesn't sound like these students were) the teacher might have supported them to remember their noticings and wonderings and some of the strategies that they mentioned but hadn't chosen.

You might compare the metacognitive coaching in this story to the hypothetical whole-group problem solving that follows. As you read it, you might consider what metacognition is being modeled, what role the teacher is playing, which decision points are made obvious, and which decision points are made invisible.

> The teacher puts the whole Charlie's Gumballs problem (which includes the question "How many gumballs did he start with?") on the projector and passes out copies to all the students. He asks students what they notice and what they wonder about the problem. As students answer things like "The friends have weird names," "He has 10 gumballs at the end," "He always gives away half of his gumballs," "How many gumballs did he start with?," "Why do some friends get more gumballs than others?," "Why did he share his gumballs?," the teacher selects certain noticings to emphasize and write on the board:
>
> - He ends up with 15 gumballs (10 for himself and 5 for his sister).
> - After each sharing he has half of what he started with.
> - How many gumballs did he start with?
>
> Then he asks, "From your noticings and wonderings, what do you think we could do to solve the problem?" One student offers, "I think we'll have to use division because Charlie divides the gumballs in half." The teacher says, "That's a good idea to think about division. What's another operation that's the opposite of division? Could we use that too?" Another student answers, "Multiplication." The teacher says, "Right, we can use multiplication to help us undo all of the division." The students are quiet. The teacher continues, "How many gumballs did Charlie have left at the end?" The students answer, "Ten."
> "Good noticing! But what happened before that?"
> "He had to give his sister 5 gumballs," ventures one student.
> "How many gumballs did he have before he had to give those gumballs away?"
> "Fifteen?" offers a different student.
> "Great. What should we do with the 15, then? What do we do next?"
> "Divide it in half?" offers one student.
> "We wouldn't divide, though, would we? Those are the gumballs Charlie has left at the end after he does all the dividing, right?"
> "Do 15 *times* $\frac{1}{2}$?" offers a different student.
> "Multiplying by $\frac{1}{2}$ is the same as dividing by 2. What could we do that would be the *opposite* of dividing by 2?"

"Fifteen times 2?" asks the student who's been the most vocal participant.

"Good thinking! We could do 15 × 2, what would that tell us?"

"Umm . . . I'm not really sure?"

"Anybody? If we take the 15 gumballs Charlie has left at the end, and double them, what does that tell us? In other words, when we *undo* the dividing in half?"

"How many he had before?"

"Right! Before what?"

"Umm, before he divided them in half? Like, um, before he split them up to share with Zack?"

"Right! So before he split them up to divide with Zack, he had 30 gumballs. Half went to Zack. How many did Zack get?"

"Fifteen," answered a handful of students.

"Right, and then the sister got 5 and Charlie got 10. How could we figure out how many Marinda got?"

"Multiply?" ventures the student who offered multiplying by 2 the first time.

"Yeah, now you're getting the hang of this. We can find out what happened before he split them with Marinda by doubling what he had left at the end. If he had 30 after he split them, how many did he have before?"

"Sixty," say several students, some loudly and confidently, others hesitantly.

"And then, for the last step, if Charlie had 60 gumballs after he split them with Jaysen, how many gumballs did he have before he split his pile in half?"

"One hundred twenty!" say most of the students.

"Right, now you've got the right answer. So basically, that's how you use working backward to solve a problem like this. You just keep asking yourself, if he had this many before he did that, how many did he have before? Good job, everyone."

I wrote this example in such a way that the teacher is making a lot of decisions for the students, and is making them invisibly. The students aren't sure why the teacher is emphasizing inverse operations, or their noticings of what happened at the end. The students in this class probably wouldn't feel like their ideas led to solving the problem. They might feel like they could solve a similar problem, but in our experience when students don't have an opportunity to participate in the decision making and discuss the reasons why a strategy was chosen or a particular noticing was helpful, they struggle to re-create independently what they experienced. Finding opportunities while modeling problem solving to record student thinking exactly as it is said, air all the noticings and wonderings, hear as many possible strategy suggestions as possible, and support students to articulate how they are solving the problem and why they are doing it that way at many points during the problem-solving process all make problem-solving facilitation more like metacognitive coaching and less frustrating for students and teachers.

The next activity offers the students more autonomy in working on the problem, as they work in small groups. The metacognitive roles have been divided up among the students, so that one student helps other students remember other ideas they had that they might want to come back to, while a second student helps the group by asking, "What are we doing? Why?," a third is in charge of asking for help if the group gets stuck, and a fourth keeps a record of what the group has done.

When students don't have an opportunity to participate in the decision making and discuss the reasons why a strategy was chosen or a particular noticing was helpful, they struggle to re-create independently what they experienced.

ACTIVITY Group Roles

Format: Students working in groups of four.

Step 0: Have students read the problem, and as a small group, generate a list of noticings and wonderings. They should also brainstorm some strategies or approaches to try and make a list of ideas, which we call the "parking lot."

Step 1: Students decide on group roles:

a. Parking Lot Attendant—observes the problem solving while looking at the strategy parking lot and the noticings and wonderings. Is responsible for helping the group use noticings and wonderings they may have missed and reminding them of other strategies they considered and what was useful. Participates when asked or when he notices something useful.

b. Trail Marker—observes the group and pauses regularly to ask them, "What are we doing? Why? What do we hope to get out of it? How will we check if it worked? What was the question again?" Participates every few minutes, plus when she notices the group making a decision or trying something new. Uses a special-color pen or marker to record the trail markings.

c. Unstuck-er—participates with the group, but has the special job of if students get stuck, figuring out who to ask for help and what to ask. Could ask the Parking Lot Attendant what's in the parking lot, or ask the Trail Marker what students were hoping to do and how they were going to check it, or could decide they need to ask another person, look something up, and so on.

d. Recorder—participates with the group, makes sure the group has a record of their problem solving (though others might write down work they do as well).

Step 2: Students begin working on the problem by choosing a strategy or starting approach from the parking lot list. The group members all work on the problem together while keeping their roles in mind (e.g., the Parking Lot Attendant checking the list of noticings and wonderings, the Recorder taking notes or making sure others write their work down). Every few minutes the Trail Marker makes them pause and they work together to answer her questions. The Trail Marker might use her special-colored pen to record students' answers on their problem-solving sheet. If the questioning prompts any changes in approach, the Parking Lot Attendant might suggest other strategies or noticings and wonderings the group considered.

Step 3: Continue this problem until students have an answer that they are confident in and have checked in some way.

ACTIVITY Roll the Tape

A colleague of ours who runs the Math & Science Education Research Center at the University of Delaware, Jon Manon, tells a great story about how he accidentally turned a group of struggling freshmen into one of the best math classes he ever taught. Jon was teaching a summer course to help students who were identified as needing extra support in math get caught up before their freshman year of college. On the morning the course was supposed to meet for the first time, Jon got a desperate call from a colleague. They were supposed to be making a video to be used with teachers, illustrating productive small-group work in math class. Their intended class had fallen through, and they needed another. Though Jon was nervous, having never met his class, he agreed to help. When the students came in that morning, he explained that they were going to be a demonstration class, helping math teachers see what effective small-group work in math class looked like. So, of course, they would need to be sure to demonstrate their best small-group work skills. As a class, students brainstormed what a productive group working together to solve a problem would look and sound like. They talked about different roles they might take, such as note taker or task manager. They talked about staying on task, listening to each other, and being polite when they disagreed. When the cameras started rolling, the students looked like they'd been working together for weeks, not less than a day. And Jon reports the best part was that the class culture was cemented, even after the film crew left. The students knew what they wanted their class to look and sound like, and they made sure it stayed that way for the rest of the term. We've used this same strategy very effectively in other math classes across the grade levels, since we're often going into classrooms and recording video to exemplify our lessons. We try to use every opportunity we have of recording students to help them reflect on what they want their actions to look like, no matter what other motivations we might have for using video in classes.

Format: Students working in groups of four.

Note. This activity takes place over two or more days, as students make a video and then review it in snippets.

Step 1: Ask students if they've ever heard of athletes watching videos of themselves as part of their practice. Ask students why athletes might do that.

Step 2: Explain that just like in a sport, you can get better at working together to solve math problems by watching your technique and noticing what you're doing well and what the areas for improvement are. Explain that today you're going to record some of their small-group problem solving and reflect together on what they're doing well and where they could improve.

Step 3: On the board or a piece of poster paper, make a list (or, if such a list already exists, review and add to it) of what a good group problem-solving session will look and sound like. Push students to be specific: "Remember, we're going to be watching this on video. What should we see? What should we hear?" *Note:* If students are focused a lot on group dynamics, push them to also think of mathematical aspects. Ask, "What specific questions might I hear?" or "What problem-solving words might I hear?"

Step 4: Give the students the problem they will be solving in their group of four. Explain the plan you'll be using for whom to record (e.g., each group in random order for five minutes each, or that you'll take volunteers, or that you're going to focus on one randomly chosen group for the whole time, or that a volunteer will record each group, etc.). Record the students solving the problem.

Step 5: Review the video. This will involve watching selected portions several times.

First viewing: Have students write down quotes that indicate good problem solving. Compare the quotes with the list of what you were hoping to hear. "Which things are you good at?" Which do students want to hear themselves doing even more of?

Second viewing: Have students make a list of everything they see students *do* during a small portion of problem solving. They should list as many verbs as they can think of. Compare the verbs with the list of what you were hoping to see. "Which things are you good at?" Which do students want to see themselves doing even more of?

Third viewing: Remind students of (or introduce students to) the steps in the problem-solving process (such as understand the problem, make a plan, carry out the plan, look back). Ask them to identify when the students are doing each phase of the process. How long is spent on each phase? Which do you want to see students doing even more of?

Variation: Debbie Wile, who teaches math enrichment at an elementary school, captures her students' group work whenever they are working on computers. Whether they're using The Geometer's Sketchpad® or online virtual manipulatives, she uses a free screen-capture program called Jing. It makes five-minute recordings of whatever is happening on the screen, as well as capturing students' voices. When the students go into the lab, they know that whenever they're about to do something interesting, they should turn Jing on and record their screen. At the end of a problem-solving session, they pick a Jing podcast or two to turn in as a record of their problem-solving process.

Each of the three activities shown helps students to develop an awareness of their thinking as they work. We hope that, as students become used to working with a facilitator, whether it is a teacher or student serving in that role, and as they review their own problem solving to become more aware of the process questions and the problem-solving stages, they start looking a little bit more like the expert mathematician that Dr. Schoenfeld observed. We hope that they will spend less time bogged down in useless calculations and more time thinking about questions like "How is this helping me solve the problem?" and "What are we trying to find out again?" In fact, you might want to give your students the challenge that Dr. Schoenfeld gave his: at any time during problem solving, I reserve the right to stop you and ask, "What are you doing? Why are you doing it? How will it help you?" At first, you might get many blank looks. But as you keep it up, students will remember to stop themselves and prepare for your questions. By the end of the year, you might hear students spontaneously asking these questions of each other, and even catching themselves before they get bogged down in dead ends.

Building Student Independence in the Problem-Solving Process

The key in this chapter for building student independence is to gradually increase the students' agency and responsibility in each of these activities. For example, after leading Facilitated Problem Solving enough times that the students can anticipate or predict the next step, choose one of the variations in which a student leads the problem-solving sessions.

The Group Roles activity uses structure to externalize some of the processes that students will eventually internalize. Students may balk at the structure, and ask, "Why can't we just solve the problem?" Let them know that you're worried they're getting stuck because they don't stop and ask, "Why are we doing this again?" or because they don't make use of their noticings to pick good strategies or get unstuck. If they feel that they can do those things without the structure, use the video activity (Roll the Tape) to let students show you what they can do on their own. Maybe they'll come to appreciate the fact that they really aren't doing a good job of monitoring their own progress or using their noticings, or maybe you'll see things they're doing informally that they can build on and keep doing whenever they get stuck.

We hope that some of the good habits will become automatic. For example, students who've experienced the group roles for several weeks might think of the role of the Parking Lot Attendant and ask each other, "What did we notice?" the next time they get stuck. You can always test this by eavesdropping on students in problem-solving situations in which they aren't given particular support in how to solve the problem or any group structure to use. You might also walk around and ask students periodically, "What strategy are you using?" "What did you notice that helped you choose it?" or "What are you doing? Why? How will it help you?" and other questions that hold them accountable for being aware of their own problem solving.

Another way to support students to internalize some of these activities is having students create posters that show what worked in problem solving. This might help students to go from asking the teacher for help, to looking around the room for reminders, to eventually just remembering some of their favorite problem-solving questions in their head.

The Problem-Solving Process and Getting Unstuck

We wanted to offer one more activity that is specifically about supporting students to use their metacognitive and self-questioning skills to get unstuck.

ACTIVITY Wonderama

> **Format:** Students working on problems in their small groups.
>
> **Materials:** Clipboard for the teacher or student leader, sticky notes for each group.
>
> **Step 0:** On the following page is a list of wonderings. Print a copy of it for the leader's clipboard.

General Questions

What does this mean?

What is this problem about?

What do they want?

Does it have to be that way?

Do I need to figure that out?

How does this situation work?

Is there another way to think of it?

How will I know if this is true?

What is a good way to express that?

When is this true?

What would happen if . . . ?

From the Strategies

What are the quantities in the problem?

What guess can I make?

How would I check if my answer was wrong?

What makes this problem hard?

How could I make this simpler?

What must be true? What can't be true? What might be true?

What are different ways I can represent this situation?

- ◆ Would a drawing help?
- ◆ Could I act the problem out?
- ◆ Could I make a graph?
- ◆ Could I make a table?

What different cases could there be?

How are these quantities related?

Which quantities can change? Which quantities don't change?

What must have happened before this step?

Step 1: Students work in small groups or pairs to solve a difficult problem. When they get stuck, they raise their hands. As the teacher, you can't *answer* any questions, you can only *ask* questions (from your clipboard or whatever you think of). Whenever you ask a question of the group, they write it on a sticky note and leave it at their desk.

Step 2: If students ask each other questions, they should also write those questions on their sticky notes.

Step 3: As group members solve the problem, they should prepare to explain how each question that they were asked helped them get unstuck. Let each group present briefly on the questions they were asked and how the questions helped.

Step 4 (optional): Each group chooses one or two of their sticky notes and makes a poster listing good questions to ask when you're stuck to hang around the room.

Variation: Use hint cards. Instead of circulating and choosing diagnostic questions for students, write each question on a large index card and leave them in a central location (perhaps on the lip of a chalkboard or whiteboard). Students go up and choose a question when they're stuck, rather than having the teacher come to them.

Variation 2: Let students take turns being the one to walk around with the questioning clipboard. You could join a group and work with them while a student helps groups that are stuck.

Finally, if you liked these questions and want even more of them, in a handy form for quick reference during class, check out the Getting Unstuck and I Don't Know What to Do handouts available online (at http://mathforum.org/pps/). Students can use them on posters, hint cards, sheets in their math notebooks, and so on or you can use them for facilitation of students who are stuck and need to do some reflecting back, progress checking, or other thinking about thinking.

Conclusion

One theme that came up throughout this chapter is the role of structured problem-solving activities to help support students to learn new habits of mind. When we notice students struggling with an aspect of planning or selecting strategies, we might choose one of these structures or activities and have students use it to solve several problems over the course of several weeks.

A more subtle theme, perhaps, has been how the teacher can use unstructured problem-solving time as well. The Roll the Tape activity, for example, has students solving problems independently while the teacher records them and then students review the videos. Several times we suggest the teacher just observing students while they are problem solving to listen for students spontaneously taking on roles or asking metacognitive questions. Unstructured problem solving is a very powerful formative assessment tool to help teachers learn about their students as problem solvers and make good choices about which problem-solving activities or structures to impose on students.

The teacher's role is very much like that of an athletic coach. She reviews her students in practice and performance situations, and then chooses from her repertoire of drills, games, exercises, and activities to provide her "mathletes" with opportunities for growth to fix difficulties they are having.

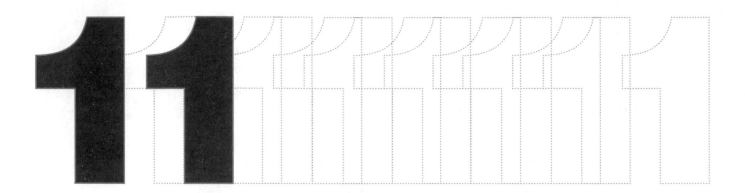

Reflecting, Revising, Justifying, and Extending

Focal practices:

6. Attend to precision.
7. Look for and make use of structure.
8. Look for and express regularity in repeated reasoning.

Ah, the end! We're reaching the end of the problem-solving process, the end of this book, and now we're thinking about what happens after students have an answer to a particular problem. For many of our students, that moment is one of relief—they have an answer, they can move on (or pack up and wait for the bell to ring). Often, the source of that relief is that students are not invested in a problem, and they aren't making sense of it, they're just carrying out a procedure and when it's done (no matter the end result) it's done.

When I see students who aren't confident in math finish a problem, heave a sigh of relief, and slam their math book shut, I wonder if they feel the way I do when I force myself to bake something. I hate baking. Baking is a series of precise, stressful steps that I don't understand and am always messing up—forgetting an ingredient, combining things at the wrong time, using a bowl that's the wrong size, beating too much or too little, and so on. By the time I'm done baking, I just want to be done. I don't even care how the food comes out.

My mom, on the other hand, loves baking. She asks for big, thick books of baking recipes and reads them even when she isn't thinking of baking things. She likes following the recipes, but she also knows how they work: when she reads a recipe she's always thinking, "What other dishes is this like? How do these ingredients usually interact? What might affect the outcome?" She has an idea in mind but she's also willing to be surprised by the results. No one enjoys messing up, but when one of her baked goods doesn't come out right, she actually likes the part of figuring out things like "Why is the texture wrong? What would I do differently next time?" as well as sharing and celebrating the results.

I hope that as you read this book and bring some of the ideas in it to life in your classroom, that the activities and philosophy are helping your students become more like Max's-mom-the-excited-baker and less like Max-the-grumpy-baker. That your students are more often in situations where they understand the problem scenario in a big-picture way (including what's interesting about it), that they have some strategies they're confident in, that they aren't following procedures that they don't understand, and that they have the habit of looking for connections between what they're solving and their prior experiences. I hope that when they're done solving a problem, they have a prediction of the answer and are eager to test their result against their predictions, other people's ideas, and (if one is available) the verifiable real-world answer, because they've become invested in the process through their understanding and connections.

Just in case you're wondering if math could ever really feel to students the way cooking a new dish feels to an enthusiastic baker, some math teachers have recently shared great stories (and videos) of students who have gotten so invested in math problems that they watch raptly as an answer is revealed, react passionately to the joy of being right and the frustration of being off by "this much," and (best of all!) want to keep doing math to find out *why* the answer is right. Sadie Estrella shared her students' reaction to seeing the answer revealed in a visual-pattern video Dan Meyer made, and Meyer wrote up the experience in a post at his dy/dan blog entry, "Watch Students Watch the Answer to Their Math Problem" (http://blog.mrmeyer.com/?p=15873). Julie Reulbach's students were so excited to see the results of their Barbie Bungee work that they made their own iMovies afterward and posted them in the "Barbie Bungee iMovies—Line of Best Fit" post on Julie's I Speak Math Blog (http://ispeakmath.wordpress.com/2013/01/03/barbie-bungee-imovie-line-of-best-fit/). Nora Oswald's students were so curious about why their predictions about the scoring system in a Mario game were wrong that they launched into an exploration of nonlinear functions, as she describes in "Super Mario Bros. Results" entry on her Simplifying Radicals blog (http://simplifyingradicals2.blogspot.co.uk/2013/02/super-mario-bros-results.html). And some of Laurel Pollard's fourth-grade students at Hanover Middle School were so intrigued by the math they had done on a Math Forum Problem of the Week about voter turnout patterns that they wrote, produced, and edited their own video of a survey they distributed to learn more about teachers' voting patterns (http://youtube/W1eFijX9esI). To view these stories and videos on your smartphone, scan the QR codes in the margin.

The Role of Revision and Reflection

One of the Math Forum's unofficial mottoes is "The goal is not to be over and done. The goal is to reflect and revise." Over the course of mentoring thousands of students in their problem solving and written communication and studying those interactions, we came to find that students learned more from the process of reading feedback and revising their thinking

Estrella

Reulbach

Oswald

Pollard

"The goal is not to be over and done. The goal is to reflect and revise."

than from attempting the original problems.[1] We had noticed informally that students who revised their work seemed to grow more and more with each problem, and when the study confirmed it, we really focused on helping students value revising and be motivated to revise their own work. The revision process isn't just about checking the answer (though that is important). We were also asking students to think metacognitively about solving the problem, such as thinking about why it was hard, where they got stuck, what a good hint for another student would be, and so on. The problem-solving rubric that we developed from the experience of crafting replies to thousands of students includes a category for reflection, and we list the following "reflective things":

- ▸ I showed how I checked my own answer.
- ▸ I explained why I think my answer is reasonable.
- ▸ I summarized the process I used.
- ▸ I connected the problem to another problem or experience.
- ▸ I explained where I'm stuck.
- ▸ I suggested a hint that I would give to another solver.
- ▸ I explained why I think the problem is easy or difficult.

The study showed that students who revised *and reflected* by doing one or more of the reflective things made big gains in their use of problem-solving strategies and their autonomy in problem solving. The online mentors were able to engage students in the process of revising and reflecting by asking students to do specific revisions that interested the students and made them feel listened to and valued, and by giving specific prompts for reflection.

Building Reflective Skills

Getting students to stay engaged with a problem scenario beyond the point when many students want to be "over and done" (i.e., getting to the end of a known process, or getting an answer) takes perseverance on the part of the teacher. Some aspects that help students with this are:

- ▸ Focus on sense making and estimating, including understanding the context of a problem and what's interesting about it, from the outset.
- ▸ Make sure students have authentic reasons to explain and compare their ideas (not just because you said it was important).
- ▸ Give students feedback that shows you understand and value the thinking they've done so far.

---

1. Renninger, K. Ann, Laura Farra, and Claire Feldman-Riordan. 2000. "The Impact of the Math Forum's *Problem(s) of the Week* on Students' Mathematical Thinking." Presented at ICLS 2000. Available at: http://mathforum.org/articles/Renninger2000.pdf.

▶ Give students specific feedback about what it might look like to revise or reflect on one aspect of their work.

▶ Provide opportunities for students to check their work against nonteacher, non-back-of-the-book sources[2] like:

  ◆ Use measurable, real-world phenomena (e.g., they use math to predict how many rubber bands will make the most thrilling bungee ride for Barbie without letting her head touch the ground and then test their predictions).

  ◆ Use purely mathematical patterns that they can watch unfold (e.g., they use math to predict the outcome of a pattern and then watch as the pattern iterates and their predictions are confirmed or disconfirmed).

  ◆ Consider other students' assertions about mathematical objects and their definitions (e.g., they must come to consensus on a mathematical debate such as "Is a square a rectangle?" or "Can six be even and odd?"[3]).

▶ Support students to think about multiple meanings for the phrase "check your work" and to decide strategically what kind of checking to use, such as:

  ◆ Make sure you answered the problem that was asked.

  ◆ Use inverse operations to make sure arithmetic results are correct.

  ◆ Use a calculator or other technology to check results.

  ◆ Use some specific values to check if a mathematical rule/number sentence/ formula makes sense.

  ◆ Check the constraints of the problem, including definitions of mathematical objects, and make sure the answer meets them all.

  ◆ Use your noticings and wonderings and ask, "Did we address all of the noticings? Did we account for everything we were wondering?"

  ◆ Plug the answer back into the original problem context and ask, "Does this answer make sense in the story?"

  ◆ Solve the problem using an alternate method and compare the results.

What Does It Mean to Check Your Work?

In our experience, students are most comfortable with the kind of checking work that is checking for *accuracy*. When we prompt them with questions like, "Does your answer make sense in the story/picture/context?" they can usually (if they understood the story/picture/context) decide if their answer is *reasonable*, though inexperienced problem solvers rarely volunteer that on their own. Students rarely independently see the value of solving

---

2. See Dan Meyer's blog at http://blog.mrmeyer.com for lots more about this idea. The tags "3acts" and "anyqs" are particularly relevant.

3. This video from the work of Deborah Loewenberg Ball shows a classic example of a class discussion around this topic: http://ummedia04.rs.itd.umich.edu/~dams/umgeneral/seannumbers-ofala-xy_subtitled_59110_QuickTimeLarge.mov

a problem they've already finished with *another method*; however, we do see students enjoying checking one another's work to confirm if different paths can somehow result in the same (correct) answer. Sometimes that's a new, interesting experience for students: two really different paths can both lead to the same outcome and both can be correct! We do see experienced problem solvers try a second method when they aren't confident in their answer, and we have many Problem of the Week submitters who have (because their teacher expects it) learned to submit two methods for every problem they solve. I think for these students, it's an interesting challenge to be able to think about the same problem from more than one perspective.

The fourth kind of answer checking that we've identified is checking *constraints*. Students' difficulties in finding and making good use of constraints vary widely, in part because there are different kinds of constraints. Some are obvious and some are much more subtle. For example, there are:

- stated clues and rules about the answer like "There are 47 heads and 122 legs"
- unstated facts and definitions from students' prior knowledge like the fact that llamas have 4 legs and ostriches have 2 legs, or the fact that if you're counting people you round to the nearest whole number and if you're counting money you round to the nearest cent (hundredths place)
- mathematical definitions, for example, if a shape has to be square, then the constraints are that it must be a regular quadrilateral (all four sides and all four angles congruent).

Most students are aware of the first type of constraint and have varying degrees of success spotting the clues in problems, depending on their experience at noticing and paying attention to details, and being on the lookout for clues when they think, "Gee, I could solve this problem if only I knew. . . ."

The second type of constraint can be so obvious students don't realize it's a constraint (like when solving problems about ostrich legs and llama legs, they don't even think of their knowledge of how many legs an ostrich or a llama has as a clue or constraint). But at other times students don't think of or don't know how to use their background knowledge. The famous stories of students giving oddly precise answers like determining that 3.5, not 4, 12-passenger vans are needed to transport 42 people, show that students don't always bring their background knowledge to problem-solving situations.

The third type of constraint—constraints put on problems by precise mathematical definitions—are by far the hardest for students to recognize and make use of. Some of the activities later in this chapter, such as Precheck and I Will Know We Are Right If . . . , help students to identify multiple types of problem constraints while making sense of the problem, and then use those constraints to check their work once they've come up with some solutions. If reasoning from mathematical definitions is a challenge you'd like to focus on more with your students, the companion website (http://mathforum.org/pps/) includes two additional games for focusing on definitions and logical constraints: Categories and Break My Rule.

Giving Students Written Feedback

One important way to help students focus on revising, reflecting, and improving their mathematical communication is through writing and responding to feedback on their written thinking. We really like the ways written math conversations can help students slow down and concentrate on their thinking and organization; how for teachers, reading students' writing can give them a chance to more carefully diagnose what the student understands and needs to work on (versus in a quick oral conversation walking by the student's desk); and how for both parties, there are just more chances to understand what's being said and respond to it thoughtfully. These next activities present some different ways to help students get good at understanding and responding to initial feedback, as well as tips for teachers on ways to respond to students that is relatively quick and keeps the agency on the students for continuing to make sense of the problem scenario and figure out how to revise their thinking.

Teacher Feedback Tips

We recommend that teachers make only two comments per student following the format:

> I notice . . .
>
> I wonder . . .

The I Notice statement notes one thing that you value in the student's solution. In other words, a sentence of praise. The I Wonder statement is a question with the intention that as a result the student will reflect on their draft, revisit it, and add more.

Here are some I Notice, I Wonder mentoring examples that Suzanne used with some students on a middle school problem:

> I notice that you had several missteps that you learned from. Thanks for sharing those!
>
> I wonder if you could explain how you decided a guess of 2 didn't work. Why did you choose to try 5? How did you check that?
>
> I notice that you have used algebra as a strategy. Nice job!
>
> I wonder if you might want to include what you mean by n.
>
> I notice you've used algebra as a strategy for this problem. You've done a nice job identifying your variable and showing how you reached your answer.
>
> I'm curious to hear more about the "pattern" you saw to help you find the answer to the Extra. Could you tell me more?

We've found that the I Notice statement is a very valuable piece of the teacher's response, as it gives the student a clue about what they did well and should keep doing. Sometimes when hesitant problem solvers are responding to written feedback for the first time, they assume everything they've done will need to be thrown out. The I Notice statement helps students become aware of what they are good at and helps them practice and keep doing those good things.

Sometimes when hesitant problem solvers are responding to written feedback for the first time, they assume everything they've done will need to be thrown out. The I Notice statement helps students become aware of what they are good at and helps them practice and keep doing those good things.

The I Wonder statements tend to get students reflecting and revising. Students often report that this kind of feedback rarely feels threatening. Instead, the I Wonder statements show that the teacher really is curious about the student's thinking and has presented the student with something new and interesting to consider. That's a good motivation to keep working!

In our experience working with students who are new to writing their ideas, no matter how old they are or how good they are at writing in other situations, it's very rare for them to respond to more than one wondering or suggestion for feedback. Restricting yourself to one I Wonder statement means that the revision you receive will be focused on the most important question you had for the student! Subsequent revisions can take care of other aspects if you invite your students to continue to revise their work.

In addition,

- Writing one I Notice statement and one I Wonder statement doesn't take very long per student.
- It reinforces problem solving as a process, not something to be over and done.
- Most importantly, the student's thinking and problem solving remain in *their* possession and are not transferred to the teacher.

When a teacher gives step-by-step feedback about everything they want a student to revise, in some way they are taking over the student's thinking, much like if they repeated and rephrased every statement a student made in class. If students are to embrace and *do* the mathematical practices, *they* have to continue to own their work. *They* have to reflect and revise!

Activities

Building Revision Skills

Even with simple I Notice, I Wonder feedback, it's still often challenging for students to think of what it might mean to revise their math work and to make sense of the feedback they're given. Some normal reactions we've seen when students receive early written feedback are,

- They don't understand what we've written.
- They don't "stick" on the feedback message long enough to read it and so they don't comprehend (*very* normal!).
- They might read it but by the time they get to their submission they've forgotten what we said (*very* normal!).

In Chapter 2 we presented one structure for students working on responding to feedback together. Following are a few other routines we've used with students to help them understand teacher feedback. We'd like to acknowledge that feedback, even nonjudgmental

I Notice, I Wonder feedback, can be scary to share with peers, and some schools even have policies about sharing work that teachers have returned to students. While this is not something we've encountered with I Notice, I Wonder feedback, we always offer the option for students to opt out of sharing their feedback with other students and allow those students to work independently, or to just share their thinking without sharing what the teacher responded. If you notice students who choose not to share teacher feedback, it might be worth checking in with them privately about how they're feeling in math class—building an environment in which wondering feedback feels inviting, not threatening, is helpful in supporting bold problem solving.

ACTIVITY Revision Buddies

Format: Students working in pairs.

Step 0: Collect written explanations from each student about a problem they solved. Write I Notice, I Wonder feedback to each student.

Step 1: Let students know with whom they will be working. Have them sit in their pairs and decide who will be Partner A and who will be Partner B. Give students their work with written feedback.

Step 2: Partner A reads his submission out loud to Partner B. Then Partner B reads the teacher's feedback to Partner A out loud to Partner A (think of Partner B as acting out the role of the teacher).

Step 3: Partner B asks Partner A, "What did you hear?" and listens to Partner A.

Step 4: Partner B reads the feedback out loud again and tells Partner A, "I heard. . . ."

Step 5: Partner B asks Partner A, "What do you think you could do now to revise your work?" and together the students make a plan for Partner A's revision.

At this point, both students could work on Partner A's revision, and next time you do this activity, both students could work on Partner B's revision. Or you could have the students switch roles and make a plan for Partner B's revision together.

Building an environment in which wondering feedback feels inviting, not threatening, is helpful in supporting bold problem solving.

ACTIVITY Peer Conferences

Format: Students working mostly independently.

Step 0: Collect written explanations from students about a problem they solved. Write I Notice, I Wonder feedback to each student.

Step 1: Choose a time when students have some different math work they could be working on, such as homework, a class activity, or a challenge. Return students' written math work and your feedback. Let students know when you would like them to finish their revisions, and how many work periods they will have before then.

Step 2: Students read your feedback and decide if they are ready to start revising or if they would like to have a peer conference. If they'd like to conference, they should indicate that in some way (e.g., write their name on the board, sit at a conference table, or politely ask a peer if they would be willing to conference).

Step 3: In their peer conferences (groups of two to three but no bigger), students read their work aloud and then read the teacher's feedback. Each peer begins with:

> One thing I think the teacher appreciated about your work was . . .
>
> One thing that you could do to revise your work might be . . .

The student should write these ideas below the teacher feedback.

Step 4: Then, the student whose work it is has a turn to add:

> One thing I think the teacher appreciated about my work was . . .
>
> One thing that I could do to revise my work might be . . .

Step 5: If the student has any questions for her peers, she asks them. Then they discuss the different revision ideas to see which they think would be most useful.

Step 6: The peers thank the student for sharing and the student thanks the peers for their ideas.

A really interesting peer-conferencing model comes from elementary literacy conferences. Teachers noticed that their students didn't always have good strategies for differentiating between giving feedback in which they focused on details like spelling, punctuation, and capitalization, and feedback in which they focused on bigger-picture elements like tone, clarity, imagery, and so on. So the teachers helped the students differentiate between these two kinds of feedback by having them sit in different configurations depending on the kind of feedback they were to give. When students talked about things like how the story made them feel, what parts were clear, what was interesting, and what left them wondering, they sat facing one another, knee-to-knee. When students looked closely at a peer's spelling, punctuation, grammar, and so on, they both sat facing the paper, side-to-side. Students could associate the different ways of looking at peer work with the different ways they were sitting and give the appropriate sorts of feedback.[4]

ACTIVITY Face-to-Face Revisions

Format: Students working in pairs.

Step 0: Students work independently on a problem and write about how they solved it.

Step 1: Students sit face-to-face with their partner and the first partner reads his writing (or tells what he did to solve the problem).

---

4. See http://writinglesson.ning.com/forum/topics/peer-conferencing?id=3025388%3ATopic%3A8667&page=3#comments.

Step 2: The second partner tells at least one thing she noticed and valued in what she heard, and one thing she is wondering about. The first partner takes notes so he can remember the feedback.

Step 3: The partners switch roles.

Step 4: Working together, the partners notice and talk about what they did that was the same and what they did that was different. They identify any places they disagree.

Step 5: The partners read the original problem together and work together to think about if their answers are *reasonable* and if they fit the *constraints* or *clues* of the story/context. If the partners disagree, they use the clues in the story to try to agree on which answer fits the *constraints* better or if both could be right. If they agree, they make sure they can both say how they know the answer is reasonable and fits the constraints.

ACTIVITY Elbow-to-Elbow Revisions

Format: Students working in pairs.

Step 1: Students sit side-to-side (elbow-to-elbow) with their partner and decide whose work they want to look at first (who will be Partner 1). Partner 1 puts her work down in front of the pair, so both students can read it.

Step 2: Partner 2 reads the work over once, and shares one thing he notices and values about the work, and one thing he's wondering.

Step 3: Both partners read through the work together, more carefully (Partner 2 can read out loud if that helps). When they come to anything that's confusing or either one wonders about, Partner 1 explains anything she can and marks it for possible revising.

Step 4: The partners switch roles and Partner 2 notices and wonders about Partner 1's work, and they mark up anything he has questions about.

Step 5: If the partners had any difference in the final answer or disagreements about each other's work, they can take turns going through step-by-step, comparing results and if they differ or wonder, using these questions:

> A partner asks, "How did you think to do that step?" and listens to see if he agrees with the other's thinking.

> A partner asks, "How can we check that step?" and the partners use a calculator, an inverse operation, plugging in, and so on to check that the calculations were accurate.

Supporting Checking Work in More Ways Than One!

It's quite common for students, when we ask, "Did you check your answer?" to tell us, "I don't have to because I used a calculator" or "Yes, I redid all of the calculations." Often, though, those students don't have a correct solution because they made a mistake in their reasoning and the calculations they are doing don't make sense. We coined the "Testing 1, 2, 3, 4" idea to support students to remember more than one meaning of checking their work.

ACTIVITY Testing 1, 2, 3, 4

> **Format:** Students working alone, then working in small groups. A student-friendly handout to support students' thinking about this activity is available online (at http://mathforum.org/pps/).

> **Step 0:** Familiarize students with four different meanings of checking work.

> **1.** Constraints: Does your result work with all of the *constraints* in the problem? Be sure to check if your answer addresses what the question was asking for! Review all of the information you noticed and make sure you have tested the result with all of it.

> **2.** Accuracy: Have a method for going over your work to test its accuracy: do the inverse operations, reverse your calculations, use a calculator or computer to check your calculations, and so on. Also check that your steps made sense: make sure you can answer "I did this step because . . ." for each one.

> **3.** Different approach: Solve the problem using a different strategy and see if the results come out the same.

> **4.** Reasonable: Can you explain why your answer makes sense in the original context or is reasonable using logic or estimates or drawing on experience?

> **Step 1:** Students work individually on checks 1 and 2 above and prepare to share their work with their small group.

> **Step 2:** In the small group, each student shares and compares their work from part A. Then they discuss check 3. Did anyone use a different strategy? If someone did, compare results. If nobody did, try to come up with a different approach.

> **Step 3:** Create a group statement about check 4: why the answer you figured out seems reasonable. Is there a way you can show that whatever the answer is, it has to be something like the answer you found?

The genesis for the next two activities was a task with a group of middle school students. They were trying to find all the lines of symmetry of a regular and an irregular hexagon. The students recalled lines of symmetry from previous years but hadn't worked with them yet this year (we were previewing a lesson). The students had drawn some lines and I was about to ask them to turn and talk with a partner, when I thought to check that the students had a way to tell if a line was, indeed, a line of symmetry. I asked, "When you work with your partner, how can you tell if their answer is wrong or right?" The students answered,

> ▸ "Look and see if they are the same or different."
> ▸ "Compare your work."
> ▸ "Check the answer."
> ▸ "Look at their work and compare it to yours."

When I followed up with "What can you use to check it?" and "What will you compare?" the students couldn't come up with any criteria. So I added, "Sometimes when math folks are stuck, they turn to their definitions. Can you remind me what our definition of *symmetry* was?" The students recalled their definition, which was "The same on both sides," but they still struggled to articulate how they could apply that to checking their work. So I drew an obviously incorrect line of symmetry on the hexagon and displayed it for the class. "How could you check if this was a line of symmetry using the idea of 'same on both sides'?" I asked the class. Suddenly, hands shot up in the air: "Fold the paper to see if they line up"; "See if the two halves are the same"; "Count to make sure both sides have the same number of lines on them." Once we'd established these ways to prove my obviously wrong line was wrong, the students had an easier time checking other subtler, possible lines of symmetry. (I still had to remind the students that if we were going to use the folding method to check one another's work, then I needed to see papers being folded as I looked around the room.)

ACTIVITY Precheck

Format: Think-pair-share.

Step 1: Present the problem scenario to students. Do a quick noticing and wondering activity, such as a brainstorm, private writing, or think-pair-share.

Step 2: Put an obviously wrong answer, including brief reasoning or steps, on the board. Ask students to think about if the answer is right or wrong, and how they know.

Step 3: Students share with a partner and compare their thinking. They should come up with a list of ways they know the answer is wrong.

Step 4: Ask partners to share one reason they knew the answer was wrong. Record the list. Encourage students to step up or step back—if they have shared, step back until everyone has had a chance, if they haven't shared, step up and try to add something to the list.

Step 5: Ask if anyone has any questions or wonderings about anything on the list. Give plenty of wait time for students to read the list and compare to their own thinking. You might say, "I'm going to give you two minutes to look over the list and come up with a wondering about it." Address any wonderings that occur by asking the original contributors to say more about their thinking and asking the class to come to consensus on the validity of the idea.

Step 6: Say to students, "Now we know one answer to this problem that definitely isn't correct. I'm going to have you solve the problem in a minute, but I want to be sure you're ready to check your work on the problem. Based on our list, what are some ways that we can check if our answer is right?"

As a follow-up question you might ask, "What characteristics will a right answer have?" or "What is a good estimate for the right answer?" or "What will definitely *not* be true about the right answer?"

Step 7: Leave the list of reasons that one answer was not correct visible throughout the problem-solving process. Have students work individually or in pairs to solve the problem (this can be done as a homework assignment).

Step 8: Individuals then find a partner, or pairs form a group of four, and check one another's work. Students can use the list to practice language like "I think you are right because . . ." or "I think this can't be right because . . ." based on the list.

ACTIVITY I Will Know We Are Right If . . . I Will Know We Are Wrong If . . .

With students who have more experience making sense of problems, we don't need to give them a sample wrong answer as in the Precheck activity and instead simply ask them to brainstorm some ways that they can be sure the answer is right.

Format: Think-pair-share.

Step 1: Present the problem scenario to students. Do a quick noticing and wondering activity, such as a brainstorm, private writing, or think-pair-share.

Step 2: Have students think for a minute and complete these prompts in as many ways as they can:

> I will know the answer is right if _____
>
> I will know the answer is wrong if _____

Step 3: Students share with a partner and compare their thinking and try to add more to the list.

Step 4: Ask each partnership to share one thing for each prompt. Record the list.

Step 5: Ask if anyone has any questions or wonderings about anything on the list. You might say, "I'm going to give you two minutes to look over the list and come up with a wondering about it." Address any wonderings that occur by asking the original contributors to say more about their thinking and asking the class to come to consensus on the validity of the idea.

Step 6: Leave the list visible throughout the problem-solving process. Have students work individually or in pairs to solve the problem.

Step 7: Individuals then find a partner, or pairs form a group of four, and use the "I will know the answer is right if . . ." and "I will know the answer is wrong if . . ." lists to check one another's work. Students can use the list to practice language like, "I think you are right because . . ." or "I think this is wrong because . . ." based on the list.

As students get better at finding constraints and articulating how they will know they are right based on the given information, you might help them notice mathematical definitions in the problems they solve and the math work they do in class. Often, when a class comes to a seemingly impossible-to-solve-with-common-sense problem in math, like "Is

0 even or odd?" or "Is a square a rectangle?" the answer can be found by considering the mathematical definitions.

ACTIVITY Math Debate

An activity that can support students' learning to look for and reason from definitions is giving students the opportunity to debate topics in math that have clear correct answers that aren't always intuitive to students, for example:

- ▸ When rolling 2 dice, are there 36 possible outcomes [(1,1),(1,2),(2,1),(1,3), (2,2),(3,1), etc.] or 21 possible outcomes [(1,1),(1,2),(1,3),(1,4),(1,5),(1,6), (2,2),(2,3), etc.]?
- ▸ Is ■ a rectangle?
- ▸ Is ▰ a trapezoid?
- ▸ Is 0 even?
- ▸ Is 1 a prime number?
- ▸ Is 0 a positive number?
- ▸ Does {1, 1, 3, 3, 5} have a mode?
- ▸ Is ◣◢ a pentagon?

Format: Whole group.

Step 0: Choose an example from the previous list (or come up with your own question that's clearly answered by a math definition but is nonetheless controversial) and poll your students to find out if it's controversial. Anonymous polls (such as put your head down and raise your hand) work best.

Step 1: Split the students into two camps based on their choice for the controversial topic. Give them 5–10 minutes in their camps to come up with their best argument for their answer.

Step 2: Have each group share its best argument. The other team should listen and plan one question the members would like to ask.

Step 3: Teams regroup and come up with one question the members have for the other team.

Step 4: Teams deliver their questions, in writing, to one another. Students have another 5–10 minutes to respond to the question.

Step 5: Team members deliver their responses to the question.

Step 6: Bring the whole class together and poll students (anonymously again) on whether or not they were convinced by the opposing arguments. Hear from multiple students about their experience.

Step 7: As a group, reflect on what was and was not convincing in the arguments. Ask the students if they could research one thing about the topic (other than "the answer") what they could look up to help them strengthen their argument, or what the other team could look up that would convince them they were wrong.

Step 8: Direct students to a reputable math source such as Ask Dr. Math®, a dictionary, Wikipedia, or Wolfram|Alpha. Have them look up one thing they wanted to find out and see if that convinces them.

Step 9: If students haven't discovered it, share the formal definition and ask students, "Based on this definition, who wins? Why?" If there are multiple accepted definitions (such as for a trapezoid), ask students "Does which definition we choose change the debate?" Reflect on the importance of careful definitions in math if you want to have good debates and the ways in which reasoning based on definitions is more convincing than reasoning based on "common sense."

Notice and Wonder, Revisited

So far, we have shared activities and feedback prompts for getting students to reflect and revise, some activities to help them improve the quality of their own work checking, and a more complex activity to introduce a key aspect of precise mathematical reasoning: using definitions. A final component of wrapping up a math problem without being "over and done" is to extend the problem, by *wondering* about what we now know, based on the results of our thinking so far. A great way to extend thinking on a math problem is to reinvite student wonderings. Often students' initial wonderings about a math problem open the door for some great extension problems, as students get to the heart of what is interesting to know about a topic. Revisiting the list of wonderings and noticing what has been addressed and what we could still try to figure out is a neat way to launch another round of problem solving.

After students have presented solutions to problems, you can ask, "What did you notice about the different solutions? What do they make you wonder?" Noticing and wondering about what just happened can be a really cool experience. It reminds students that problem solving is a process and one that can be rich for exploring! By bookending the problem-solving process with an I Notice, I Wonder routine, we help students realize that while we might have solved and finished one problem, we can always look for more mathematical ideas and connections.

Building Student Independence

Our research at the Math Forum has shown that reflecting and revising can support students to become more independent problem solvers. In fact, when researchers studied students who were submitting to the Problems of the Week over time, weaker students who reflected and revised were performing identically to their stronger peers at the end of the study![5] The conferencing activities in this chapter support students to begin to learn how to reflect and

---

5. Renninger et al.

revise. As students become more proficient at reading written feedback and revising written work, they can do more of these activities without peer oral support.

The Testing 1, 2, 3, 4 activity and the Elbow-to-Elbow and Face-to-Face Revisions activities support students to use peer support to help them get better at key mathematical habits. It's important for students to be aware of and know how to use fine-grained checks for accuracy, but also bigger-picture checks for reasonableness, as well as to learn techniques for checking the answer that focus more on the problem-solving process, such as using multiple methods and being aware of all of the constraints.

In helping students get good at checking-work activities, it's important to strike a balance between requiring that students practice good habits (the way they practice their musical scales, their athletic drills, their drawing figures, or their acting diction) and supporting students to be strategic in choosing different ways to check their accuracy. Should all problems be solved using multiple methods to ensure their accuracy? No, it's probably not necessary. But all students should be aware that whenever they aren't confident in an answer or a method, they have the option to try to solve the problem a second way to confirm their thinking, and when the stakes are high they should probably do so even when they are confident. You can support this strategic checking by helping students to reflect on the different kinds of errors made across the class and the different kinds of checks that caught those errors. What is checking for constraints good for? What kinds of mistakes are caught when you redo your work? Has anyone ever had an error sneak through that they only caught when they did the problem using a second method?

A further way to engage students in checking their work strategically when using the peer-conferencing techniques is to collect student work the day before and pair them up for peer conferencing after you've had a chance to skim through each student's response. Pair up students with different answers to give students a purpose for comparing one another's work. The job of the pairs, then, becomes not just helping each other check work that may or may not be right (and how frustrating when you go through all that work to painstakingly check it and you were right all along!) but sleuthing out where the discrepancy came in. If they are thinking strategically about checking their work, a face-to-face pair might choose to become an elbow-to-elbow pair as students realize they made the same assumptions and thought about the problem in the same way but disagreed somewhere in the details of the calculations. Or a group doing Testing 1, 2, 3, 4 might decide to pool one another's results before going through the accuracy testing, on the grounds that if members agree on the results, they were probably all at the same level of accuracy. However, they still might want to check the constraints, because a small group could all have misinterpreted the problem in the same way.

Conclusion

Each of these activities relies pretty heavily on students working together. This is because one of the best ways to learn to check your own work is to have a lot of experience with others' feedback on your work. We've found that students who repeatedly compare their work with others and have conversations with others about their work become better at having those "Does this make sense? Have I used all the information? Is this right?" conversations internally as well. Everything you can do to support your students working together to solve problems whose context they fully understand, and to put them in situations where they need to compare answers and come to consensus, makes them stronger problem solvers. If they can then compare their consensus-based answer to some objective answer that's out there in the world, well, what an awesome way to help them tap into and appreciate the value of their own mathematical reasoning skills!

Conclusion

This book is unique in that it is not a collection of problems designed for students to learn content, nor a collection of problems of particular types or structures designed to expose students to a variety of problem-solving strategies. It is also different from books that focus mostly on the *why* and theories of problem solving and how problem solving fits into the math classroom. Instead, we've tried to create a book that is full of hands-on activities, stories, and tips for the classroom teacher that focus on *how* students can be supported to get better at the kinds of thinking that problem solvers do. We wanted to go beyond one-strategy-at-a-time presentations of problem solving to unpack the problem-solving process and mathematical practices into activities for the elementary and middle school classroom. We hope that this book has inspired feelings of "I'm going to try that tomorrow!" as well as "There's a lifetime worth of stuff to keep getting better at in here!" because that's how we feel about supporting students to become better problem solvers.

Final Thoughts

I asked my colleague Annie Fetter what should be in the conclusion and she said, "They should take away three things: Struggle is really important. Methods are good. Students' ideas are the lifeblood of the classroom."

Struggle is really important.

In Chapter 9, I talked about the idea of productive struggle, that students often learn best from having the opportunity to struggle with an idea and come up with their own representations and methods for thinking about it, before having formal instruction in the concept. In

Chapters 8 and 9, we described the importance of teachers not making decisions for students; if they do give students support by making a problem simpler, changing the representation, using abstraction, and so on, teachers should make that thinking very explicit so that students understand the reasoning that's happening. When we say that struggle is really important, we mean that students need opportunities to make sense of math *for themselves*, and that inherently involves some degree of frustration or struggle.

In Chapter 7, you met some second-grade girls whose teacher wanted them to learn some new problem-solving strategies. She started giving them what she called "juicy problems," and soon all her students were begging her for more juicy problems! The problems took more than one day's math session to solve, and the students reported that the problems were hard to make sense of. Their scratch work is full of cross-outs—these problems are not easy for the students! But they keep asking to do them. Something about struggling to make sense of a problem and then figuring out a plan, carrying out that plan diligently, and getting an answer they're confident in is inherently motivating to these students. It helps that their teacher loves juicy problems too, and shows how much she values their hard thinking. She snaps photos of them hard at work and encourages them to write up their thinking to share with the world—the girls know that they are working hard and that hard work is valuable. Struggle is a good thing in their classroom.

We hope the activities in this book help you find ways to support students by making their struggle as productive as possible. It may be by finding ways to ensure that they understand the context and have some good estimates before they begin working on the problem so they can feel whether they're on the right track. Or it could be training them in some organization habits so that when they do Guess and Check their work helps them see patterns quickly and get to the answer efficiently. Or perhaps you support them to struggle productively with math problems by helping them understand good group work and communication skills so that when students work together, their ideas build on one another's and two (or more) heads really are better than one. When students have the opportunity to struggle *productively*, they're invested in sense making and they are ripe for learning—any math teacher's dream!

Something about struggling to make sense of a problem and then figuring out a plan, carrying out that plan diligently, and getting an answer they're confident in is inherently motivating to these students.

Methods are good.

As we described in Chapter 1, a lot of debate and energy in mathematics education has focused on concepts and procedures. We think of general problem-solving strategies or habits of mind like the ones in this book as the *methods* that students use to apply their concepts and procedures, and to make sense of new concepts and procedures. Whether you are using a problem-solving curriculum or a more traditional one, students need to be able to understand mathematical ideas, whether it's a problem to be solved or notes about a concept. They're being asked to solve the same type of problem over and over and look for patterns they can develop into procedures. They are being asked to use visual reasoning or physical models and connect them to abstract ideas like numbers and operations. Students are expected to reason by analogy to simpler problems, to use logical reasoning, and to consider specific cases.

When textbook authors choose, for example, to teach students about negative numbers by having them first think about temperature change on a cold winter day, they are expecting that students will be able to read or listen and make sense of the quantities in that mathematical situation and the relationships of adding and subtracting. They're expecting that students can transfer from a visual model of a thermometer to working with "naked numbers." If students haven't had a chance to engage in the mathematical practices of making sense of problems, if they haven't noticed and wondered and named quantities and relationships and talked about what degrees below zero might feel like, then they will have a hard time understanding the analogy well enough to reason from it. If they haven't had experience solving problems first with visuals and manipulatives and then representing their ideas with number sentences and then thinking about patterns and rules in the calculations they've done and using them to answer more problems of the same type, they may have trouble moving from the concrete, "What is the temperature if it was 8 degrees out but then it got 10 degrees colder?" to "What is $8 + -10$?"

Or consider the students we described in Chapter 5, who had learned about right triangles, understood the basic concept that missing side lengths in right triangles can be calculated, and had mastered the procedures for finding those missing sides. They nonetheless struggled to solve word problems involving missing side lengths. They didn't have a *method* for approaching problems and thinking about "What quantities are in this problem? What shapes are in this problem? What are the relationships?" They barely noticed the triangles in problems, even when the diagrams were given to them, and they definitely didn't notice right triangles with missing sides. The students needed support to get better at their problem-solving methods to make use of what they were learning in their curriculum.

I hope that this book begins to make methods as central in classrooms as concepts and procedures, and that you have some resources now to pay attention not just to students' knowledge or skills with math procedures, but also to how effective your students are at things like:

- noticing mathematical aspects of stories or images
- wondering or conjecturing about quantities, shapes, and relationships
- visualizing and making connections among different representations of scenarios
- using their number sense to make estimates and guesses
- organizing information to see patterns and regularity
- describing mathematical situations in ways that are sharable, transportable, and reusable
- looking for opportunities to use, and using, problem-solving strategies like Solve a Simpler Problem, Use Logical Reasoning, Work Backward, and Look at Cases
- being deliberate, planning, and being aware of their thinking as they solve problems

- ▸ checking their work

- ▸ learning from their work through revising and reflecting

- ▸ using math reasoning to explain why their thinking makes sense by appealing to definitions, experience, reasonableness, alternate verification methods, and so on.

I also hope that you now have a framework and initial activities for supporting students to be aware of these skills and start to make them part of their regular math habits.

Students' ideas are the lifeblood of the classroom.

As you read this book, you may have noticed that there hasn't been a lot of explicit instruction. Yes, we've introduced some vocabulary words to label students' noticings (quantities, relationships, constraints), helped them learn specific techniques to organize or check their work, and occasionally modeled specific problem structures and strategies, but we haven't given teachers or students too many step-by-step problem-solving skills to remember or advice on what to do when they see this type of hard problem versus that type of hard problem versus some other type of hard problem.

Instead, what you've seen us doing is encouraging students to carry out an activity or game and supporting them to do so using their own good thinking. We expect different approaches, and we expect some students to come up with more effective or efficient ways to do the task, even in the most homogenous of classrooms. Then, we encourage reflection and generalization based on the differences and similarities we notice. Finally, we ask students to take away one concrete thing they've learned, appreciated, or want to explore or develop more—and then give them opportunities to do more applying, exploring, and developing their different thinking skills!

We set up the activities that way because we believe that people learn from testing and using their current ideas and encountering others' ideas or new experiences that challenge them or introduce a new point of view, and then, through reflecting and generalizing, they come to a new or more complete understanding. This idea about how students learn is similar to many other educational approaches, from Experiential Education[1] to Model Building[2] to Accountable Talk.[3]

For many students, especially students who struggle in math or feel defeated or silenced already, this kind of sense making is outside what they see as possible for themselves. One of our most important jobs as math teachers is to unsilence our students' mathematical voices.

1. Kraft, Richard J., and Michael S. Sakofs. 1988. *The Theory of Experiential Education*. Boulder, CO: Association for Experiential Education.

2. Lesh, Richard, and Helen M. Doerr, eds. 2003. *Beyond Constructivism: Models and Modeling Perspectives on Mathematics Problem Solving, Learning, and Teaching*. Mahwah, NJ: Lawrence Erlbaum Associates.

3. Michaels, Sarah, Mary Catherine O'Connor, Megan Williams Hall, and Lauren B. Resnick. 2010. *Accountable Talk˚ Sourcebook: For Classroom Conversation that Works. Version 3.1*. University of Pittsburgh. Available at http://ifl.lrdc.pitt.edu/ifl/index.php/download/index/ats/.

Whether it's their actual voice as they share ideas in math class, their written voice as they communicate their thinking on paper, or their mental voice that helps them monitor their own thinking and check their assumptions, we hope the resources in this book help your students find their voices.

When all children are encouraged to communicate and learn from each other, we see teachers make moves like:

▸ Keep a public record of the noticing and wondering that has been done, and refer back to it repeatedly as students begin to calculate.

▸ Ask, "What did you notice that made you think to do that?"

▸ Listen to students whose reasoning doesn't match our own or doesn't make sense, to understand what that child is thinking.

▸ Ask questions like "What happened in the story?" and "Did that match what you thought was going to happen?" and "Have you ever had an experience like the person in the story?" and "Can you visualize a movie of the story in your head?" rather than "What are the important clues?" or "What information is extra?" or "Underline the key words."

▸ Repeatedly refer back to the story and context of the problem when questioning or supporting students, rather than push students to think abstractly without referring to the context.

▸ Encourage students who have ideas about the problem, even incorrect ideas, to fully play out their ideas. We hear statements like, "I see what you're thinking and I understand why you thought that." And then questions like "How do you account for . . . ?" or "What happens if . . . ?" or "What do you think about so-and-so's idea?"

▸ Support students to talk peer-to-peer to resolve different ideas and interpretations of the problem, rather than intervening to correct them.

▸ Let students share their ideas as often as possible, even if it means having very little teacher talk at all. Students might share in writing, in peer-to-peer conversations, in small-group conversations with the teacher while other students or groups work independently, as well as during whole-class conversations.

▸ Hear from a wide range of students before offering our own information or questions; encourage students to ask questions directly of one another.

▸ Stop small-group or independent work periodically for public check-ins in which students can hear different viewpoints or talk through what they notice and are thinking about, making reasoning public and building shared understanding.

▸ Encourage noticing and wondering during and after problem solving, to look for patterns, make and test conjectures, extend problems, and more.

Whether it's their actual voice as they share ideas in math class, their written voice as they communicate their thinking on paper, or their mental voice that helps them monitor their own thinking and check their assumptions, we hope the resources in this book help your students find their voices.

▸ Support students to *reflect*, to notice what they are doing well and articulate what they want to get better at, and then provide more opportunities for them to get better. Taking time after successes and failures to think about what happened supports students to turn an experience into a learning tool they can apply again.

Making student ideas the lifeblood of the classroom, and showing that their thinking matters and is valuable to you and others, is personal for me. I went through most of my formative years believing I was bad at math and would never be good at it. I thought that I had no math ideas because I couldn't answer all the subtraction and multiplication problems right the first time—and those were the only math thinking anyone had asked me about. I gave up on myself as a math thinker when I was seven years old! Then, in fifth grade, I was lucky enough to be in a class where we solved problems that asked for more than right answers, and where the teacher was always asking students to share how they thought about problems and inviting other students to notice and appreciate different ways of thinking. I vividly remember being asked, for the first time ever, to explain to other students how I thought about a problem (I even remember that I used the green marker to write my calculations on the overhead transparency!). I hadn't solved the problem correctly, but no one cared. They cared about the ideas I had about the problem—and they thought my ideas were cool! From that moment on, I was hooked. I sought out more math to do and I wanted to tell people my ideas all the time! And I've noticed it doesn't take much—often listening to a student for a few minutes and showing how much you appreciate their thinking will turn them into math friends for life. As we mentioned in Chapter 2, students at a school Annie worked with came running up to her in the hallway weeks after she visited their classroom to tell her how they figured out a way to add 40 + 70—and she had only visited their classroom once! They just knew that she valued their ideas and they liked that feeling. If that's all it takes to start students on a path that can lead them from hating math to writing a book about problem solving, then it's worth the time to turn your classroom into a place where everyone's thinking is valued and no one's math voice is silenced.

Finding More Resources and Support for Teaching Math Through Problem Solving

Throughout the book, we've suggested different ways to find community for supporting you to include more explicit focus on students' problem-solving methods. Here are a few more concrete ideas of ways you can collaborate with others to make problem solving a more explicit classroom focus and a bigger part of your overall math curriculum.

Online Community

Being Part of the Math Forum Community

The companion website (http://mathforum.org/pps/) isn't intended to be just a static resource for finding more Math Forum materials. It's intended to be a portal for community conversation about the activities, stories, and themes in this book. Some ways to engage with us through the website are:

- ▶ Follow my blog about problem solving and mathematical habits of mind, and blogs of other Math Forum staff members, and engage in discussion in the comments.

- ▶ Participate in scheduled chats about themes in the book.

- ▶ Ask a question raised by the book in the Teacher2Teacher Q&A service and I, other Math Forum staff, or a classroom teacher will respond to you.

- ▶ Explore the videos of math teaching and learning and explore possibilities of learning through video and sharing video across math classrooms.

- ▶ Contribute to the Community Resources area.

- ▶ Find out about opportunities to collaborate with the Math Forum online and in person on projects for supporting teachers and students to do more problem solving.

Being Part of the "mathtwitterblogosphere"

More and more teachers are using social media for their own professional learning, and math teachers are leading the pack (just ask *Education Week*![4]). Reflective blogging and receiving friendly feedback from comments and tweets can help you improve your professional practice, support you when you try new things, and bring a steady supply of good ideas.

- ▶ Visit http://mathtwitterblogosphere.weebly.com to learn how and why to get a Twitter account and start following math educators on Twitter.[5]

- ▶ Check in regularly on the blogs of math educators who inspire you. Use a feed reader to see all of the blogs you follow in one place and when there are new posts waiting for you. You can find links to blogs that we follow on the community portal of the companion website.

- ▶ Find one of the regular (live) online sessions where teachers share their ideas with one another. You can find links to some of them on the website.

Face-to-Face Community

As teachers, there is nothing better than having supportive colleagues down the hall, in your building, or in your city or town. I encourage you to reach out and use this book for formal and informal professional development: Read this book with your colleagues, friends, or professional learning community, book-group style. Try a lesson study approach using the activities in the book. Or join or start a Math Teachers' Circle. (Math Teachers' Circles are a

---

4. Reich, Justin, "The Math Blogotwittersphere Is the Best Blogotwittersphere," July 17, 2012. Available at http://blogs .edweek.org/edweek/edtechresearcher/2012/07/the_math_blogotwittosphere_is_the_best_blogotwittosphere.html.

5. And for another introduction to Twitter, you can watch a short video I made called "Tweet Me, Maybe?" that you'll find on the website.

program of the American Institute of Mathematics, aimed at middle school teachers; you can learn more and find one near you at www.mathteacherscircle.org.)

Unsilencing Your Voice

We close the book with a call for finding community and ongoing conversations because we believe that adults learn just like their students. Exploring ideas and improving our practice involves risk. Just like we can build a supportive environment for our students to take risks to challenge their current thinking about math, we know that teachers need supportive colleagues to help them take risks as they try new things and work to improve their own practice. Every day in front of a classroom is a fresh opportunity to try something new, something that may be awesome or may feel like a disaster, just like every math problem we give students is an opportunity for them to feel like awesome problem solvers or totally dumb. It takes a community that values the thinking that went into the apparent success or failure, and opportunities to reflect and revise with feedback, to make each experiment into a larger learning experience. Please take advantage of the resources we've shared and all the resources you've found around you to help you feel supported and be reflective as you engage with the ideas in this book.

All of the ideas in this book are evolving models of learning math, which evolve through conversations with students, teachers, researchers, Math Forum colleagues, and math educators, online and face-to-face. This model will get better as we share the ideas and listen to others' thoughts, comparing and contrasting our work with theirs (sounds like a familiar process!). Math education in every classroom will improve as teachers make more opportunities to share their teaching practices, their models of teaching and learning, their favorite activities, and their stories across their departments, districts, cities, and the entire online world. We hope you'll join us in these conversations to help strengthen this model of student learning through, and teacher facilitation of, problem-solving activities and that you find many places to share your own ideas.

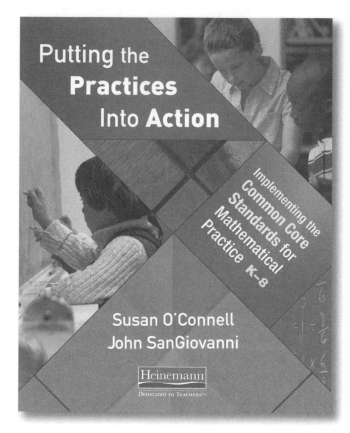